ACCLAIM FOR TERRI BLACKSTOCK

" . . . [*Last Light*] is in league with first-rate adventure fiction and bodes well for the series to come."

—*Publishers Weekly*

"A popular suspense author, Blackstock combines fast pacing with relationship threads in the fourth series entry (after *True Light*). This title should find its way onto public library shelves."

—*Library Journal* (on *Dawn's Light*)

"The Restoration series comes to a dramatic end. Blackstock is absolutely masterful at bringing spiritual dilemmas to the surface and allowing readers to wrestle with them alongside her characters. This is a fitting conclusion to this unique series."

—*RT Book Reviews*, 4.5 stars (on *Dawn's Light*)

"*Truth Stained Lies* is the first in what's likely to be a very popular new series for Blackstock. Her characters are flawed, faltering in their faith, and ultimately human. They're the kind of people you wish you had as friends. This latest novel should appeal to millions of existing fans and millions of new fans who just don't know it yet."

—*CBA Retailers + Resources*

"Short chapters and terse dialogue propel the fast-paced action . . . [and] the mother-daughter relationship strikes true emotional notes; the redemptive arc of evangelical Christian fiction is natural and resonant in a story of addiction. Blackstock's many fans will be pleased, and this story will also speak to families dealing with addicted children."

—*Publishers Weekly* (on *Intervention*)

D0189191

"The second in Blackstock's Intervention series is a fast-paced thriller . . . the portrayal of the dangers of drug abuse and the effects after rehab are fascinating."

—*Romantic Times* (on *Vicious Cycle*)

"Crisp prose, an engaging story, and brisk pacing make this thriller another home run for Blackstock. Recommend it to readers who enjoy material by Lynette Eason and Erin Healy."

—*Library Journal* (on *Downfall*)

"*Shadow in Serenity* from *New York Times* best-selling author Terri Blackstock won't disappoint. It features page-turning suspense, believable characters, a straightforward but non-preachy Christian message of redemption, and just enough romance to satisfy without being sappy. Blackstock is a masterful writer; highly recommend this excellent title to fiction fans."

—*CBA Retailers + Resources*

"Blackstock's superior writing will keep readers turning pages late into the night to discover the identity of the culprit in this amazing mystery. The unique setting and peek into the Nashville music scene are fascinating. Suspense lovers are in for a delightful treat."

—*RT Book Review*s, 4.5 stars TOP PICK! (on *Double Minds*, 2009 Nomination for Best Inspirational Novel)

NIGHT LIGHT

ALSO BY TERRI BLACKSTOCK

QG 12-17-15

NIGHT LIGHT

A RESTORATION NOVEL I *BOOK TWO*

TERRI BLACKSTOCK

ZONDERVAN®

ZONDERVAN.com/
AUTHORTRACKER
follow your favorite authors

ZONDERVAN

Night Light
Copyright © 2006 by Terri Blackstock

This title is also available as a Zondervan ebook. Visit www.zondervan.com/ebooks.

This title is also available in a Zondervan audio edition. Visit www.zondervan.fm.

Requests for information should be addressed to:

Zondervan, *Grand Rapids, Michigan* 49530

Library of Congress Cataloging-in-Publication Data

Blackstock, Terri.
        Night light / Terri Blackstock.
            p.   cm. – (A restoration novel ; bk. 2)
        ISBN 978-0-310-25768-4
        1. Regression (Civilization)–Fiction. I. Title.
PS3552.L34285N54   2006
813'.54–dc22   2006007197

Published in association with the literary agency of Alive Communications, Inc., 7680 Goddard Street, Suite 200, Colorado Springs, CO 80920. www.alivecommunications.com

Cover design: Michelle Lenger
Cover image: © *Guy Grenier / Masterfile*

ISBN 978-0-3103-3779-9 (2013 repackage)

Printed in the United States of America

13 14 15 16 17 /QG/ 20 19 18 17 16 15 14 13 12 11 10 9 8 7 6 5 4 3 2 1

*This book is lovingly
dedicated to the Nazarene.*

DEAR READER

Thank you for reading my Restoration Series. I got the idea for these books as the world was preparing for "Y2K." The world was expecting a huge catastrophe as the clocks turned from 1999 to 2000. Computers were expected to crash, power grids to shut down, and the world as we knew it might come to an end. We all sat around our televisions the night of New Year's Eve, bracing ourselves for darkness. That darkness never came, and the catastrophe didn't happen. But the thought of what might have happened continued to germinate in my brain.

I asked a physicist friend of mine what kind of event could knock out our power grid and fry all our technology, and he told me to research electromagnetic pulses. These pulses could be caused by different things—solar flares, celestial events, E-bombs, and nuclear weapons exploding in our upper atmosphere. As I read and studied these situations and their repercussions, I became more and more aware that these things were real threats to our way of life.

At the same time, I was troubled spiritually by the cultural decline in America. Families (including my own) seemed to be eating most meals in their cars between ballet and soccer practice, the children were glued to video games and television, and parents were distracted by their smart phones. Our comfort had numbed us to the things God wanted to do in our lives. I became convicted that He was going to have to do something drastic to America to get our attention. What would that be? Would it be war? Famine? A nuclear attack?

That's when I decided to flesh out the idea for the Restoration Series and challenge a spoiled American family with a massive global power outage. The Brannings, who'd been used to fast food and take-out, now have to grow their own food and find water. Their cars don't run, their jobs are gone, the banks are closed, there's no communication . . . and this family has to decide if they will hoard what they have or share with their neighbors, when sharing might lead to their own starvation. All around them are desperate people, some willing to kill for food or the opportunity to get ahead.

Since I wrote these books years ago, there have been variations of this theme in television series and books by other authors. Mine are different because I chose not to focus on the military aspect, but on the changing character of the people suffering through this disaster. I fell in love with these characters as I wrote the four-book series, and so did many of my readers. Several years since the series was first released, people are still buying the books and sharing them with their friends. For that reason, we've decided to give the series a second life with new covers and a re-launch that will give new readers an opportunity to discover them. It's my hope that "rehearsing" this catastrophe with my characters will help prepare readers for catastrophes in their own lives. And if it gets the attention of God's people *before* He has to give us a wake-up call . . . well, that would be my idea of true success.

If you like the books, please tell others about them. And if you enjoy the way I tell a story, there are many other books where these came from. Learn more about all of them at http://www.terriblackstock.com/books.

Thanks again for reading my books!
Terri Blackstock

CAST OF CHARACTERS

Branning, Doug—forty-seven, father of four and husband to Kay Branning. He's a successful stockbroker who's never known failure until technology comes to an end, and he's forced to provide for and protect his family from the dangers surrounding them. Though the circumstances of life threaten to defeat him when the power goes out, he manages to find the character and strength to do what needs to be done.

Branning, Kay—forty-five, Doug's wife, mother to Deni, Jeff, Beth, and Logan. She was a spoiled soccer mom before the outage, living in a four thousand square-foot home with all the bells and whistles and driving a brand-new Expedition. Now she faces a daily struggle to feed her family and help those around her who have less than she does.

Branning, Deni—twenty-two, Doug and Kay's spitfire daughter. Just before the outage, she graduated from Georgetown University in broadcast journalism and landed an internship at the NBC affiliate in the Washington, D.C., area. She is engaged to Craig, an attorney who works for a prominent U.S. senator. Just before the outage, she comes home to Crockett, Alabama (a suburb of Birmingham), to plan her wedding. When the power goes out and transportation and communication are shut down, along with all electronics, she feels trapped. She misses her fiancé and longs to hear from him.

Branning, Jeff—sixteen, Doug and Kay's son. He's the star pitcher on his high school baseball team, a true jock, and a popular kid at school. But he doesn't much like hard work. He's a Christian kid but has moments of rebellion. Saddled with a lot of adult responsibilities since the outage, he finds the weight of the world on his shoulders as he tries to help protect his family from the evil surfacing around them.

Branning, Beth—twelve, Doug and Kay's daughter, who looks up to her older sister. She's sensitive to the needs of the neighbors and tries to help when she can. But with her siblings, she gives as good as she gets, and the constant arguing and name-calling drives her parents crazy.

Branning, Logan—nine, Doug and Kay's youngest child, who was raised on PlayStations, computers, DVDs, and television, and finds their new way of life boring and unfair. But he's enjoying spending more time with his dad now that he's home all the time.

Caldwell, Brad—the Brannings' next-door neighbor, an attorney, a good man but not a Christian. He sets up a neighborhood watch in Oak Hollow. An African American, he was initially blamed for the murders and robberies in the neighborhood and was beaten up and almost killed.

Caldwell, Judith—wife of Brad, a nurse, who begins to attend Doug's house church.

Caldwell, Drew and Jeremy—Brad and Judith's sons, nine and seven, friends with Logan.

Horton, Chris—twenty-two, Deni's best friend from high school, a nurse.

Green, Mark—twenty-two, another of Deni's friends from high school. He's good looking, strong, inventive, and skillful. He skipped college and went to work in construction. He's disliked in the neighborhood because of his father's reputation. But Deni and her family know that Mark is all that he appears—a good Christian man who puts others before himself.

PROLOGUE

CIVILIZATION AS WE KNOW IT ENDED ON MAY 24, AND NO
one knows why.

Some mysterious force has caused all electronics on the
Earth to fail. Plumbing doesn't work because the water treatment plants run on electricity. Trucks and trains don't run,
so stores run out of food. Generators no longer work. In this
major meltdown of life, people are left stranded where they
are, with no transportation, no power, no communication.
People are left with a choice: will they hoard what they have
until it all runs out, or will they share with those around
them who are in need?

The Brannings are a Christian family who pride themselves on their righteousness. But in the wake of this disaster,
they respond like everyone else at first: they hole up at home,
hoarding their food, paranoid that interacting with others will force them to share the few provisions they have.
The children are angry that their lives have been disrupted.
They're bored without visual and audio entertainment.
Deni, the twenty-two-year-old, explodes at the idea that she
won't be able to get across country to start her new job on
time. But word is slowly making its way to them that the
power outage is far-reaching.

After a couple of days waiting for this to pass, Doug
reluctantly concludes that this may not be temporary. He
breaks down before God, realizing that he's not equipped to

function without technology. How will he support his family? How will he provide food? How will they survive?

Time passes—and the Brannings, along with all of their neighbors, try to learn to survive with what they have. Everyone works hard just to eat. Everyone is on edge. The Brannings start a church in their home. Doug, who's been a stockbroker for twenty years and has never even taught a Sunday school class, suddenly becomes the preacher.

Oak Hollow, the upper middle-class neighborhood where the Brannings live, where neighbors barely know each other, gradually becomes a close-knit, cooperative, and supportive community. But not without hardship. There is, in fact, a near-total breakdown of society. There are killings, robberies—and a family's most important possessions become their firearms.

Tension grows between Deni Branning and her parents until she runs away to join her fiancé—and instead finds herself in the clutches of a psychopath.

Finding food and clean water continues to be a daily struggle.

Government barely functions, and although rumors abound, information is hard to come by.

And still the power outage continues, without explanation ...

ONE

STEALING CAME EASY TODAY.

Most days, breaking and entering was harder than this for the boys, requiring hours of watching and waiting for families to leave their homes so the two of them could slip in and out, arms full of loot, without being noticed.

At nine and seven, Aaron and Joey Gatlin knew how to blend in. They had a system. They would case the ritzy neighborhoods while bouncing a basketball or tossing a Frisbee back and forth, looking like any other kids out playing on a summer day. No threat to anyone.

The massive power outage that had set technology back over a hundred years, knocking out everything from cars to electricity, had left millions hungry and desperate. But not Aaron's family. He made sure his brothers and sister had something to eat every day.

Some of those who lived in this neighborhood called Oak Hollow had begun plowing up their front yards, and vegetables were growing there instead of grass. Word around town was that they were digging a well, which meant they would have fresh water soon. The lake in the middle of the neighborhood already made them rich, since they didn't have to walk far to get water, and most of them had fancy barbecue pits in the backyard where they could boil the lake water to sterilize it.

"The Br-an-nings." Joey, Aaron's seven-year-old brother, sounded out the name on the mailbox. "They have a big

3

family—they were all working out here in their garden yesterday. Bet they got a lot of food."

Aaron remembered seeing them. "Nobody around today. They're all at the lake, just like the message board said."

The big wooden message boards were a major source of information in every neighborhood around town, since there weren't any newspapers and people couldn't talk on the phone. According to the boards, Oak Hollow was having some kind of big-deal meeting. The mayor was coming to tell people about something. Most of the neighborhood would be there. There would be bicycle patrols up and down the streets during the meeting, but it was easy for the boys to work around them.

If they'd had more boxes and a way to carry them all off quickly, they could have swept a dozen houses clean in Oak Hollow today. As it was, they'd hidden their empty boxes in the woods surrounding the neighborhood. They would hit one house, fill the boxes to the brim, then roll their loot home in their rusty wagon. Then they would come back and do the same with the next house, and the next. The problem was that few of the homes had much of what they wanted, so it took a lot of hits to gather enough to call it a day.

The Brannings' house had two stories, with a double front door and a big porch with white wicker rockers and a cushioned swing. It was the kind of house Aaron's mother used to dream about on her good days. She would cut pictures out of magazines and tack them to the walls—glossy-paged shots of colorful rooms with soft, clean furniture and shiny floors. As if she had a chance of ever owning such a place.

There was no one around. The street was quiet. Aaron couldn't have timed things better. He hoped they'd left their windows open, inviting in whatever breeze there was in the sweltering month of August, as many families did since air-conditioning became a thing of the past. He and Joey had easily gotten into most of the houses they'd hit today and found treasures they hadn't expected. This morning, he'd even managed to find nearly new tennis shoes for Sarah and Luke, who'd been barefoot since they'd outgrown their own. His three-year-old sister had stepped on broken glass last month, and it had been a mess trying to get it healed. Now that it was, he didn't want to let her play outside till she had shoes. Luke, his five-year-old brother, was wearing an old pair that Aaron and Joey had both outgrown—they were so holey there was almost no point in wearing them.

They went around the house and through the wooden gate to the backyard. No one was there. The gate at the back of the property was open, offering a view of the yard behind them, but there was no sign of anyone there, either.

"Okay, Joey, I'll look for a way in. You run back and get the wagon. And watch for the bike patrol. Wait till they've gone by before you cross the street."

Joey complied, as always. Aaron glanced around again, then went to the back door and tested the knob. It was locked, as he'd expected. These people weren't stupid.

He backed up into the yard, stepping on some of the plants, and surveyed each of the windows. The ones on the ground floor were all closed ... but one on the second floor was open a few inches.

Perfect. There was a trellis with vines on it leaning against the house—as good as a stepladder to reach the second floor. He shook it to make sure it would hold him. Carefully, he climbed up, testing each foothold of the white lattice before moving higher.

At the top, he balanced carefully on the steep roof and stepped across the shingles to the open dormer window, pulled it up, and slipped inside. He looked back out—Joey was stealing back into the yard, two big cardboard boxes in the rattley wagon he pulled behind him.

Aaron grinned down from the window and flashed Joey a thumbs-up. His partner-in-crime grinned up at him, revealing his two missing front teeth.

The room looked like a teenaged boy's room, with a framed baseball jersey with Mark McGuire's number on it hanging proudly on the wall, an autographed picture beside it. Aaron lingered in front of it for a moment, wishing he could snatch that and hang it on his own wall. But it would be too hard to carry. No, he hadn't come for that.

The bed was unmade. Several pairs of large, muddy shoes lay on the floor. A computer sat in one corner on a desk, looking like it could boot up any time. A television with a DVD player and a PlayStation sat on shelves facing the bed, coveted items before the outage on May 24. But they were useless now.

He tiptoed out of the room and down the stairs, staying quiet in case they were wrong about no one being home. As he'd hoped, he saw and heard no one. Quickly, he opened the back door, letting Joey in. "Anybody see you?"

His brother shook his head. "Nope. They're all gone."

"Yeah, well, we better be fast. That meeting could break up any minute."

His brother rolled the wagon in behind him, its wheels rattling across the ceramic tiles. Aaron ran into the kitchen and threw open the cabinet doors. Worthless stuff: dishes and small appliances—a mixer, a blender, a coffeepot. He opened the dark refrigerator and saw nothing but recycled plastic containers, a stack of books, and some folded towels. He turned to the floor-to-ceiling pantry next to the fridge and opened it.

"Score!" Joey cried at the sight of the food on the shelves. The Brannings had a bag of apples and a loaf of homemade bread wrapped in plastic wrap. A paper sack full of potatoes sat on a shelf with a dozen or so jars of vegetables.

"We'll be eatin' good tonight!" Aaron began loading everything he could reach into the boxes in the wagon. He glanced at the kitchen counter. There were several jugs of water lined up there. Someone had written *drinking water* on the side of a plastic milk jug. They'd struck gold! "Go get that water," he told his brother.

Joey's grinning eyes widened. "Do you think they cooked it?"

"Prob'ly. Throw it in, quick."

Joey found the caps and snapped them on, then carefully placed them in the box. They'd have to remember this place, Aaron decided, so they could give the family time to restock and hit them again.

Joey helped him empty the shelves, then rolled the wagon around the open pantry doors.

"Careful, now. Those jars'll break."

"Mom?"

Aaron froze at the sound of footsteps coming through the back door. He grabbed his brother's hand and stopped him. The pantry door hid them as the footsteps entered the kitchen.

"That you?" It sounded like a girl or a young boy. Aaron looked down at his feet, wondering if she could see them under the pantry door. She was coming toward them.

He looked for somewhere to hide, but there was no place. Joey's eyes were huge, fixed on Aaron's, silently asking what they should do.

Suddenly, the door swung back. A blonde girl of about twelve faced them, her eyes wide with shock. She screamed, her voice an alarm that would resound across Oak Hollow. Any second a police task force would surround the place with AK–47s, gunning them both down and taking back the food.

Sarah and Luke would be twice abandoned.

Aaron couldn't let that happen.

TWO

Beth Branning gasped and stumbled back from the two boys, her heart slamming against her chest. But the littlest one looked more afraid than she. His dark hair strung into his eyes, as he stared at her. These were kids, no older than her brother Logan. "What are you doing?" she cried.

The boys looked at each other and threw the box they'd been holding into a wagon, jars clanging. Their wagon rattled as they dragged it around the island at the center of the kitchen.

The little creeps had stolen their food! Beth's shock turned to anger as the fear of starving became greater than any danger. "Stop!" she screamed, trying to cut them off before they got out the door. "Give it back!"

"Run, Joey!"

The boys dashed out the door, but she caught up to the wagon and grabbed it to stop them. "That's our food! You can't have it!"

The oldest boy spun around and leveled a gun at her face. Sweat dripped from his dirty brown hair into his dark eyes. "Get back!"

She sucked in a breath and let the wagon go. The boys raced around the house and into the street, with Beth following at a distance. "Help!" she yelled. "Somebody stop them!"

Her brothers—part of the bike patrol—rounded the corner of their street, Jeff pedaling and Logan on back.

"Go after them, Jeff!" Beth called, pointing. "They broke in and stole our food!"

The boys were just disappearing into the woods, dragging their wagon.

"They won't get far!" Jeff yelled, turning up a neighbor's driveway and cutting through his yard toward the path into the woods.

Beth had no doubt her brother could stop those brats. He had to. If he didn't, the Brannings would go hungry tonight.

THREE

"JEFF, THEY'VE GOT A GUN!"

Jeff heard his sister's cry behind him as he followed the boys into the woods. He tried to push through the tangle of vines and brush. "Get off, Logan!"

Jeff's nine-year-old brother jumped off the back, lightening his load. No way would Jeff let those little rug rats take away the food he and his family had slaved over. He would not go hungry because those two didn't want to work for it themselves.

Thorny bushes tore at his clothes and fallen branches slowed him down. He thought of jumping off his bike and tearing after the boys on foot, but he couldn't take the chance of leaving his bike to be stolen.

One of the kids turned and threw a limb in his path. He tried to lift his front wheel over it as he rode, but the rear wheel skidded on the dirt path and he fell. Getting up, he tried to mount his bike again, but the branches were tangled in his spokes.

The kids kept running as he worked his wheels free. They disappeared into the trees, but Jeff knew he could overtake them. They didn't know who they were dealing with. At sixteen, he was one of the best athletes in his class. If it had been a straight shot, he could have overtaken them easily. But they clearly knew the woods better than he did, and used it to their advantage.

He got back on his bike and went after them. He found the beaten path they had gone down. Now he would catch them.

He heard the wagon up ahead and saw the kids breaking out of the trees and running across a parking lot. Perfect. If he got them on level ground, they'd never outrun him.

But they'd thrown more limbs across the path.

And they were fast, really fast. Still fifty yards or more behind them, Jeff chased them as they crossed an empty lot and cut behind a church. Then they vanished again. Jeff stopped as he came to the church, balancing the bike with his foot on the ground, trying to catch his breath as he looked around for some sign of them. He heard the wagon rattling, then a gate slammed.

Taking off toward the sound, he came to a tall fence. He tried to push the gate open, but they had bolted it. He rammed it with his shoulder, but it wouldn't budge.

Reluctantly leaving his bike, he scaled the fence. Jumping down, he saw the back of an apartment complex. Garbage was piled waist-high behind the building, and the stench almost made him gag. He saw the boys disappearing around the far corner of the building.

Wiping the sweat out of his eyes, Jeff followed. The sign said Sandwood Place Apartments. There were the boys—running up the stairs, slowed by the weight of their boxes and the neighbors in their way. They got their loot to a door and disappeared inside.

Jeff ran up the stairs two at a time—past people sitting on the steps—and banged on the door he'd seen them go in. "Open up!"

No answer.

He pounded again. "I'm not leaving here until you open this door, you little thieves!"

Still nothing.

Rage exploded inside him. Kicking the door, he shouted, "Give me back my food!"

But there was nothing but silence behind the door.

FOUR

THE DOOR TO THE NEXT APARTMENT OPENED AND A WOMAN looked out. She was pale and skinny with long, stringy black hair and yellow teeth. Even so, she looked young—not that much older than Deni. "Hold it down out here, would ya?" she said. "I'm trying to sleep!"

Jeff banged again, determined to get to the children inside. "Some kids in there broke into my house and robbed us."

The woman looked mildly interested. "What'd they get?"

He raked his hand through his light brown hair. "Our food, that's what," he bit out. "And I'm here to get it back."

"Careful, they got a gun. They wave it around at everybody. Somebody would have strung them up by now if they didn't have it."

"So I heard," he said. "Is it loaded?"

"Don't know for sure. But if you want to find out, bust that door in. We haven't had any good entertainment around here in months."

He noticed the curtain on the front window being pulled back, someone looking out through the bottom of the miniblinds.

What would his father do? Probably weigh the danger and walk away. But there was no way Jeff could do that. They had worked for weeks tilling the yards, cultivating the

12

garden, and taking care of the plants; they had bartered everything they had of any worth. They'd traded an ax for a bag of
potatoes. A shovel for some beans. Two of their flashlights for a
couple of loaves of homemade bread. And these little thugs were
not getting it.

But they had a gun. And that meant he had to be smart about
this.

In a voice loud enough to be heard through the door, he told
the woman, "Well, I guess they're not coming out. I'll have to come
back later."

The woman stepped back into her apartment and closed the
door as Jeff started back toward the stairs. But he didn't go down.
He waited just around the side of the building at the top of the
stairwell, watching for the door to open.

He hadn't noticed the parking lot before, he'd been so focused
on getting to the kids. Like every other parking lot in town, it was
full of cars that hadn't moved since May 24. Several people on the
stairs stared up at him. No one looked inclined to interfere. If they
felt as bitter toward the brats as that woman had, maybe they'd be
glad to see them get theirs.

He sat for half an hour or so, watching people bringing sloshing
buckets of dirty water home. Where did they get it? There wasn't
a lake nearby.

And how could they grow food when everything around them
was paved? How did they cook with no electricity or gas? And what
was up with that garbage piled up in the back of the buildings?

Men clustered out in the parking lot as if they had nothing else
to do. Women supervised children playing on the pavement. The
smoke from a grill rose nearby. At least they had that.

Finally, the door at 4B opened, and the two boys stepped cautiously out.

Jeff watched, hidden, until they turned away from him, then
launched himself and ran toward that door. The boys didn't see
him until he shoved their door open behind them and pushed his
way into the apartment. The younger one shouted, "It's him!"

A little girl screamed.

Undaunted, Jeff walked through the filthy, dark apartment, trying to look as threatening as he could. At five-eleven, he towered above the skinny children. The living room was smaller than his family's laundry room, and the place smelled almost as rank as the garbage outside. Through an open doorway, Jeff could see a little red-haired boy sitting at the cruddy kitchen table, eating squash out of a jar with his fingers. Next to him, the screaming girl of about three stood on her knees, holding a carrot. Snot had dried under her nose and her hands were filthy.

"Get out of here!" the oldest boy shouted.

"You stole my food, you little punk! I want it back." Jeff bolted into the tiny kitchen and saw that some of the jars of vegetables had already been opened and eaten. They hadn't wasted any time. The boy at the table started to cry, and the preschool-aged girl screamed in a higher pitch.

Jeff suddenly felt like *he* was the criminal, here to torment innocent kids. But they were anything but innocent. "I'm not turning you over to the police," he said, quieter now. "Just give me back what you haven't eaten and we'll call it even."

"We're not giving nothing back!" the kid cried.

The second child—the other thief—emerged from a bedroom with a gun. "You better leave, Mister."

Jeff lifted his hands, palms out—placating rather than surrendering. "Chill out. I don't want to hurt anybody. Put the gun down."

But the boy wouldn't lower the gun.

"Look," Jeff said, "I don't care what you do. You can steal from everybody in town. Just give me back my food and from now on leave our house alone."

"Give it to me, Joey." The oldest took the gun, keeping it aimed at Jeff. "I ain't afraid to use this," he said through his teeth.

Jeff's breath caught in his chest. What would happen if they shot him? Would that detached, bitter neighbor next door leave him to bleed to death? Would they drag his body out and leave him in the garbage? Would someone go for the police?

The two little ones at the table quieted, as though the gun brought them comfort. Sweat dripped into Jeff's eyes.

"Shoot him, Aaron," Joey bit out.

Jeff latched onto his name. "No, Aaron. You don't want to shoot me. Then you *would* be in trouble."

If there was any doubt that the gun was loaded, Joey's attitude almost banished it. Yet Jeff was standing in front of the little ones. If the gun was loaded, wouldn't Aaron fear killing them?

Ammo was hard to come by, since all the stores that had once carried it had been robbed and shut down by now. With no transportation to bring new merchandise in, few of the stores had reopened.

Besides, what kind of parents would leave four children with a loaded gun?

He decided to take a chance. Lowering his hands, he said, "Where are your parents? I want to talk to them."

"I'm in charge here," Aaron said.

"Right. Just tell me when your mother'll be home. I want to talk to her."

"She's not comin' home," the little girl cried in a distraught, lilting voice. "Is she, Aaron?"

Aaron shook his head. "Our mother is none of your business."

Jeff frowned. "Then your dad. Where is he?"

"We don't got a dad," the youngest boy said.

"Shut up, Luke!" Aaron moved closer with the gun.

"Well, you can't be living here by yourselves."

Aaron grabbed one of the jars that hadn't been opened, handed it to Jeff while keeping that gun on him. "Take this and go. I don't want to shoot you."

Jeff took the jar. "I don't want you to, either. So just put the stinkin' gun down."

"No! Not until you leave!"

The other boy, the one who had hung behind Aaron, thrust the bag of potatoes at him. "Here. Now go."

Jeff gladly took them. He saw an empty cardboard box on the floor and loaded them into it. When he rose up, he looked for the rest of it. Some of it was on the filthy kitchen counters. Roaches feasted openly on the counter crud. How did they live like this? The smell alone was killing him.

And the kids were so skinny, as if a gust of wind might break them in two. The girl looked like that little good-ship lollipop kid in those black-and-white movies—only with brown hair and dirt everywhere. And she wasn't much bigger than a toddler.

Despite his anger, his heart softened. "Look, I can see that you guys are hungry. You probably only steal so you can eat. Am I right?"

The little girl wiped her wet eyes, smearing dirt across her cheek, and deferred to her brothers. But none of them answered.

"You can't go breaking into people's homes and stealing their food," he said. "That could get you killed. Does your mother know that you do that?"

The kids all just stared at him. Aaron kept clutching the gun.

"Look, just let me talk to her. When will she be home? Is she at work?"

"We don't know where she is," the boy who looked around five piped in. "She left and never came back."

Aaron shot him a dangerous look. "Luke, don't tell him nothin' else."

But Jeff tried anyway. "How long ago did your mother leave? Hours? Days?"

Silence.

"*Weeks?*"

Joey, the second little thief, nodded.

"Did you look for her?"

"Yeah," Aaron said. "But we didn't find her. We don't need her, anyway. We get by just fine by ourselves."

"By stealing?"

"If we have to," Aaron said.

Jeff started to suggest that they work for their food, or grow it, like everybody else. But these were little kids. They had no place to dig, to till, to plant. Where did they even get the water they needed each day? With no one to take care of them, he couldn't imagine what kind of life they were living.

Gathering some of his unopened jars from the counter, he reached for the bag of apples. But the food didn't matter so much anymore. Maybe the kids needed the apples more than his family did. Leaving them on the counter, he lifted the box with the meager things he'd salvaged and backed toward the door. Aaron kept the gun trained on him.

"I'm going, okay?" Jeff said. "Just keep the rest of it, but don't break into my house again. I know where you live, understand? I'll come after you, and next time I'll bring *my* gun."

No one said a word. He backed out the door, and Joey slammed it shut. He heard the dead bolt clicking.

Jeff looked around at the neighbors who had come out of their apartments to see the show. As he passed, they eyed the things in his box. Everyone here seemed hungry. He felt a sudden need to get out of there fast. He jogged down the stairs and back the way he'd come, around behind the building, through the garbage heap at the edge of the woods, and back to the fence. He unbolted the gate and went through. His bike was still there.

Making his way back through the woods, thoughts of those kids haunted his mind. Somehow, he'd have to convince his parents to help the thieves that had robbed them.

FIVE

THE WARM AIR RIPPLED WITH ANTICIPATION AS THE OAK Hollow residents waited for government news. But Deni Branning's anticipation was greatest of all. She'd heard that the postmaster was bringing mail today. She'd been waiting weeks for word from Craig, her fiancé, in Washington, D.C. If it didn't come today, she might just drown herself in the lake.

She pulled her dark brown hair out of its ponytail, finger-brushed it back up, and bound it again. The heat was already oppressive. Oh, how she longed for air-conditioning! Her friend Chris looked even hotter than she. Instead of wearing shorts, as Deni had this morning, Chris wore her nursing scrubs. Her shoulder-length, wavy blonde hair was pinned into a bun, but perspiration glistened on her neck.

Even in the sweltering August heat, almost every able-bodied citizen in Oak Hollow had turned out to hear the mayor's announcements. Kit Arboghast, who'd been elected last year when the main problems of their small suburb of Crockett were the need for more restaurants and the traffic flow from Birmingham, hadn't done much since the outage. Now that she had news from the government, she'd chosen to reassert herself. Because there was no PA system, and being heard over a large crowd was difficult, she was making the mystery announcements in individual neighborhoods rather than having a huge town meeting at the high school football field.

The mayor had ridden over with Sheriff Scarbrough in the 1963 VW van the government had given him. Only vehicles built before 1970, before microchips were built into the systems, still ran. There weren't many of those around, but occasionally you could hear one of the old, rattletrap engines passing by where the roads had been cleared of cars that had stalled on that first day.

Besides the regular Oak Hollow residents, some from other subdivisions had come just to listen in. Their own meetings would be held later today, but many of them couldn't wait. Deni understood. She would have done the same thing if theirs hadn't been the first meeting of the day. But the added people made it difficult for the ones who belonged here. These neighborhood meetings usually filled the empty lots by the gazebo at the lake, but this morning they spilled over into the street.

The mayor stepped up into the pickup truck that had been rolled onto the grass to provide a platform, and the crowd hushed. Mayor Arboghast had tried to dress up for the occasion — she wore a short-sleeved golf shirt that already had sweat rings and a khaki skirt with bare legs and sandals.

"Good morning, ladies and gentlemen," she said, in her best politician's voice. "Thanks for coming this morning. As you all know, I've come today to bring you some very important announcements. Over the last month, the United States government has been meeting with leaders across the country, as well as consulting with experts in various fields, to figure out exactly what has caused the problems plaguing us today and to come up with solutions to them.

"First of all, the government has been able to conclusively determine that this event, which they're calling the Pulses, is global and is caused by a pulsar, which is a rotating neutron star. This pulsar was created from a supernova that occurred in 1999."

"Speak English," someone yelled. "I don't know a supernova from super*man*."

"A supernova is an exploded star. I don't understand enough about it to explain better than that, but Mabel Litchfield assured me she'd be opening the library today, and she's pulled all the books that explain this in more detail. They're calling the pulsar SN1999.

"Until recently its pulses had no effect on our planet. But on May 24, this pulsar's gamma rays began to reach the earth. These produced electromagnetic pulses that knocked out all of our electronics."

"So is it gonna kill us?" Gary Emory called over the crowd.

A rumble went up, but the mayor quieted them. "As far as scientists can tell, there doesn't seem to be any harm to humans."

"So far," Amber Rowe said, bouncing her baby on her hip. "But from what you've said, things could change, right? Couldn't the radiation get stronger?"

Alarmed, Deni looked up at the mayor, waiting for an answer.

Kit looked frazzled by the question. "My understanding of this whole thing is limited, believe me, but nothing I've been told so far suggests that the radiation might increase. And the good news is that pulsars eventually die out after a few months ... or a few years."

A roar erupted, and Deni looked at Chris. "Then this could be over in a few months? We could actually go back to the way things were before?"

"Don't count on it," Chris said. "She said it could be years."

The mayor raised her arms to silence them. "The pulse effect happens because the pulsar is emitting these rays as it rotates. So every few seconds we get a pulse. It's like a lighthouse beacon, rotating around and hitting us with rays every time it passes us. That's why even new equipment is destroyed once it's turned on. Even the military's equipment, designed to withstand any manner of attack during wartime, isn't defensible against it.

"If and when the pulsar dies out, most of the high-tech equipment that isn't working today will have to be rebuilt or repaired. It's destroyed."

If? Deni shuddered at the idea that it might not end.

"Simple electricity will resume working, however," the mayor continued, "once the electrical plants are up and running."

"You mean we'll have to replace *everything?*" someone shouted from the back of the crowd.

"That's what I'm being told. But who knows—maybe science will find a way to salvage some of it."

A man a few feet away got to his feet and swore. "Are you telling me that in our whole government, with all the science and all the telescopes and computers, nobody knew that this was gonna happen?"

"We should have been warned!" Roland Gunn yelled. "There should have been systems in place!"

The mayor held up both hands to stem the protests. "They *didn't* know, Roland. Nobody knew this could happen, or I guarantee you there would have been something in place to protect the economy. It surprised all of us ... even the scientists. But listen—we've all known this event was catastrophic. It doesn't take a rocket scientist to figure that out. The letter from the White House a few weeks ago said as much. The only difference now is that it has a name, and it's official."

A low roar of complaints waved through the crowd.

"Guess we won't know it's over until the lights start coming on," Chris muttered. "If we aren't all dead first."

Deni searched for the bright side. "At least we won't have to rewire our homes."

The mayor clapped her hands and raised her voice again. "Now, I have several things I need to cover today—some new decisions that have been made at the highest levels of government. These decisions have been difficult, but they've been made in the interest of preserving our country, so that it will be possible to recover economically if and when this is over. Some of these are bad news, some are good news. I need you to hear me out before you react. This situation is difficult for all of us. Remember that I'm a citizen just like you. I'm having to work my fingers to the bone to survive just like everyone else."

"Get on with it," someone shouted.

The mayor paused, as if dreading what she was about to say. *It must be really bad*, Deni thought.

"As you know, the government is extremely concerned about the banking system. To protect the investments you have in the bank, they have chosen not to reopen the banks at this time."

A yell went up from the crowd, and several people sprang to their feet. Chris was one of them. "No!" she cried with the others.

"You can't do this!"

"It's our money!"

The mayor raised her hands. "Hear me out! That's all I ask!"

"Maybe we need to break in and get it out ourselves!" a man yelled.

"We can't live without cash!"

Sweat trickled down the mayor's face. "Don't shoot the messenger!" she cried. "Let me finish! We've made provisions for getting you some cash! Please, hear me out."

The volume of the protests lowered somewhat, but already some were crying. Mumbling continued around them. Many who'd been sitting were standing now, as if preparing to lynch her.

"The president has decided to call in FEMA to handle disaster relief."

"FEMA?" the crowd shouted.

"FEMA can't get anything right," Roland Gunn yelled. "We can't depend on them!"

"Frankly, I'm willing to accept help wherever we can get it," the mayor said. "If you'll listen, I'll tell you how it works."

The crowd grew quiet.

"Since this disaster affects everyone, and not just a region of the country, they can't just set up offices in every town. For the last few weeks they've been trying to decide the best way to help Americans. But it hasn't been easy. There's never been a disaster on the scale of this one—not since Noah's flood, anyway. FEMA's resources are limited, especially without transportation or communication. To help us with our immediate needs, they've concluded that our economy will need a massive restructuring. That means that prices need to temporarily drop drastically, on everything."

"How will that help?" an angry woman cried. "It doesn't matter how cheap things are. I don't have a dime to my name."

"We're going to help with that," Kit said. "Here's how we'll do it. FEMA will disburse twenty-five dollars to every American—adults and children alike—and they'll continue it every three months—"

The crowd erupted again, but the mayor kept talking. "They'll continue it every three months until the Pulses stop or our economy can take over."

"Twenty-five stinking dollars?" someone shouted. "How is that gonna help?"

"Just listen. As I said, adjustments will have to be made to pricing. The government is recommending that prices be reduced by 95 percent for the duration of the Pulses. That means that what used to cost one hundred dollars should now cost five dollars or less."

James Miles, who owned one of the local hardware stores, almost knocked someone down as he tried to get to the front. "The government can't tell me what to charge for my merchandise!"

"No, they can't," the mayor said. "You're right. They can only make recommendations. But if you want to open and stay in business in the current economy, you'll have to make these adjustments. People are dead broke, James. The twenty-five dollars won't change that. As long as the banks stay closed, your money is protected, but everything's going to have to scale down to get things moving again."

James let go a string of curses that made Deni cringe, even though she was used to such language in her college dorm.

"Many of you have already been bartering to survive," the mayor said. "That will have to continue. But it's our hope that giving you this infusion of cash will allow you to make purchases so that you can find ways to make more money. For instance, you might be able to make things that people need and will buy. Yes, you'll have to price them low, but if *everything* is priced low, then you can afford it. And if you go from being a consumer to a merchant, you'll be a step ahead of the game. Hopefully, this will help some of the stores to reopen. We're working on getting steam locomotives running to bring products across the country, so stores will have new merchandise sometime in the next few weeks. With the FEMA disbursement, a family of five will have 125 dollars. That doesn't sound like much, but it's more than you have now."

"When do we get the money?" Deni recognized her father's voice and saw him standing next to her mother in the crowd. He looked pleased with the news, a good sign. He knew the inner workings of the economy better than most. He would know if this was a lame idea.

"We'll have what we're calling the Disbursement on Saturday, August 14, twelve days from today. In Crockett, we'll distribute the money at the Crockett High School football field, beginning at seven a.m. Now this part is very important. You must bring each member of your family with you to receive your disbursement. Everyone must be present. Children must be accompanied by parents or legal guardians. You'll need to have proof that you're a Crockett resident, as well as identification for every member of your family. When you get your disbursement, your hand will be stamped with a special ink that can't be washed off for several days, so we can make sure that no one comes through twice. But let me say again, you must be present to get paid." Her voice cracked, and she reached for a jug of water.

The crowd grew noisy again as the news was absorbed. Mayor Arboghast used that time for a slow drink of water. By the end of the day, Deni thought, she wouldn't have a voice.

Mark Green, another friend from Deni's high school days, came toward her through the crowd. At every neighborhood gathering in the last few weeks, he'd hung on the outskirts of the crowd, as if he didn't belong. It was no wonder. Most of the neighbors treated him like an ax murderer since his father had been implicated in a string of murders that had almost included Deni.

But Deni remained his friend, and hoped the neighbors would soon follow her lead.

He'd recently gotten a haircut, and it made him look older than twenty-two. He had grown so much from the skinny track star he'd been in high school. With all the hard work of the last few months, his shoulders had grown broader. He even seemed taller, but she supposed he'd stood around six-foot-two, even before the outage. He stooped next to her as the crowd continued to roar. "Twenty-five measly bucks," he muttered. "I have five thousand in the bank. That's pitiful."

Chris dropped back into her lawn chair. "It's better than what we have now, which is zilch. I'll take it."

The mayor raised her hands again. "Listen up, please—there's more. And once again, this is a bad news/good news scenario. Please bear with me. As you know, car engines built before the 1970s—before microchips—have not been affected by the Pulses. Unfortunately, there aren't that many around. For that reason, the government has found it necessary to conscript all cars, trucks, and vans that do run, so that they can be used by emergency personnel in our towns and cities, the post office, and for other essential government uses. If you own an antique car, we ask that you drive it to the sheriff's office immediately and turn it over to him."

"How'm I gonna do that when I can't get gas?" Lou Grantham cut in. He had a 1968 Porsche that had been sitting in his garage. He had used it once a few weeks ago to drive to Birmingham, but it had run out of gas half a mile from home, and there'd been no way to get more.

"Let the sheriff know and he'll come get it. He's having to siphon gas out of stalled cars, just as some of you have. We realize that this is bad news for those of you with valuable old cars, but trust me, it's good news if you have a fire, need an ambulance, or have some kind of emergency. You'll want your emergency workers to be able to move faster than they're able to by bicycle and horseback."

"We can't even call them, Kit! By the time we send someone to get emergency workers, the sick person could be dead."

"It's better than nothing, Lou! At least they can take them to the hospital if they need to."

"And what can they do for them there without electricity and equipment that works?"

"Shut up, Lou," Hank Huckabee yelled. "I think it's a good idea."

"Yeah, that's because you don't have to give up anything!"

Kit sighed and tried again. "Because of the nature of the problems created by the Pulses, the government recognizes the value of mechanics across the nation. For that reason, we have no choice but to conscript all licensed mechanics to help with the effort to restore transportation across our land, as well as some engineers being selected according to their expertise."

Again, a roar went up, and Deni looked at Mark. "What does that mean?"

"It means they're reinstituting the draft, and the mechanics are the ones they're drafting."

Her mouth fell open. "They can do that?"

"Sure, they can." He got up and looked over the heads at the frazzled mayor. "Wish I was a mechanic."

The mayor went on. "Some of those conscripted, depending on your skills, will be sent where you're needed to help the government build engines, revamp existing engines, and develop technology that will work during the Pulses. Others of you will be able to stay in this area. But your services are greatly needed right now. We will have a table set up at the Disbursement for all of you to register for this draft and receive instructions on how to proceed."

As the mayor went on, Deni saw her little sister running toward the crowd. She was crying, and she searched the crowd frantically. Deni stood up and watched as the twelve-year-old spotted her parents and pushed through the people. "What's wrong with Beth?"

Chris and Mark both looked in her direction.

Beth talked to her parents, and suddenly they rushed off toward home.

"Probably nothing," Deni said, sitting back down. "She's probably ratting out Logan for something." She pushed Beth's distraught face out of her mind and looked at her watch. When would they start distributing the mail?

When the noise died down again, the mayor answered a few questions, then stepped down from the truck bed. Hank Huckabee, the homeowner's association president, took her place. As he began updating them about the plans to start a neighborhood school in mid-September, run by several of the teachers in Oak Hollow, and went over the progress on the well being dug by the men in the neighborhood, Deni's eyes swept the crowd, searching for the postman who was supposed to have brought the mail. She saw a scrawny middle-aged woman in a postman's uniform and a baseball cap. On the truck bed, several boxes were stacked. Could Craig's letter be there?

Her foot jittered as she waited, wishing they'd get on with it. But there were too many questions.

Finally, Hank introduced Mrs. Lipscomb, the postmaster. She'd bound the letters according to address, so she called out each family one by one, in no particular order. Couldn't she have put them in alphabetical order? Even if she'd sorted them by address, Deni's family would be at the top of the heap.

Her heart raced as she waited...

Finally, the postmaster called, "The Brannings, at 220 Oakhurst."

Deni flew out of her chair and almost knocked down several people as she made her way up. She took the bundle from the poor bedraggled woman and, still standing in front of the crowd, flipped through the letters.

There it was! She jerked it out, almost dropping the others. Tears rushed to her eyes as she went through the rest, hoping for a dozen more. There was one from her grandparents in Florida, another from the ones in Louisiana. Something from her dad's head office in New York. A few other letters whose origin she didn't recognize.

Nothing else from Craig.

But that was okay. She had one!

She held it to her heart as she went back to her seat. Chris and Mark looked as happy as she was. "I told you there'd be one from Craig."

"Well, open it! Let's see!" Chris cried.

"No, not here. I want to be alone when I read it." She folded up her chair. "I'll see you two later."

Mark laughed. "Yeah, maybe when your feet touch earth again. I'm glad you got it, Deni. I hope it says everything it should say."

She pushed through the crowd, hurried between the yards and through the open gate into their backyard. Racing up to the door, she burst in. Her parents were standing in the kitchen.

"Guess what!" she shouted.

"Our food's been stolen!" Beth cried.

The wind whizzed out of Deni's sails, and she stood there with the letters in her hands, gaping at her angry family.

SIX

"How could this happen?" Kay slammed the pantry door. "How did they even get in? I locked the doors myself!"

Beth brooded at the kitchen table. "Jeff's window is open. Maybe they came in that way."

Kay let out a frustrated yell. "When that boy gets back here, he'd better have his hands full of food, or he's going to face some consequences."

Doug sat down and studied his daughter. "Do you think the boys were violent? Could Jeff be walking into trouble?"

"Well, they had a gun."

Kay swung around. "*What?*"

Deni came in and sat beside her sister. "You saw them?"

"Yes!" Kay shouted, sweeping her dark hair behind her ear. "They could have killed her! And now Jeff is facing two guys with a gun!"

"Not guys," Beth said. "Boys. Logan's age or younger."

"So you weren't exaggerating when you said they were kids," Doug said.

"Doug, what are we going to do?"

He rested his face on his hands, then raked his fingers through his brown hair. "I don't know, honey. Just let me think a minute."

WHILE HER DAD WAS THINKING, DENI STOLE UPSTAIRS. As upset as she was about the food—and she *was* upset,

29

since they barely had enough to fill their stomachs each day as it was—she didn't want to wait another minute to read her letter.

She sat down on her bed and slid back against her pillows. Crossing her legs beneath her, she tore into the envelope. Her heart raced as she pulled the folded papers out.

Two pages? That was all, after all this time? When the post office had opened again three weeks ago, she'd sent him a stack of letters she'd been writing all along. Swallowing her disappointment, she started to read.

"Dear Deni," it said. She had hoped for something more personal, like "My dearest Deni" or "Hi babe." But this was fine. He was a lawyer, not a poet.

I've missed you so much.

Isn't this power outage unbelievable? I was at the Senate Building when it all went out. You should have seen the havoc. At first there was a lot of confusion as people kept working with only window light. You know how it is. There's not much rest for lawmakers, and Senator Crawford wasn't all that bothered, until he picked up the phone and realized it was out too. Then he tried his cell phone. No dice. It was about then that we started thinking "terrorist attack." So we gathered up our laptops and rushed out of the building, only to see the traffic stalled in the middle of Constitution Avenue. We were certain it was a terrorist attack, and before we knew it, rumors were flying about it being an electromagnetic pulse. And sure enough, when I tried to boot up my laptop, it was dead too.

She wished he wouldn't give her a travelogue right off the bat. She had hoped for some declarations of love, some promises, some longing.

It was horrible. I had to walk home, fifteen miles, in my Gucci loafers. I didn't know what to do with myself. Stranded in that townhouse and having to find water and food, with all the stores closed. You should see me. I've lost fifteen pounds. For the first few days I just walked around nibbling on Cheez-Its and drinking bottled water.

Then we learned it was a worldwide event, not just confined to the states. We really had our work cut out for us, trying to decide what to do about the banking system, law enforcement, communication, and Homeland Security. If you think I worked long hours before, you should see me now. I practically live in this building, because it's so tough getting from one place to another without a car. I've found myself wishing I still had that 1967 Plymouth Belvedere my dad kept for twenty years. But even if I did have it, the government would be conscripting it. Senator Crawford was one of the lawmakers that introduced the legislation to do that.

If there were some way to get to you, I would.

She stopped reading. *If* there were some way? There *was* a way, and she knew because she had tried it a month into the stinking outage, and she'd almost gotten herself killed by the murdering maniac who'd offered her a ride in his horse-drawn wagon. When she'd finally managed to get a bike, she could have ridden on to D.C., but she'd chosen instead to head home to warn her family before the killer could get back there. She hadn't had the courage to launch out again.

If he'd wanted to see her badly enough, he could have made it by bike in just a few days. He still could. The letter continued:

I guess our wedding isn't going to come off like we planned. But if it's meant to be, I guess we'll wait for each other.

Her heart sank, and her jaw dropped. What was he saying? That he wasn't even going to *try* to get to her? That the wedding date they'd set for October—just eight weeks away—wasn't going to happen? No declarations of love, no sweet verbal caresses. Not even a sad romanticism. Just a matter-of-fact mention of their aborted wedding, and their future boiled down to an *I guess, if.*

Were they even still engaged?

She almost couldn't read the last line through her tears.

I really miss you. Hope this will all be over soon and we can get together again.

"Get together," like they were acquaintances hoping to do lunch. Did he even realize how cold that sounded? Or did he care?

As grief stole over her, she read the letter again, looking for something she had missed, something between the lines ...

Did he still love her? He said he missed her, but it sure didn't sound like it.

Her mother knocked on her door and leaned in. "Deni, somebody'll have to go get water and start boiling it, since they took all we had. Your dad has a shift at the well, and I need to stay here in case Jeff comes home."

Deni turned her wet face up to her mother. "Mom, I can't go right now."

Her mother saw her tears and came to her bed. "Honey, what's wrong?"

Deni held up the letter.

"From Craig?"

"Oh, yeah."

Kay took the letter. "What does it say?"

"Oh, just the basics. I'm fine, how are you, the weather's great, how 'bout them Yankees ..." She crumpled into tears.

Kay sat down on the bed and quickly read it. "It doesn't say that. Well, look. Here he says he's missed you."

"Look at the travelogue, Mom. Ninety percent of the letter is his play-by-play of his own drama the day the outage happened. Did it not even occur to him that I was on a plane ten minutes before the Pulses started? That I could even be dead? No! He didn't mention that at all."

"Honey, I'm sure that occurred to him. But he's a man. They don't express themselves that well. That doesn't mean they don't feel it. Cut him some slack."

She snatched the letter back. "Mom, he blew off our wedding!"

She knew she had her mother there. Even in all her optimism, she couldn't soft-sell that one.

"Maybe that's not what he meant. Maybe he has every intention of marrying you, but he's just not sure it'll happen on that very day. Things are complicated now. They're not predictable."

"Don't defend him, Mom. There's no way you can turn this business correspondence into a love letter." She slammed her fist on the mattress. "The e-mails he used to send me were warmer than this. I'm losing him. I may have lost him already. There's probably some senate intern who's cooking for him and pampering him."

"Deni, don't let your mind go there. You're making things up and making yourself miserable. Think of him as a man who doesn't express himself well in letters. That doesn't mean he's not sick over your separation."

Deni knew that wasn't true. She folded up the letter and put it back in its envelope, then tossed it into the drawer in her night table. She pulled her shoes back on. Roughly smearing her tears, she said, "I'll go get water. Just let me wash my face so no one will know I've been dumped."

"You haven't been dumped, Deni. You're still engaged. It's not like he asked for the ring back."

"That's because it's worthless now. It wouldn't do him any good."

"You're still engaged, Deni, until the man tells you he's not going to marry you."

"Or until I tell him I'm not going to marry *him*!" Deni didn't want to talk about it anymore. She just went into the bathroom where her mother kept a bowl of water and washed the tears off her face.

KAY WENT DOWN THE STAIRS AND ACROSS THE HOUSE TO HER bedroom. Doug was changing into his work clothes. "That jerk!" she bit out.

"What jerk?"

"Craig Martin. He finally sent her a letter, and it broke her heart."

Doug stopped before pulling his shirt over his head. "No way."

"She's up there crying. I'd love to get my hands on him."

"What did it say?"

"It said that he didn't see how the wedding would come off, but if it's meant to be, they'll wait for each other."

Doug finished putting the shirt on. "That's not so bad."

"Yeah, well, he couched it between all this stuff about how hard the outage has been for him. After she almost got killed going after him—"

"He didn't know that when he wrote the letter."

"Don't defend him, Doug."

He bent over to pull on his work boots. "I'm not defending him. Frankly, I don't want to see her hurt, but if they break up, it won't break my heart. I never liked him to begin with. He's not good enough for her. Not by a long shot."

Kay sank down onto the bed. "You're right, but I don't want her hurting. She's been through enough. How much more can she take?" She let out a long breath. "How much more can *I* take? *Where* is Jeff?"

"He's okay. He's a tough kid. He'll be back soon. Probably with our food."

"He could get shot."

"He won't."

She watched as he bent over and tied his boots. He had changed in the last few months. Her husband, whom she had believed was handsome before, had grown more attractive as the harsh sun and backbreaking labor did its work on him. She wished it had done the same for her, but she was a mess. She'd had to let her brown hair grow out, since she couldn't style it without electricity, and the sun had deepened her wrinkles. No amount of moisturizer would be able to erase the damage.

Finally, Doug straightened. "Look, there's no point in losing it before we know the situation. If he doesn't come back soon, *then* we'll panic. For now, let's just have faith that God is taking care of him."

She lay back flat on the bed and threw her arm over her eyes. "I'm tired, Doug. I try to be tough, but sometimes I just have to explode."

"Yeah, me too."

She moved her arm and looked at him. "So what do you think about this pulsar, or whatever it is?"

He thought for a moment. "It makes sense. I'm gonna swing by the library as soon as I get a minute and read up on it."

"Do you think she's right about the radiation not getting stronger? What if it moves closer to us? It started suddenly. Couldn't it suddenly get worse?"

He stared at the floor, shaking his head. "I honestly don't know. But there's no use borrowing trouble. For now, we should probably just be thankful to be alive." Patting her leg, he got up and started to the door. "I'm going to work at the well. Send Logan to get me as soon as Jeff gets home."

Kay sat up and took a deep breath. She'd pull herself together and stay busy until Jeff got home.

Only then would she fall apart.

SEVEN

Doug had drafted the work schedule for the well and lectured the neighborhood men about the importance of showing up, so he couldn't very well skip out himself. The plan was to keep the digging going every daylight hour, and the ones on the shift before him couldn't leave until he got there. They had limited patience when someone was late.

He and Jeff were digging partners, but since Jeff had gone chasing after thieves, Doug had asked his next-door neighbor Brad to fill in. Jeff could take Brad's shift later. Working outside the hole were Mark Green and Zach Emory, charged with mixing the mortar and lowering the bricks for the walls of the well. Judith and Brad's oldest child, Jeremy, had the job of raising the buckets of dirt out when they were full, dumping them, then lowering them again.

They'd dug the well in a square shape, eight feet by eight feet, but it was tight quarters for him and Brad down in the hole. They'd had to make it wide enough that two men could work side by side with a pick, a shovel, and a long steel rod used to break up rock, but the work was filthy and backbreaking. It would be worth it, though, when they finally struck water. Everyone working at the hole knew that it could literally be months before they dug deep enough through the soil, limestone, sandstone, and shale to hit the water table. The Pulses might very well end before they ever finished the task. But whether the Pulses lasted for months or years, the well would make their lives easier for the duration.

That was why it was so important to keep the digging going every hour of daylight. There was no time to waste.

The well-digging was going slowly. Doug and the other men in the neighborhood—those who'd agreed to a cooperative work schedule to get this done—had been digging for almost a month. They'd only made it fifteen feet down, since digging wasn't the only component of this monumental job. As they dug, they had to reinforce the walls with bricks to prevent a cave-in. The process was laborious—dig two feet down, stop, brick the walls, then dig some more. And it wasn't like they could make a run to Home Depot for the bricks, since the home improvement store had long since closed, empty of merchandise and unable to pay its employees. No, they'd first had to scout around for abandoned buildings that could be demolished for their bricks and lumber.

Most of the men working on the well had been reluctant to use their much-needed tools on this job, unwilling to dull their sharp ax blades or break their picks hacking through layers of rock. So they'd managed to come up with several steel rods that they hammered to fracture the stone.

It would all be worth it when they hit the water table. Doug had prayed often over the last few weeks that when that happened, the water would be clean enough for drinking—not rusty water from iron-rich earth, or sulfur-contaminated water they couldn't drink.

Brad thrust his shovel into the dirt and leaned on the wooden handle. Soil covered his brown skin, and he glistened with sweat. "What time is it?"

Doug looked at his windup Timex. "One-thirty. Thirty minutes more." He was thankful that the neighborhood men had seen the wisdom in their taking only hour-long shifts and rotating the schedule so that no one had to continually work in the hottest part of the day. Today he and Brad had started at one, and tomorrow their shift would be at two. By the weekend they'd be shoveling during the late daylight hours, when it would be cooler.

Brad wiped the sweat off his forehead, then opened his milk jug of water. Taking a long drag, he looked up to see how much progress they'd made.

They'd at least deepened the well by another foot. It was time to stop and lay some more bricks.

"Hey, Dad."

It was Jeff's voice, and Doug looked up to see his son's face at the top of the hole. Relief washed through him. "Jeff, did you catch the thieves?"

"Yeah, kind of."

"So you got the food back?"

Jeff hesitated. "Well ... some of it."

Doug braced himself. "Some of it? Why didn't you get it all?"

"Because they were four kids living by themselves in a hole-in-the-wall apartment. The oldest didn't look more than nine, and the littlest was three or four. No parents. They've been fending for themselves. They stole to eat, Dad. I don't really know what choice they had."

Doug looked at Brad. His friend rolled his eyes and shook his head. "Don't believe that, man. It's a con if I ever heard one."

Doug agreed. He looked up at Jeff. "Son, four kids living alone would probably have starved to death. No neighbors in their right minds would let that happen."

"Dad, I'm telling you, they didn't have any adults in that apartment. They said their mother took off weeks ago and never came back. The neighbors know they have a gun, so that's probably why they haven't bothered them. That and the fact that they can barely feed themselves, much less four more kids."

Their mother was probably the one who'd come up with that cockamamie story to keep from having to work hard like everybody else. Anger tightened his chest. "So are you telling me you didn't get our food back?"

"I got some of it, but they had already eaten some. And I didn't want to take everything. How will they eat?"

If Doug could have gotten out of the hole easily, he would have throttled his son. He wiped his forehead on his arm, and longed for some water. But those deadbeat kids had taken all the sterilized drinking water they had, so he hadn't been able to bring any.

"All right, we'll talk about it later. For now, just help Deni get water, and as soon as it's filtered and boiled, bring me some."

"Okay, Dad. But I really think we need to do something about those kids."

Brad picked up his jug and thrust it at Doug. "Here, drink some of mine. Our shift'll be over before yours is boiled and cooled enough to drink."

Gladly, Doug accepted the jug and took a long swig.

Above him came his son's voice again. "Dad?"

"I heard you, son. We'll discuss this later. The Boxcar kids can wait. They've survived this long."

Jeff disappeared from the mouth of the well, and Doug went back to digging.

EIGHT

WHEN DOUG GOT HOME, COVERED WITH THE DIRT AND CLAY he'd been shoveling out of the hole, he went into the bathroom where Kay had a bowl of water waiting for his cleanup. What a day! First the meeting and the bad news about the banks, the promise of the measly disbursement money, the thieves walking away with their food, then the miserable work at the well ...

Now he had to prove to his son that those kids were nothing more than pawns of sick parents who'd trained them to burglarize from those who actually worked for their food.

He splashed water on his face, soaped up, then rinsed. The water was brown, just from his filthy hands. He sighed. Sometimes he thought he would never be truly clean again. Two months ago, dirt under his fingernails would have been a shocker. Now it seemed tattooed there.

He did his best to wash off the sweat and grime, then got dressed. He found his family sitting around the patio table. Jeff had Kay's rapt attention. Great. As if she wasn't stressed enough about the pulsar, now Jeff was giving her those kids to worry about.

"Doug, we've got to do something," she said. "Those poor children!"

He dropped into the chair. "How much food did you get back?"

"A few jars of vegetables. A bag of potatoes. But I left them the apples."

Doug gritted his teeth and looked at the sky. They'd worked hard for those apples. In exchange for two bags of them, the entire family had had to ride five miles to the Hortons' orchard and spend the day harvesting the fruit. It was the Hortons' way of maintaining the orchard while keeping up the daily drudgery of surviving. For two bags of apples, a family had to work several hours. Now they were gone.

"Doug, he says they're all alone. Orphaned children, living there with nothing to eat."

"I'll believe it when I see it."

"Good. Then let's go," she said.

He sat up straighter and turned his troubled eyes to his wife. "Go where?"

"To see for ourselves. Doug, if this is true, we have to do something."

He could see in her eyes that there would be no talking her out of it. He let out a heavy breath. "All right, but I want the sheriff to go with us."

"Dad!" Jeff said. "You can't arrest a bunch of little kids!"

"Not to arrest them," he said, sliding his chair back and getting up. "I want him to be there to see what's going on with the parents. Sounds like it's a case of neglect, maybe even child abuse. He should be aware of it."

"Do you want me to come with you?" Jeff asked.

"No," Doug said. "You and Deni stay here and do your chores. What's the apartment number?"

"4B, Sandwood Place Apartments. They're a block south of the bank, or you can cut through the woods."

"I know where it is. When we get back, you and I are going to talk about that window you left unlocked."

NINE

KAY'S FIRST REACTION TO THEIR FOOD BEING STOLEN HAD been pure rage. Though they often shared with their neighbors, their resources had been stretched unbearably thin. The family had shared in the work of growing the food and canning it, and they'd bartered and baked and built and babysat to stock their pantry.

But now, as she pedaled her bike to the sheriff's department, she didn't know who to blame. Starving children didn't deserve her wrath. But someone must.

How she longed for the days when she could whip over to McDonald's in her SUV and get the kids combo meals. Would those days ever return?

It wasn't all bad, of course. Strange as it seemed, the Pulses had brought about some good. Before the outage, she'd only had a waving acquaintance with most of her neighbors. Time spent with her kids was in the car to and from soccer tournaments, baseball games, and ballet lessons. Doug was rarely home, and when he was, he was on his computer. The kids were always lost in PlayStation games or IMing their friends. She TiVo'd her favorite programs to watch at her leisure—Oprah, Dr. Phil, 24, ER and a number of sitcoms she was too ashamed to admit she watched.

Since the Pulses, so much had been different. Her lazy children were turning into hard workers who understood that if they wanted to eat they had to do their share. Their situation left no room for slackers. Over the weeks since the outage, the whole family had come to recognize the value of home as they never had before, and she'd seen Doug transformed into a new man—spending time with his kids, providing for them with his hands rather than his head.

The darkness in the house at night had even become a blessing. Instead of separating to their rooms at night for their favorite but solitary activities, they now spent evenings together in one room, talking and playing games, or reading aloud under the light of the oil lamps.

Though her children still complained and plotted to get out of their work, they seemed healthier, if skinnier. Their skin glowed, now that they'd all been detoxed from their high-fat supersize diets, food additives, trans fats, and soft drinks. And the truth was, the hard work had toned her body as no Pilates class could, and made her healthier than daily aerobic workouts. Weight was no longer a problem.

Life moved at a slower, more deliberate pace, and that had profoundly affected Kay's character as well as her family's. No more instant gratification. The Pulses had fostered patience in all of them, and made them think more of others than themselves ...

Most of the time.

Now she swung between anger and compassion at the children who'd disrupted her day.

Four children that young, living alone? It was criminal. If it was true, someone was going to pay.

Doug was quiet as he rode beside her.

"Doug, I know you're upset about having to do this," she said. "But imagine if something had happened to us when our kids were small, and our children were living alone."

"Kay, you'll see that it's not even true. They probably lied to Jeff, playing on his sympathy. They've taken enough of our resources already. I don't like that they're taking more of our time. I have work to do."

"But what if it's true?"

They sailed around a corner. "That's why we're going, Kay. On the off-chance that it's true."

His attitude worried her. Though the outage had brought the family closer together, her relationship with Doug seemed more distant than ever. They rarely had a private moment, and when they did, they were so exhausted that they fell into bed and went to sleep. Intimacy had been exchanged for efficiency.

It was her fault as much as his. They were each too burdened by life to make intimate time a priority. Sometimes she longed to slip into her husband's arms and lay her head against his chest. But his constant preoccupation dissuaded her.

They turned down the road leading to the sheriff's office and saw Scarbrough's van sitting out front.

"Good," Doug said, "he's here. Maybe he'll give us a ride and we can make this quick."

"He won't give us a ride, Doug. They've said over and over the cars are not for personal use."

"It's not for our personal use," Doug said. "We're reporting a crime and leading him to the perpetrators."

She sighed. "They're not perpetrators. They're children."

Doug wasn't buying it.

Carrying their bikes inside, they found Scarbrough at his desk. He heard them out, then agreed to go with them. After loading their bikes into the van, they headed for the Sandwood Place Apartments.

They pulled into the apartment complex Kay had driven past so many times in her pre-outage days. She'd hardly given it a thought. But now she saw the people loitering in their doorways or standing out on the hot pavement.

"Jeff said it was apartment 4B." Doug's eyes scanned the buildings. "There," he said, pointing. "It must be that one right there."

All eyes were on them as they got out of the car. Scarbrough locked the van that had the words "Sheriff's Department" painted on the side. The sign and the uniform produced an instant aura of suspicion among the residents. Some stepped back into their open apartments. Clusters of people spoke in low voices, staying out of his way.

But he headed toward one of those clusters. Doug and Kay followed him at a distance. He asked about the children in 4B. "We've heard rumors they live up there alone. Any truth to that?"

"They have a mama," a man said. "But I ain't seen her in a while."

A skinny woman with a bandana on her head spoke up. "Come to think of it, I haven't seen her in weeks."

"She's probably laid up somewhere with a needle in her arm," the man said.

Kay met Doug's eyes. So the mom was a drug addict. That explained a lot.

The sheriff questioned a few other neighbors as they made their way to 4B. All confirmed that the mother hadn't been seen in weeks.

"Not sounding good," Scarbrough said as they reached their door.

"No, it sounds like Jeff got it right." Kay glanced at her husband. His frown lines cut more deeply into his brow as they moved closer to the door.

Scarbrough was getting angry. "I ought to arrest the whole bunch of them for letting this go on. Four children, all alone. And when I find that sorry excuse for a mother ..."

He banged on the door.

The curtain was snatched back from the window and a little girl looked out, apparently the three-year-old Jeff had described. Her face was dirty and her mop of curls was tangled and unbrushed.

No one answered the door, but the sheriff had seen the little girl peering out too. He banged harder. "Sheriff's department, open up!"

The door cracked open then, and a small boy peered out.

He didn't look much older than the girl, and his face was just as dirty. "We didn't do nothing," he said, looking fearfully up at the sheriff.

Behind him, a voice yelled, "Luke, I told you not to open it!"

Luke looked back. "But it's the sheriff!"

Kay peered into the dark apartment and saw two older boys—perhaps the ones who'd broken in.

The oldest one came to the door. "Our mom's not home," he said. "She's at work. But we didn't do anything wrong."

Scarbrough pushed the door open so they could look into the apartment. Kay took it all in. The place looked like the back room at a Goodwill shop, where people dumped their discards before they were sorted. The floor was covered with clothes and items of all sorts, and on the table she saw the bag of apples the boys had stolen from her house earlier that day.

A sewage smell wafted out of the apartment, making her want to cover her nose. She shot Doug a distraught look. This time, he returned it.

The sheriff led them inside, and the picture grew more grim—as did the smell. How could anyone live in conditions like this—much less children?

"Where's your mama?" the sheriff asked.

"She's at work," the second oldest said. "She'll be home late tonight."

"Where does she work?"

"At Western Sizzlin'."

Kay and Doug looked at each other. The Western Sizzlin' hadn't been open since the day the Pulses began.

Aaron saw the exchange and quickly corrected his brother. "No, that's where she *used to* work. Now she works for that family in Birmingham. Cleaning houses. I can't remember their names."

That didn't even make sense. Hardly anyone had cash for the bare necessities. Even the richest person in town was probably cash poor by now and wouldn't spend what they had on domestic services.

"So why did the neighbors tell me they haven't seen your mama in weeks?"

Aaron just stared at them. "They lie, some of them. They don't know anything."

Doug moved a box off a chair and sat down, putting his face on an eye level with the boys. "Look, kids, we're not here to hurt you. If it's true that you're living here alone, we just want to help. Our son was here earlier, and he told us some things about you."

Aaron swallowed. "We gave most of the food back. He said we could have the rest."

"It's not about that. We're worried about the conditions you're living in here, and how you're getting food and water. Four kids shouldn't be living alone."

The little girl, thumb in her mouth, looked up at Kay. Despite her filthy face, Kay could see that she was a little doll. She smiled at the girl, who pulled her thumb out for a second, as if considering the small kindness. Then she shoved it back in.

"We're *not* living alone," Aaron said. "I told you that's a lie."

Scarbrough sighed. "Fine. Then tell us where we can talk to your mama, and we'll leave you alone."

There was a long pause, and all three younger children looked at their brother ... waiting.

Emotions tugged at Aaron's face, and for a moment, Kay wished they hadn't pushed him into a corner. Defeat hung over him as powerfully as the apartment's horrible smell.

"I don't know where she is, okay? She left a while back."

"Did she tell you where she was going?" Scarbrough asked.

"No. We've looked all over for her. Nobody knows where she is."

Scarbrough let out a long breath, and suddenly the hardness went out of him. In a softer voice, he said, "Son, why didn't you tell the authorities?"

His face flushed red. "Because I knew what you'd do. You'd want to put us in foster care. Only nobody'd wanna take all four of us. Sarah has bad dreams, and Luke walks in his sleep. I have to be there to take care of them."

That was all it took for Kay to lose it. Her eyes filled with tears, and she stooped in front of the little girl and put her arm around her. The thumb came out again. "Aaron, I'm sure something can be worked out," she said. "You know it's not healthy for you to live here like this."

"We live fine," he bit out. "I take good care of us."

There was pride in his voice, and she didn't want to shoot it down.

"I can understand your fears," the sheriff said. "Maybe I can keep you four together. We'll see what we can do to make that happen."

"Yeah?" Aaron cried. "Who do you think is gonna want to take in four extra mouths to feed when they can't hardly feed their-selves? I know what'll happen. When nobody shows up, you'll *have* to split us up!"

He was right, Kay knew. That was exactly how it would happen.

Joey's mouth curled as his own emotions took over. "We'll run away if you do that!"

Sarah started to cry. "I don't want to go! I want to stay here!"

Kay tried to hug the little girl, but she pulled away and went to Aaron. He stroked the child's curls. "It's okay, buddy. Don't cry."

"But I want to stay with you!" she wailed.

Kay looked at Doug. She saw something in his eyes, but it wasn't compassion. How could he not be moved?

The sheriff cleared his throat. "Kids, all I can say is I'll do the very best I can. But this is not negotiable. You have to come with me, period. You've broken the law, and I can't let you keep doing it. No way can I let you stay here. I'll try to keep you together, or at the very least place you in pairs, but at this point you're lucky I'm not locking you up."

Kay imagined her own children—what if, when they were small, they'd lived in squalor or been farmed out to foster care?

She looked up at Doug, her eyes pleading. But he wasn't biting.

The words flew out of her. "We'll take them!"

Doug's mouth fell open. "*What?*"

She got to her feet and turned to the sheriff. "I said, we'll take them. All four of them."

Scarbrough's eyebrows shot up. "Really? Are you sure?"

Kay saw the dread on Doug's face. He had enough problems feeding the six of them. She knew what he was thinking: How would he feed four more?

But she was ready for a fight if it came to it.

"Kay, I know what you're trying to do, but we're not equipped—"

"Doug, we have to take them. Just until the sheriff finds a home for them."

"We got a home, lady," Aaron said. "We don't need anybody else messin' things up."

Kay sighed. "Aaron, you don't have much choice right now. The only way you've been surviving is by stealing, and now that the sheriff knows, that has to stop. We'll help you until your mother is found. Or a grandmother or another relative who can take care of you."

Doug's tension was growing. "Kay, that could be a long time."

Her eyes flashed. "Doug, we are not leaving these children!"

He swallowed hard, then looked from one to the other of the urchins lined up before him, his struggle plain on his face.

But when he turned back to her, the struggle had turned to resolve. "All right. Let's get them packed."

Kay knew he wasn't happy about it, but she didn't care. She would convince him later that it was the right thing. "Okay, come on, kids, I'll help you get packed, and the sheriff can drive us home."

"In a car?" Sarah asked.

"A van," she said, smiling. "It's one of the only ones in town that runs. How about that?"

Sarah jumped up and down, delighted at the interesting turn of events. But the three boys brooded. And when the sheriff found and confiscated their empty revolver, they looked even more distraught. Kay could see this was going to be a challenge.

She hoped her marriage was up to it.

TEN

Deni's parents had been gone way longer than she'd expected, so the task of preparing dinner on their outside grill fell to her. The choices were slim, and the food Jeff had salvaged from the thieves would have to last. She had just started boiling six potatoes, one for each of them, when Brad next door brought several fish he'd caught that day. Her unbelieving neighbor didn't even realize he'd been used by God today. She had quickly cleaned the fish and put them on the grill.

Three months ago, she hadn't known how to boil water. Now she could bake bread, can vegetables, clean fish—and her father threatened that she'd soon be skinning animals, a talent she'd rather not foster. But a lot of good all those domestic skills did her, since she'd probably be fifty before she saw Craig again. By then, he'd probably be married to some cute intern. Deni hated her already.

"Smells good." Jeff came out of the house, still filthy from working at the well. "I wonder if I should go looking for Mom and Dad. I'm getting worried about them."

"Maybe you should. They may have gotten conked on the head in that neighborhood."

The words were no sooner out of her mouth than they heard an engine turning onto the street. Since it was such a rare sound, one that usually meant bad news, she scooped the fish off of the grill and ran to see who it was.

It was the sheriff's clunker van, pulling into her driveway. Her chest tightened. Was he coming with bad news about her parents?

She breathed in relief when she saw her dad in the passenger seat. "It's about time," she said as he got out. "Where have you been?"

Her dad opened the back door, and her mother got out. Behind her, a scrungy-looking boy filed out, followed by three other filthy children.

Her jaw dropped. "Dad, don't tell me ..."

Her mother flashed her an overbright smile. "Deni, this is Aaron, Joey, Luke, and Sarah. They're going to be staying with us for a while."

Deni wanted to scream. This couldn't be happening. How had the burglary of their house turned into an opportunity to feed four more? "Mom, you've got to be kidding!"

Doug shot her a stern look, then turned to the children. "Are you guys hungry? Looks like Deni's got fish."

The four nodded, but Deni quenched the urge to remind them that they couldn't be hungry since they'd probably pigged out on a couple weeks' provisions they'd stolen out of her pantry.

Sheriff Scarbrough opened the back of the van and began unloading. There were bags of filthy, reeking clothes for the kids, and a couple of boxes. When he set one of the boxes on the driveway, she saw its contents. They'd brought back a few more of their jars of vegetables, but not all of them. That was probably her dinner hardening on the little ones' faces.

Kay herded the children inside, as Doug and Jeff helped the sheriff unload. Deni grabbed her dad's arm. "Dad, this is a joke, right? They're thieves!"

"They're abandoned children, Deni. They've been stealing to eat. They don't even know where their mother is. She's been gone almost since the outage."

Okay, so they had a story. That didn't mean Deni was responsible for them! Lowering her voice, she said, "Dad, we can't feed them!"

"Tell it to your mother," he whispered. "She's dead-set on keeping them until we can find their relatives."

Deni watched, stunned, as they unloaded more bags of stinking stuff. "Why do we have to take them?" she whispered harshly. "Do I need to remind you that they broke into our house today? They can't be trusted. They might slit our throats while we sleep."

He shot her a look. "Deni, they're little kids."

"I don't care how old they are. They're criminals."

Jeff walked up behind her. "Get over it, sis. Mom did the right thing. They have to stay somewhere."

"Why not with a neighbor?"

Her dad sighed, and she got the feeling that he'd already made the same arguments. "If someone at the apartments could have done that, they would have by now. But those people are in squalor. They don't have gardens, they don't have yards. I have no idea where they're getting their water."

She couldn't believe it. "How long do we have to keep them?"

"Not long, I hope. I'll start looking for relatives tomorrow. Meanwhile, God will provide, like he always does." He nodded to the fish on the plate. "Looks like he already has today."

Deni looked down at the fish. God *had* provided for them for three months. He'd even provided for her in her deepest stupidity, when she'd been on the road with a killer. She had surrendered her life to Christ on that horrible journey, and she was learning to trust him.

But she hadn't expected this.

She followed her family in and watched as her mother lined the children up at the sink to wash their hands in a bowl of water. They looked like unwilling captives. The two older ones looked around as if taking inventory of things they could snatch when the family went to sleep tonight. These kids would surely clean them out by morning.

The two younger ones, with swollen eyes and streaked cheeks, looked more innocent. As her mother washed the dirt off, they didn't look so evil anymore. Just scared. The little girl was still sniffing and holding her brother's hand. He kept patting her, like it was going to be all right.

Deni's heart softened a degree.

Logan and Beth came in from outside and gaped at the crowd in their kitchen. "What's going on?" Logan asked. "Are those the crooks who stole our food?"

"Logan!" Kay set her hand on the little girl's shoulder. "They're our guests. They're going to be staying with us tonight."

Beth sucked in a breath. "Where are they sleeping?"

Her mother's voice was soft, markedly cheerful. "You'll stay in Deni's room with her, and Sarah and Luke will sleep in your bed. Logan, you'll sleep with Jeff, and Aaron and Joey will take your room."

Logan grunted. "No way those creeps are sleeping in my bed! No way, Mom!"

Aaron's lips compressed in a sneer. "Don't worry. I'd rather sleep on the concrete than in your stinking bed."

Logan took a step toward him. "Speaking of stinking—"

Kay slapped her hand over Logan's mouth, her eyes shooting daggers, then turned his face up to hers. "Logan, that's enough."

Doug grabbed Logan's shoulder and turned him around. "Outside, son. You and I need to have a talk."

Logan stormed out of the house, and Doug followed. Logan was in trouble now, Deni thought, because he was the only one with the guts to speak out.

Her mother looked as if she could spit nails. "Now," Kay said, trying to put a happy face on their chilly reception, "let's finish washing our hands so we can eat."

Hands, feet, legs ... Those kids had weeks' worth of filth on them. Deni bit her lip and began to set the table.

Beth looked about to cry.

Kay stood the little girl up on a chair and dipped her hands in the bowl of water. "I'll wash up in the back," Jeff muttered.

Deni eyed the boys as she finished setting the table. The two older ones stood like hostile prisoners, their arms crossed in defiance. Maybe, if she were lucky, these kids would run away tonight and be done with it. The little boy, though, wasn't showing such bravado. He held his eyes wide, as if he didn't know whether to cry or smile. Quietly, he awaited his turn at the sink.

Deni watched as her mother talked softly to the little girl, gently washing the filth off her hands. It was going to take more water than they had ready. She'd only filtered and boiled enough for drinking water to replace what they'd taken, but it wouldn't be enough to wash with.

"After supper, you'll all need baths." Kay finished washing little Sarah's hands and dried them on a clean towel. "All right, sweetie. You can jump down."

Sarah got down from the chair.

"Your turn, Luke!" Sarah had a cute little voice that lilted with energy, and when she turned her face to Deni, she saw that the voice matched the face. Holding her hands up proudly, she said, "See? Clean."

Luke compliantly got up on the chair and dunked his hands into the water. Kay spoke softly to him as she scrubbed the dirt off. "How old did you say you are, Luke?"

"Five."

"Do you go to school?"

"I'm gonna be in kindergarten. I was real smart in preschool, wasn't I, Aaron?"

Aaron's arms came unfolded. "Yeah, Luke. You were the smartest kid in the class."

Deni's hostility toward the oldest boy faded a little. He seemed to care for his younger siblings. Maybe he wasn't a total loss.

Luke looked more human as he jumped down from the chair with a clean face and hands. Joey stepped up and moved the chair. "I don't need to get up there. I'm tall enough. I can wash myself."

Kay backed off and let him soap up, then waited until he'd rinsed. Then he got a handful of water and smeared it on his face, doing a haphazard job of wiping it clean. She handed him a towel. "That's better. Don't you feel better now?"

He shrugged.

Aaron stepped up next. "It's not that I don't make them bathe," he said like a father embarrassed about his poor parenting skills. "It's just that we never have enough water."

Kay looked into his face as she talked to him. "I don't know how you did it, Aaron. Taking such good care of your brothers and sister without any of the things you needed."

He glanced at her suspiciously, as if questioning her sincerity.

"I'm serious, Aaron. Your mother is going to be proud of you when we find her."

"You won't find her," he muttered.

Kay frowned. "What makes you say that?"

"Because she doesn't want to be found. She took off for a reason, you know."

"And what reason is that?"

"She always thought there was something better somewhere else," he said. "Maybe she went to find it."

Deni's heart plummeted.

Sarah pulled the thumb out of her mouth. "Mama's favorite color was green."

Joey turned on her. "You don't know what her favorite color was."

"Do too!"

"*Your* favorite color is green."

Sarah smiled then. "Yep. I like green too."

As much as Deni wanted to nurse her anger, she was having a hard time maintaining it. She finished setting the table. "Time to eat," she said more softly. "Jeff and Beth, go get some chairs from the dining room."

As her brother and sister headed out, Logan came back in with red eyes. Doug followed him in and nodded to him.

Logan slid his hands into his pockets and looked at the floor. "I apologize for being rude," he said to the children.

A canned speech if Deni had ever heard one.

The four just stared at him, then took their places at the table as Jeff and Beth brought the extra chairs in.

ELEVEN

DENI HAD TO HAND IT TO HER MOTHER. SHE WAS determined.

Beth did kitchen detail while the rest of the family went to the lake to bring back as many barrels of water as they could. The cursory washing of the new kids' hands and faces had gotten them through dinner, but now her mother was dead-set on getting the kids completely clean. She'd washed them out in the backyard, where she could scrub without making a mess.

Her dad had helped, turning it into a game of sorts, making the younger three kids feel like they were playing rather than bathing. Aaron, however, looked as if he couldn't believe the indignities. He brooded like Huck Finn being scrubbed by the Widow Douglas.

What kind of mother would abandon her four children, especially at a time like this? Deni couldn't even imagine, but tomorrow she planned to find out. She was going with her dad to Sandwood Place Apartments tomorrow morning to look through their things, hoping to find some clue as to where their mother could be.

But what would they do if they found her? Drag her back and force her to be a mother? No, the kids' best hope was to find grandparents, or aunts and uncles, who could raise them. Their mother was unfit.

Deni's mother was soaking wet by the time she came into the house after scrubbing the kids' clothes clean. Since it was almost dark, she brought the wet garments in and hung them over the shower stall in the bathroom. Hopefully, they would be dry by morning.

While Deni worked on Sarah's tangles, her father held a pow-wow upstairs with the boys, trying to get as much information as he could about who their mother was and what friends she might be staying with.

Sarah seemed more than content with all the attention being shown her. She sat on Deni's lap, turning the pages of a children's book that Beth had pulled from her bookshelf.

"Your house is pretty," she said. "And your TV is big!"

Deni glanced at the forty-eight inch television sitting in the corner. "Yes, it is."

Sarah looked up at her. "Can we watch it?"

Deni smiled. "It doesn't work."

The child's face fell. "Neither does ours."

"Nobody's TV works right now."

Beth got down on her knees in front of them. "Sarah, if the TV worked, what would you watch?"

"Wiggles," Sarah said without blinking. "I have a tape with all their songs, but it don't work, either."

Deni knew the Wiggles were like a rock band for preschoolers—four silly men dressed in bright colors, singing songs that children loved. She wished she'd watched that show even once, instead of surfing past it. "Can you sing me one?"

Sarah slid off Deni's lap, turned to face her, and launched into song, complete with hand motions. She was cuter than Dakota Fanning in *I Am Sam*.

If Deni ever found this little girl's mom, she would personally ream her. A woman like that didn't deserve the love and respect of an innocent child like Sarah.

"You know what?" Beth said. "I've been thinking about writing a play. All the little kids in Oak Hollow could be in it. We need some entertainment around here."

"Luke was in a play one time," Sarah lilted. "Aaron took us. His teacher made him a tree!"

Aaron took them. Why hadn't their mother? That angry, belligerent street kid had cared for his siblings all this time. Deni was the oldest child in her family. What if she'd been responsible for her siblings at age nine?

Shame beat through her for thinking of these kids as trash. Aaron had kept them alive and together. Deni had known something about desperation herself, when she was on the road. Given the same set of circumstances, she might have become a thief too.

Surely there were relatives who could love kids like this.

UPSTAIRS IN LOGAN'S ROOM, DOUG HAD HIS HANDS FULL with Aaron and his brothers. He knew that when the family went to sleep, the boys were likely to rob them again and return home. For the past four months, since the killer in the neighborhood had been found, Doug had been able to sleep with relative peace. But tonight was going to be a long night. He had to convince the children it was in their best interests to stay.

But Aaron was having none of it.

"Look, Mister, I know you're trying to help us and everything, but we don't need your help. I can take care of my sister and brothers."

"You can't take care of them by stealing, Aaron. That's wrong, and it's dangerous. You could get shot."

"I'm not afraid," Aaron said.

Jeff sat on the bed, staring at the angry kid. "Guys, wouldn't it be better if you were in a clean house on decent beds without all that junk around? Without that smell? If you didn't have to go scrounging for water and food? If you had somebody looking out for you so you didn't have to leave those little kids by themselves while you go out stealing?"

"What about Sarah?" Doug added. "She likes being fussed over. Don't you think she deserves that? And little Luke hasn't seemed too repulsed by Miss Kay's affections. He needs somebody, even if you don't."

Luke hung his head, as if he'd betrayed his brother. Doug could see the distrust in Aaron's eyes.

"I know what you're gonna do," Aaron said, the corners of his mouth twitching. "Now that the sheriff knows about us, you're gonna get him to get us into foster homes. You don't want us. You'll probably dump us on the first person who'll take us. You only took us because your wife made you."

The boy was more perceptive than he thought. "I brought you home because it was the right thing, Aaron."

Aaron breathed a mirthless laugh. "I'm not stupid, you know. Nobody here wants us, and that's just fine."

Doug rubbed his face, hoping that he hadn't just brought danger into his home. The kid was hostile, and desperate or not, he broke laws without batting an eye.

But what else could Doug do? He couldn't very well send them home, and turning them over to the sheriff was out of the question. Kay would never forgive him. He'd just have to stay on guard tonight, to make sure they didn't clean them out. "Look, I know we got off to a bad start, but it was only because you took our food. We just need to start over. We brought you home because we care, but I can't put you in a cage. If you decide to leave, I want you to think hard about whether you're going to something better than I'm offering you."

Joey sat down on the carpet, crossing his legs in front of him. The boy had dark circles under his eyes. He looked weary with the burden of life. He looked up at Aaron with a pleading face. "We could stay here for a little while, Aaron," he said. "It was good to have hot food tonight."

Aaron just looked at the floor.

As tough as the kid was, he was scared. Whatever Doug had against him, Aaron did care for his siblings.

Sighing, Doug set his hand on Aaron's shoulder. "Aaron, I promise you, no foster homes, period. Trust me. The sheriff isn't going to take you away from us until your relatives are found."

"That could be a long time," Aaron said. "You don't even know what you're getting into."

Doug felt like he was talking to a peer, a grown man made stronger through suffering. It was hard to believe this was a little kid.

"Why do you say that, Aaron? I have four kids. Why do you think I don't know?"

"Because I told you, you won't find my mama. If she wanted to come home, she would. And we haven't seen our grandma and pop since before Sarah was born. Mama kept moving us so they couldn't find us."

"Why?" Jeff asked. "Were they mean?"

"No, they were real nice," Joey piped in.

Aaron shot his brother a withering look. "Mama said they were trying to get her arrested, and if they did, we'd be split up."

So their mother had put that idea in their heads, making them fear it worse than being alone. "Why would they have wanted your mother in jail?"

Aaron kept his eyes fixed on his feet. "She mighta stole from them or something. I don't really know."

"Do you know where they live?"

"They used to live here, but they moved before I was born. They used to come visit us, but they'd fight so bad with Mama that they quit coming. And she never took us to visit them after that."

Doug hoped he could find an address in their apartment tomorrow. "I'll bet they've missed you and wanted to see you."

"Bet they haven't," Aaron said. "And if you don't find them, you won't be able to keep that promise you made."

This kid might not be afraid to break into homes at the risk of getting shot, but he was terrified of losing his family. Doug respected that. "I know you're worried about your family, and I admire you for that, Aaron. You've had a hard row to hoe these last few months. Despite your methods, you've done a good job of keeping your brothers and sister fed, but I'm going to ask you to do something that doesn't come naturally for you. I'm going to ask you to trust me."

The boy looked up at him, studying his eyes.

"Just hang around here for a few days, and if you don't see that life is better for you, then you're free to go."

"Besides," Jeff said. "The sheriff knows where you live now. If you go home, he'll put you into foster care for sure."

Aaron clearly hadn't thought of that. His ears reddened. "You shouldn't have brought him. We'd have given the food back, what was left of it."

"Don't you get it?" Jeff asked. "You just can't go around breaking into people's houses! And four little kids shouldn't be living alone!"

Doug quieted Jeff with a raised hand. He was tired, so tired. But these children needed him, like it or not. "Look, I believe this was all a God thing. I think he was looking out for you when he led you to our house this morning."

"God didn't lead us nowhere," Aaron said. "We came here ourselves because we knew it was a rich neighborhood and most of the people would be at the meeting."

Doug smiled. "That's what you think, but I believe God's involved in everything in our lives, and this happened so we would find you and take you in. I'm not saying it's going to be easy. Nothing's easy these days. You'll be expected to work in the garden and help us do our chores to keep things going. I'll expect obedience from you like I do from my own children. But in return, I'll give you food, water, and a nice safe place to live. You won't have to worry about people taking things from you or hurting you. And where you were living was not a very safe place."

"Tell me about it."

"For the sake of your brothers and sister, just try to settle in. I can see that your family is the most important thing to you. Can I trust you to stay?"

Aaron just stared at him.

"Just for a few days," Doug said. "Give me a chance to try to find your family. I'll treat you like my own kids if you'll treat me with the same respect they do. And you'll always have the option of running away later if you decide to. Can I trust you to do that, Aaron?"

Joey and Luke looked up at the boy, their eyes full of hope. He looked from one to the other. Finally, grudgingly, he shrugged. "Don't see a choice. We'll give it a try, but I'm not making no promises."

"That's good enough for me," Doug said.

TWELVE

DENI HELPED TUCK THE TWO SMALLER CHILDREN INTO bed in Beth's bedroom that night, while her father helped the older two settle in. She felt the need to lock up everything she had that she didn't want stolen, but something told her not to. Maybe these kids would respond to being treated more like treasures than trash. She would try it with the younger two, anyway.

The two seemed content as she tucked them into bed, and Sarah, who had pulled a nasty little teddy bear out of her backpack, clutched it against her as she sucked her thumb. She looked so sweet lying there with her hair combed and those tendrils falling into her eyes.

Deni led them in a prayer, something the children seemed unfamiliar with, then kissed them both goodnight and left them with smiles on their faces. Then she and Beth got into her own bed.

"She's so cute," Beth whispered. "I hope we get to keep her."

Deni pushed Beth's blonde hair out of her eyes. "What about the other three?"

"Luke is cute too, but I don't know about Joey and Aaron. They're kind of scary. I keep thinking of when I came in and found them today. They looked so evil."

"You gotta hand it to them, though. They do seem to care about each other."

"Think they'll stay all night?"

"I hope so, for Luke and Sarah's sake," Deni said. "But who knows what Aaron and Joey will do?"

Beth got up on her elbow and looked at the doorway. "Let's lock it, Deni."

"No, we have to leave it open so I can hear if one of them cries."

"Or if they sneak out?"

"Yeah. If they try, we need to stop them. Mom and Dad can't hear from downstairs." She blew out the lamp. "I doubt I'll sleep much tonight."

A NOISE WOKE DENI IN THE MIDDLE OF THE NIGHT, AND SHE SAT upright. She heard a child crying. Beth lay beside her, undisturbed.

The crying grew louder, so Deni slid out of bed and felt her way through the doorway. She moved into the dark hallway. As her eyes adjusted, she saw little Sarah standing there, hand against the wall, lost in her new surroundings.

Deni stooped in front of her. "Sarah? What's the matter?"

The child's screaming went up an octave. "Aaron!"

"I'm here, Sarah." Aaron emerged from the darkness of Logan's room, and he picked her up. She was too big for a boy of his size to hold like that, but her weight didn't seem to faze him.

"I'm scared!" Sarah cried.

"Don't be scared." His voice was a gentle whisper. "We're at those people's house, remember?"

Her crying quieted then, as if it had taken his reminder to put things into context. She looked up at Deni.

"What scared you?" Deni asked.

Sarah sniffled and whimpered.

"She has bad dreams," Aaron said. "She's used to sleeping with us, so when she wakes up nights I'm usually real close."

Deni stroked the child's curls. "Well, why don't you come sleep with Beth and me? I have a nice big bed."

Sarah rubbed her eyes.

"It's okay," Aaron said. "I can take care of her. She can come sleep with me."

"No, I want to sleep with Deni!"

Deni smiled and took her from her brother's arms. "We girls gotta stick together, don't we, kiddo?"

Aaron clearly didn't like it.

"It's okay, Aaron. Let her sleep with Beth and me. It'll be all right."

"But what about Luke? He doesn't want to sleep by hisself."

"Then you can go sleep with him," Deni said.

He sighed as if he'd been forced to give in, and finally Deni took the little girl back to her room and put her on the bed between herself and Beth. Beth turned over. "What's going on?"

"Sarah had a nightmare," Deni said. "She's going to sleep with us."

"Cool." Beth moved over so Sarah could share her pillow, then she put her arm around the little girl. "I like having sleeping buddies."

Sarah put her thumb in her mouth and grinned again. "I like having sleeping bunnies too," she said around the thumb.

Deni and Beth grinned as the little girl closed her eyes and drifted back off to sleep.

THIRTEEN

THE CHILDREN WERE STILL THERE THE NEXT MORNING, ALL three boys piled into their bed. In Deni's bed, Sarah lay like a little ball between herself and Beth.

The four kids devoured breakfast as if it might be their last meal for a while. Then, as they all cleaned up, Deni rode with Aaron and her father to the Sandwood Place Apartments to look for clues about the kids' mother's whereabouts and find the grandparents' address.

The apartments didn't look quite as threatening in the morning light as her parents had described. It was too early for most of the loiterers to be out, though one woman cooked eggs on a griddle on the grill. The smell from the garbage piled behind the place overpowered the scent of the eggs.

"You won't find nothing," Aaron said. "I know everything that's there." But reluctantly, he gave Doug the key.

Doug unlocked the door, and they stepped into the rancid apartment. An overpowering smell of human waste almost knocked Deni over. She covered her face.

"You all right?" Doug asked.

She nodded, trying not to gag. "They *lived* in this?"

"Yeah. Pretty bad, huh? It looks like the commode is stopped up, but they kept using it anyway."

"It's not my fault." Shame colored Aaron's face as he went to close the bathroom door. "It wouldn't flush."

Deni coughed. "You could flush with water."

"We never had enough. Plus, the neighbors' toilets were backed up too. They said the sewage system wasn't working."

Deni turned her astonished eyes to her dad. "How come ours works?"

"Because we have a septic tank."

Deni stepped over the piles of items the kids had stolen and discarded to look in the two bedrooms. There was a double bed in one room, and a mattress on the floor in the other. "Five people lived in this apartment. Where did everybody sleep?"

"We slept fine. Don't worry about it."

Aaron was taking her reactions personally, as if he were responsible for providing for the family. She felt sorry for him.

She went around the boxes and into the mother's bedroom.

The kids had clearly taken over that room, and it too held plunder they'd looted from people's homes. Their mother's room had a set of beaten-up bookshelves with a few books on them; her closet was piled high with wadded clothes. She clearly didn't own a hanger.

Deni picked up a pair of jeans and held them up to herself. "She must be about my size."

Aaron took the jeans out of her hands and returned them to the closet. She glanced down at him. The corners of his mouth quivered, as if he was trying not to cry. Only then did she realize that this was difficult for the kid. They had barged in to rifle through his mom's things—things that the boy probably held dear. She would have to be more sensitive.

Deni went to the bookcase and perused the titles. "Hey, look. That's my yearbook."

Her dad turned and regarded the book in her hand. "Crockett High? She must have been a student there."

"She was," Aaron said.

Deni sat down on the rumpled bed and opened the book. "This was my sophomore year. What's her name again?"

"Jessie Gatlin." There was a note of dread in Aaron's voice.

That sounded familiar. Frowning, Deni turned the pages. "When did she graduate?"

"She didn't," he said. "She dropped out in the tenth grade."

"Then she was in my class." She found the G's and saw Jessie's picture. "Oh, wow. I remember her now."

"You do?" Doug took the book and studied the picture.

Deni swept her hair behind her ear and looked up at Aaron. "She was pregnant that year, wasn't she? That's why she quit."

Aaron shrugged.

"But that was only seven years ago," Doug said. "Must have been with Joey."

Aaron didn't answer.

Deni's eyes rounded. "Oh yeah, I remember." There had been another pregnancy ... when she was in eighth grade and Jessie was in ninth. It had caused quite a scandal.

That must have been Aaron.

She'd come back the next year to repeat the ninth grade and wound up in Deni's class.

She took the book back from her father. "Aaron, can we take this home with us? I want to read the notes her friends wrote in here. Maybe some of them are still around and know where she is."

"I don't care." He turned and left the room, his hands crammed into the pockets of his baggy jeans. She watched him cross the hall to the other room and begin sorting through his things.

Doug sat down next to her. "What else do you remember about her, Deni?"

Deni kept her voice low so Aaron wouldn't hear. "She hung around with a rough crowd, Dad. They did a lot of drugs. Most of them never graduated."

Doug studied Jessie's picture again. "That's a shame. She was a pretty girl."

"Yeah, that's why her kids are so cute. But 'pretty' wasn't the image she was going for. I think she was into shock value. Black lipstick, thick black eyeliner, piercings, tattoos ... It was hard to see through all that stuff."

"Maybe she's still friends with some of that group. Do you think you can find them?"

"Maybe," she said. "I'll ask Mark and Chris to help."

They put the book down and began rummaging through her chest of drawers. Finding nothing helpful, Deni looked under the bed. "Oh no. Dad, look at this."

When her dad turned, Deni held up a Ziploc bag of new syringes and several little white slips of paper.

"It's heroin," Deni said.

Her father shot her a look, as if asking how she knew.

"A girl in my freshman dorm was an addict," Deni said. "She flunked out that semester. But they peel the heroin off these papers. They don't throw them away because when they run out, they scrape whatever is left off the papers for one more fix."

"So Jessie was an addict."

"I'd say so."

"Maybe that explains her disappearance. When the outage happened, it was hard enough to find food, much less drugs—especially with no money. A lot of addicts probably had to detox without wanting to. It could have been bad."

Deni nodded. But could that have killed her? It seemed unlikely.

Her father waded toward the closet. "Here's her purse," he said, and lifted it from where it hung by its strap from the doorknob. He opened her wallet. "License ... credit card ... she sure didn't take anything with her."

He dug through the purse's contents, then held up a marijuana joint and a bottle of prescription painkillers, plus something rolled up in tinfoil. Deni watched as he unwrapped it. Another syringe. This one had been used. "Right here where any of the kids could have found it," he said. "Unbelievable."

Deni glanced into the other room. Aaron was on his knees sorting through the contents of a box. "Dad, if she disappeared intentionally, don't you think she would have taken her purse with her? Especially if she had dope in it?"

"Seems like it. But the kids are under the impression she left on her own. Maybe it was typical of her to leave without her purse. It's hard to predict what an addict might do. You never know if she was sane when she made the decision to leave."

"Yeah, but would any mother really leave her kids alone at a time like this? Could anybody be that selfish?"

"Of course, they could," Doug said. "We've already seen what people are willing to do out of selfishness. It's no surprise. And addicts neglect their kids all the time. That's why Human Services stays so busy."

She opened a cabinet and bent down to look. A stack of papers sat on a shelf. Deni pulled out the top few. They were brochures about drug rehabs. Had Jessie been looking for a way to break her addiction? Deni flipped through the stack: page after page of medical records, prescriptions for painkillers, xeroxed copies of other people's driver's licenses and credit cards.

It looked as if Jessie's drug-buying operation was a full-time job.

She flipped through the xeroxed identities and stopped when she came to a Gatlin. "Bingo."

"What?" Doug asked.

"Looks like this might be a relative." She handed him the xeroxed page with a woman's driver's license. "And there's an address."

He studied the card. "Yeah, but this expired five years ago. Tuscaloosa address."

"Maybe they still live there."

He crossed the hall and took the page to Aaron. "Aaron, do you know who this is?"

The boy took the page. "My grandma."

"Great," he said. "Then we've got an address."

Aaron said nothing.

Deni pulled more papers out of the cabinet and a handwritten letter fell out. She picked it up and skimmed it. It was from Jessie's parents, dated three years before. The paper was limp and wilted, as though it had been handled often. "Dad, come here."

Her dad came back into Jessie's room.

"What?"

"A letter from her parents," she said in a low voice.

He looked over her shoulder. "What does it say?"

Deni read quietly.

Dear Jessie,

We can't watch you ruin your life anymore. These drugs are killing you and you know it. It's one thing to do that to yourself but another thing entirely when your children are involved. Your kids deserve better than a drug-addicted mother who can't love them enough to clean herself up.

Your father and I have decided to file for custody. It breaks our heart to have you declared an unfit mother, but that's what you are. We've turned our heads over the years when you've stolen from us, lied to us, abused us, even been violent against us, but we cannot turn our heads when our grandchildren are suffering. We've tried offering you treatment, wasted thousands of dollars trying to get you help, and believed your lies so many times. But nothing has changed. It's only gotten worse. If you care anything about your children, you can surrender them to us now before we have to get the state involved. We love you and pray for you, but we realize there's nothing more we can do for you. It can't be all about you anymore. It has to be about your children for once. Please do the right thing.

Mom and Dad

Doug sat down on the bed and glanced toward the other room. "Man."

"They sound like decent people, Dad. Like they love the kids. It probably would be good for them to raise them."

"So why haven't they come for them already?" Doug folded up the letter. "I'll take this to the sheriff and let him try to contact them."

"I think you and Mom should do it. Sheriff Scarbrough is way too busy right now. He might not get around to it for a long time."

"But he might have ways to get in touch with them faster. Maybe he could send a messenger by car. The sooner we reach them, the better."

IN HIS BEDROOM, AARON FOUND A GARBAGE BAG AND PACKED more stuff they would need to take back to the Brannings'. He threw in a ragtag Barbie doll with tangled hair and a torn dress for Sarah to play with, Joey's favorite baseball cap, a Superman cape for Luke ...

Peering across the hall, he made sure Doug and Deni were busy. Then he went to the hallway and opened the cover for the air conditioner filter. A small revolver lay there, right where he'd hidden it. It had been his mother's hiding place for both of their guns. The sheriff had taken the other one from him. But he hadn't found this one. He took the gun out and stuffed it into his garbage bag. Now he'd feel a little more in charge.

And if anyone messed with his family, he would be able to stand up to them. The guns had always protected him before.

He started to close the vent, but something sticking out from the bottom of the filter caught his eye. He pulled the filter out and looked behind it. A stack of letters was bundled there, bound in a rubberband. He grabbed it and glanced through the envelopes. They were all from his grandparents. Why would his mother have kept them hidden? They must have been important to her. He thought of telling Doug, but decided not to. He'd read them first. Then, if it sounded like his grandparents were good enough to take care of his brothers and sister, he'd hand them over.

But if they were like his mother said, then he'd toss them into the fire ... and no one would ever find them.

FOURTEEN

WHEN THEY GOT BACK HOME, DENI WENT TO THE LAKE TO get water. The empty lot where everyone came to get water from the lake was bottlenecked with the morning rush. So much would change when the well was finished. Already, the neighborhood association had forbidden people from washing their laundry in the lake, since the place was getting so polluted.

Leaning on the rolling garbage can she used to carry water, she waited her turn. She saw Chris at the water's edge, dipping a bucket into the water and dumping it into a rolling garbage can of her own. Chris's nursing scrubs were soaked. She worked for the one doctor in the neighborhood—Derek Morton. He'd set up a clinic in his home, and Judith (Deni's next-door neighbor) and Chris took turns working as his nurses. He paid them with whatever he bartered for his services —vegetables, bread, eggs, and sometimes meat from patients who hunted. Once Chris had gotten a chicken. Whatever she earned helped her family.

As she waited for Chris to finish, Deni saw her friend Mark coming up the street with a barrel on wheels. As he passed, the crowd parted, as if he carried a machete and intended to use it. Deni had tried to tell everyone that Mark had had nothing to do with his father's crimes, but most considered her naive. Still, she knew Mark's heart. He'd been devastated by his father's actions, and the shame had kept him home for two weeks. But then he'd emerged to help

73

with the work on the well and his family's chores. He still had his bad days, and the smiles he'd once worn were fewer and farther between. The neighbors' cold shoulders only made things worse. But Deni and Chris had made sure the entire neighborhood knew the two of them were still his friends.

As he approached, Chris finished filling her container, dropped her bucket in, and began trying to roll it over tree roots and grass to get it back to the street. Mark left his barrel and came to help her. He easily lifted her garbage can up to the street. He'd gotten so much stronger since the outage. Though he'd already been doing manual labor as a carpenter before the outage, the hard work post-outage was so much more strenuous than anything anyone could have expected. His arms and shoulders had developed a bulk they hadn't had before, and his skin was tanned dark from the time he spent outdoors. He wore his hair a little shorter than he had before, to combat the heat. He looked like a mature man now, rather than the teenager she'd grown up with.

Deni joined them at the street. "Chris, I hope you're not going to work in those wet scrubs."

"As a matter of fact I am," Chris said. "As soon as I get the water home, I have to report for work." She wiped her blonde waves back from her forehead. "But it's so hot they'll probably dry before I get there." She shaded her eyes in the sunlight and looked at Deni. "Hey, did I hear right? Someone said your parents took in four extra children."

"You heard right."

"Four children?" Mark asked. "What's up with that?"

She launched into the story, ending with this morning's search of the apartment. "Do you guys remember a girl named Jessie Gatlin?"

Chris frowned. "I don't think so."

"Yeah, you do," Mark said. "Remember the girl who got pregnant in eighth grade?"

"Oh yeah." Chris's eyes widened as the memory came back. "Talk about a scandal. She came back to school after the baby, didn't she?"

"Not until the next year. She repeated ninth grade and wound up in our class."

"Then she got pregnant again the next year."

Mark nodded. "I don't remember seeing her after that."

"I think that was the end of her education," Deni said. "But she's the kids' mother, and now she's disappeared, so we're trying to find her. I've been trying to remember who her friends were."

Mark looked at Chris. "Didn't she hang out with John Carrigan and Lacy Frye and that group?"

"Yeah," Chris said. "Druggies, mostly."

"You got that right," Mark said. "Carrigan's in prison now for dealing."

Deni's mind raced as memories rushed back. "I wonder if she still hangs around with those guys. Anybody remember where Lacy used to live?"

"She lived across the street from the high school," Chris said. "I have no idea if she's still there. Remember the house with the gnomes in the front yard?"

Deni remembered. The kids had teased Lacy mercilessly about her yard. "Well, that's a place to start. I think I'll go over there today. See if she still lives there, and if she knows where Jessie is."

"If you ask me," Mark said, "a woman who leaves her four children to fend for themselves at a time like this—she should probably just stay lost."

"But what if something happened to her?" Chris asked. "I mean, wouldn't that be sad if she was in trouble somewhere and no one ever came looking for her?"

"Who knows?" Deni said. "If there's ever a time she could get clean, it would be now, wouldn't it? I mean, drugs aren't any easier to get than anything else. She certainly doesn't have any money. I'm going to go try to find Lacy Frye today and see if I can get any information."

Mark took off his baseball cap and raked his hair back. "I'll come with you."

"Great," she said. "Dad has his well shift, so he can't go, and I really didn't want to go alone."

Mark helped Deni get her water, then she rolled it back home and waited for him. He rode his bike over a little while later.

Though Mark was one of the first ones in the neighborhood to convert his Volkswagen into a horse and buggy, he preferred to take his bicycle on short jaunts like this one. Deni rode her bike alongside him as they headed toward their old alma mater to look for Lacy Frye.

Mark seemed quiet as they rode.

"Are you okay?" she asked.

"Yeah, I'm fine. Don't worry about me." He forced a smile and changed the subject. "So, how was that letter from the Craigster yesterday?"

Deni didn't answer for a moment. Part of her wanted to slap on a happy face and pretend the letter was all she'd hoped. But she didn't have to pretend with Mark. "It was a little ... disappointing. I had hoped for poetry, but I got a travelogue instead."

"A travelogue? What do you mean?"

"I mean, it was a play-by-play of what happened after the outage. Not much about him missing me, or our relationship. And he left it a little open-ended, saying if we're meant to be together, we will be."

Mark rode quietly for a moment. "Well, that's true, isn't it?"

"If?" She shot Mark a look. "I wouldn't have said *if*. I made up my mind that we were meant to be together the day I said I'd marry him."

"Well, you know, he is a guy. Words aren't always our best thing."

"They are for him. He writes brilliant legal briefs, and he's a fantastic debater."

"That's not the same, and you know it."

Her mouth was dry. "I just wish he'd written me more than one letter. I sent him a whole stack."

Again, silence. Mark slowed down as they came to a stop sign. "You care if I read the letter? Maybe I could read between the lines, give you a guy's interpretation."

Well, maybe he could shed light on it. She stopped at the stop sign and pulled the folded letter out of her pocket. She'd already read it six times that morning, but her feelings hadn't changed.

He got off the bike as he read. "Well, see? He said he missed you."

Deni sighed. "Keep in mind that we haven't talked to or seen each other since May. That I was on a plane just minutes before the outage, and for all he knew I could be dead."

He went back to the letter. For several moments, he read silently. As he did, his face grew harder, as if he saw the lack of feeling that had crushed her.

So it wasn't just her.

"He says if there were some way to get to you, he would."

Deni looked at the words again. "Yeah, that really hurt. There *is* some way, and I know it, because I tried it. He just doesn't want to."

"Come on — that may not be true."

"Oh no? Read the rest."

Aloud, Mark read, " 'I guess our wedding isn't going to come off like we planned. But if it's meant to be, I guess we'll wait for each other. I really miss you. Hope this will all be over soon, and we can get together again.' "

She blinked away the tears threatening her, determined not to cry in front of Mark. Mark sat down on the curb, resting his wrists on his knees. "Well, I can see how you would be disappointed, but he might have written it in a hurry. He also may have been a lot more emotional about this than it seems."

"Yeah, right."

"No, I'm serious. You know how guys are when they're emotional, and instead of talking more, they talk less. Like they're afraid any extra words will get caught in their throat, and they might start crying like a wimp. Well, maybe he was writing like that. Afraid if he got too emotional in the letter, he'd get emotional in real life, and maybe he was in the office and didn't want anyone to see him like that."

Mark's eyes were sincere. She wanted him to be right. She took the letter back, and scanned it again. *Was* there hidden emotion there? Some kind of necessary restraint? "Do you really think that could be it?"

"Sure, I do. I bet you get another letter in a few days, and you'll see. He'd probably been wishing he could talk to you all this time, saving up all the stuff he wanted to tell you about his experiences with the outage. And let's face it, it was pretty exciting stuff. When the post office opened, he probably rushed to get it all down. It's kind of like he had to get all that out before he could get down to feelings. Those'll come later. You'll see."

It made sense. Maybe she was jumping to conclusions. The pain in her heart gave birth to hope. "He is like that. I mean, he kind of has a one-track mind. He does always blurt out everything he's saved up whenever we talk."

"See? That's all it is, Deni."

She blew out a sigh and sat down next to him. "I feel like a bratty schoolgirl who hasn't gotten her way."

"Don't," he said. "I'm sure he loves you and misses you like crazy. He'd be insane not to."

The sweet words took her by surprise, jolting her heart. Her lips softened into a smile. "Thank you, Mark."

"I'm just saying, you've agreed to marry the guy. He's gotta know how lucky he is. No way would any guy in his right mind just blow that off. Trust me, he's thinking about you constantly."

Drawing in a deep breath, she held his soft gaze for a moment before he looked away. Smiling, she folded the letter back up. She hadn't thought that anyone could make her feel better about this—but Mark had done it. "You're a good friend, Mark."

He smiled. "Yeah, well, tell that to the neighborhood lynch mobs."

As they resumed their ride, Deni wished she could return the favor and make him feel better too. But the neighbors' disdain for him was obvious. There was no way to sugarcoat that.

FIFTEEN

THE GNOMES WERE STILL IN LACY FRYE'S YARD, THOUGH they looked older and more fragile. The high schoolers across the street used to have names for them, and occasionally one would get stolen and turn up at a pep rally or a football game, or on the principal's desk. Usually the perpetrator returned it to its yard the next day. Who would want to keep it, after all?

Poor Lacy. She must have been constantly embarrassed.

Deni and Mark pulled into the driveway. They rolled their bikes with them up the sidewalk to the front door. Mark knocked. A woman in a cotton housedress answered the door.

"Yeah?"

Deni recognized the woman. She was the one who was always out tending the haphazard garden.

"Mrs. Frye?" Mark asked.

"Yes."

Deni spoke up. "I'm Deni Branning, and this is Mark Green. We went to high school with Lacy and were wondering if she still lives here."

Her mother turned back and yelled over her shoulder. "Lacy! For you!"

Deni looked at Mark. They'd hit pay dirt.

They heard footsteps coming down the stairs, then Lacy came to the door. Her eyes were dull as she regarded her visitors.

She had changed. In high school, she had dyed her dishwater blonde hair black, but now it was bleached to a platinum color. Her gold roots had grown out about an inch, giving it an interesting two-tone color. She was skin and bones—not the hard-work kind of skinny, but the kind that accompanied sickness.

"Yeah?" she asked.

"Lacy, do you remember us? Deni and Mark from high school?"

"Yeah, I remember. What do you want?"

Her tone was hostile, suspicious. For a moment, Deni wondered if she'd ever been rude to the girl. She probably had, back when her head was bigger and she thought more of herself than she should.

"We were wondering if you still hung around with Jessie Gatlin," Mark said.

Lacy's expression tightened. "Why do you want to know?"

"We're worried about her," Deni said. "My family found out that her four children have been living by themselves since right after the outage. Jessie's disappeared, and we think something might have happened to her."

Lacy peered at them from between her long bangs. "How do you know she wants to be found?"

Deni stared at her. "We don't. But she has a responsibility to her children. If she doesn't want them, we need for her to designate a relative that we can get in touch with. Do you know where she is?"

Lacy glanced back over her shoulder. Her mother was listening from a few feet behind her. "I haven't seen her since before the outage."

Deni wasn't sure she believed her. She glanced at Mark and saw doubt on his face as well. She turned back. "What was she like the last time you saw her?"

"What do you mean, what was she like?"

"I mean, was she still on drugs after the outage? Was she withdrawing?"

Lacy glanced back again, then stepped outside and pulled the door closed behind her so her mother couldn't hear.

Now maybe they'd get somewhere.

"It was bad," Lacy said in a quiet voice. "She woulda gnawed off an arm for a fix."

Deni tried not to linger on that image. "We found syringes in her purse. What was her drug?"

"Crank," Lacy said.

Just as Deni had thought. Crank was one of the street names for heroin. Besides her acquaintance with a classmate who used the stuff, she'd done some research on the drug for a speech class in college. Heroin was one of the most difficult drugs to detox from.

"So, let me ask you this," Mark said. "If she was addicted to heroin when the outage happened, and she couldn't get anymore, what do you think she did about it?"

"Same thing the rest of us did," Lacy said. "She spent whatever cash she still had on getting what she needed, and then she ran out. And like the rest of us, she was out of luck."

"What happened?" Deni asked. "Did you get sick?"

"Sick isn't the word," Lacy said. "It's painful and miserable. Your bones and muscles hurt, you vomit, you can't sleep, and you think you're going to die. Nothing better get between you and the needle."

"How long does it last?"

"A week really bad. Some of the symptoms go on for weeks. Months, even."

Clearly, Lacy was still in bad shape. "You said you found syringes?" she asked, desperation tightening her face. "Did she have any dope?"

If she had, Deni knew Lacy would have done whatever it took to get her hands on it. "No," she said. "We didn't find any."

Lacy shrugged. "Figures. Nobody has any."

"So the outage basically saved your life," Mark said.

"Or ended it, depending on how you look at it."

Deni tried to imagine what that meant. Did Lacy really feel that her life as an addict was more real than this one? How sad. She hoped Lacy could stay away from drugs long enough to think rationally again. "Jessie's kids say she hasn't been seen since two weeks after the outage."

"Sounds about right. She probably had some dope on her or was able to get some for the week after the outage. After that, with no transportation to bring the stuff in, the dealers were running out, and there was no cash to pay for it. She probably got sick."

"Do you think she would have put herself in harm's way to get more heroin?"

Lacy started to laugh. "Of course. She would have sold her body ... one of her children ... *all* of her children. Those cravings, they control you, and a lot of people I know were in dire straits when the drugs weren't coming anymore." She studied their faces, then flipped her stringy hair back. "You know, people like you think they're so much better than us. But you're not."

"I wasn't thinking that."

"Yes, you were. You're judging me just like you're judging her."

Deni swallowed. She didn't want to fight with the girl. Lacy looked beaten down enough. "I wasn't judging you, Lacy. I feel bad for you. As much as I drank my first year of college, I could just as easily have been in your shoes."

"You?" Lacy breathed a disbelieving laugh.

"Yeah, me. It just happened that my cravings for being a big shot were stronger than my cravings for a buzz. So I quit drinking."

Mark looked down at her, clearly surprised.

Lacy seemed moved too. "You were always a big shot," she said.

Deni swallowed. "Well, I'm trying to change."

Lacy crossed her arms and looked down at her feet. "Jessie was raped by a neighbor when she was fourteen. She got pregnant, and everybody turned on her."

Deni hadn't known that. Everyone had just thought she was easy. If someone had just told them...

But who was she kidding? It wouldn't have stopped the gossip.

"So she started using to numb the pain?" Mark asked quietly.

"Something like that."

"She was pregnant again in tenth grade," Deni said. "She never came back to school."

"No, her folks took her and moved to Tuscaloosa after that. They wanted her to start over clean. But she was in too deep. She kept running away. She loved her kids, though. She always brought them with her. Some guy was always willing to put her up ... for a while, at least."

"Then you don't think she would have left her kids intentionally?"

"Not for more than a few hours, or maybe a night."

Deni pulled the notepad out of her back pocket. "Could you tell us some of the guys who've taken her in? Maybe she's with one of them."

"Doubt it. Most of them dumped her after she got pregnant. They always wanted her to get rid of the babies, and she would say she was going to, then before you knew it her stomach was growing. Some of them got real hot about it. One dude beat her to a pulp, but it didn't hurt the baby."

"Who was that?" Deni asked.

"Moe Jenkins, though he'll deny it if you ask him. He's the little girl's daddy."

"Sarah's?"

"That's right."

"Can you tell us where he is?" Mark asked.

She shrugged. "He's a jerk. I don't know where he lives. I see him around sometimes, so I know he's still in town."

Deni wrote his name down. "Lacy, did she keep using during her pregnancies?"

"She said she didn't, but I never knew for sure. They all came out all right, though, so maybe it was true."

As Deni and Mark rode back home, Deni turned the conversation over in her mind. "So what do you think?"

Mark shrugged. "I think when we find her, she probably won't be in any condition to take care of those kids."

"I don't get it," Deni said. "If she loved her kids enough to stay clean while she was pregnant, why wouldn't she love them enough to take care of them? My mom would lay down her life for me."

"Mine too."

"But instead, Jessie winds up so addicted that she'd leave her children to fend for themselves with absolutely no resources."

"It happens all the time," Mark said.

Deni knew that was true. She'd had friends in college who had succumbed to drugs and dropped out, ruining their lives, changing their ambitions, their personalities, their character. But there was always hope for redemption. Hadn't God redeemed her, when she was wallowing in a spiritual pit after her own rebellion? If he hadn't given up on her, maybe there was hope for Lacy Frye and Jessie Gatlin.

"Deni, I have to go work at the well. But don't go visit that Jenkins guy by yourself."

She shook her head. "I'll give his name to my dad and the sheriff, and let them handle that. I'm not brave enough to visit him alone. But I have thought of another way to get the word out that we're looking for her. I've been thinking about starting a newspaper. The *Crockett Times* has been down since the outage, and the *Birmingham News* probably has too. I was thinking I could do one that focused on human interest stories. Like these kids, for instance."

Mark laughed. "That's a great idea. But how would you produce it without Xerox machines and printers?"

"I'd have to handwrite it. Maybe post it on the message boards around town."

"Okay, I can see that."

"I could call attention to the poverty in some of these apartment complexes. Those people don't have any place to get water. I don't know how they're surviving. They have one grill to cook on and they line up for it. Your guess is as good as mine where they're getting their food. They have no place to grow it. All they have is a paved parking lot. Maybe if I called attention to it, people would try to help them."

"I like the idea, Deni. Somebody needs to help them."

"And there are so many other things to write about."

"Wouldn't be any money in it, but it would sure be a great service to the community," Mark said. "I think it's an awesome idea. Sounds like the kind of thing that's right up your alley. And it'll keep your journalism skills fresh."

It would also help keep her mind off Craig, she thought. Busyness was the best medicine she knew.

SIXTEEN

THE WORK THAT AFTERNOON WASN'T AS HARD AS AARON had expected. It was even kind of fun. The Brannings had sent him and Logan to fish for supper, and since he didn't much like Logan, he sat down the pond from him behind a big tree. He tied his pole to a lower branch that hung out over the water, so he had his hands free to read through the letters he'd brought from home. He took all of them out of their envelopes and tried to figure out which letters came first.

His grandma's cursive was small and as neat as a teacher's. She had dated each letter at the top corner. The oldest one was on the bottom, dated six years before.

> *Dear Jessie,*
>
> *I'm sending this to your old apartment in hopes that the post office will forward it. You need to know that as soon as you're found, you'll be arrested. We've filed charges against you for stealing from us.*
>
> *I don't know what you've done with the boys, but I pray you're taking care of them. If you have any sense of right and wrong left inside you, you'll turn them over to us. They don't deserve what you're putting them through.*

He scanned to the end of the letter. There was more of the same. As much as he'd wanted to believe that his mom was wrong about them, he could see that at least some of what she'd said was true. No wonder she wouldn't talk to them. If they were going to have her locked up and take her children away from her, then he didn't blame her for running.

Maybe the endless trail of apartments and live-in arrangements with her boyfriends had been necessary, after all.

He flipped through and found a longer letter.

Dear Jessie,

I pray for you all day long and into the night, then I wake up and pray some more. And I pray for your boys. The guilt eats me up nights, and I go back over every event in your life, thinking where I went wrong, what I should have done differently, wondering how I can get you to see reason. How did it come to this?

He could feel the pain in the words, and he understood the guilt. He'd struggled with it himself, thinking that if he'd just been a better kid, his mother might not have needed to take so many drugs. He thought of the grandmother he remembered—the one who always had a sweet smile for him and baked him cookies and read to him and his brothers at night. The things his mother said about his grandparents had never quite fit with the memories he had of them. Maybe she had lied. Maybe they really were nice like he remembered.

Jessie,

If you'd just come home, we could get you some help. You could get off drugs and get your life on track. You could be the mother that your children deserve. You could stop destroying yourself.

If you don't, I'm afraid you're going to die.

He held the letter in his hand and looked into the warm breeze blowing across the pond. Down the way, he heard a splash, and Logan cried out, "Got another one!"

Logan was way ahead, but Aaron didn't care. His memory drifted back to the grandparents he remembered. He'd seen them since this letter was written, so apparently they'd found her that time. She'd disappeared for a few days after that, while she was pregnant with Luke. Had she been in jail? When she came back, she'd been bitter and angry, and hungry for her dope.

His pop had played softball with him and talked about signing him up for T-ball. His grandma made him a birthday cake, and they'd celebrated his fifth. It had been a good day.

Then sometime that night, his mother woke him and Joey up and whisked them out into the night. A man with a car was waiting for them, and she threw them into the backseat and laughed like a lottery winner as they drove off. He hadn't seen his grandparents since.

"They want to lock me up and give you away! They're hateful, selfish people, and if they find us you'll never see me or Joey again."

He could still remember his crushing disappointment. He'd never had a birthday party before. And he really wanted to play ball.

But his mother's threats loomed over him.

He turned to the next letter. The handwriting was different, more angular and bolder. His grandfather had signed it.

Jessie,

How did such a beautiful, bright little girl, who loved to dance and sing, turn to a life of drugs? I know the abuse changed you, and I'd give my very life if I could undo it. But it happened. We should have handled it differently. We should have gotten you a counselor to help you work through it. We should have seen how much pain you were in.

But drugs? It doesn't even seem possible.

And now here we are, with you walking in complete bondage, and your children suffering as a result. The abuse that was done to you is now being turned on them.

He read back over that sentence. Had his mother been abused by her parents? Was that why she thought they were evil? Was that why she refused to let the four of them see their grandparents, even when she didn't want to take care of them herself?

These pregnancies, the arrests, the failed treatment ...
all leave me baffled and bewildered, and very, very sad. The
only thing I know to do is get the state involved, and have
those children taken from you.

There it was again. Their goal was to get the kids away from
their mother. His mom had always mentioned "the state" in the
same breath with those foster homes that would split the family up.
Was that what his grandparents had planned? He tried to think of
Grandma and Pop as evil, but it just didn't line up with the picture
he had in his mind of them.

Still, nice people turned mean all the time. His mother proved
that. That's why he couldn't trust the Brannings.

And if the Brannings found Grandma and Pop, they'd turn
them over to them, and they might hurt Sarah, Luke, or Joey. They
might turn them over to the state. They might split them up.

He bit his lip until he drew blood, then ripped up the letters.

Who needed them? His brothers and sister had him, and he'd
already proven that he could protect them. As soon as the time
was right, he would get them all out of the Brannings' house, and
they'd be free again.

Freedom. It was what his mother always wanted.

But if he had anything to say about it, his freedom would be
different than hers.

SEVENTEEN

THE WORK HAD GONE SLOWER ON THE WELL FOR THE PAST twenty-four hours, since one of the shifts late yesterday had struck another layer of bedrock. What Doug wouldn't give for a working drill, or some dynamite to help them break through it. Since they couldn't get their hands on either, they'd had to get creative. Scrounging for objects that were heavy enough to drop into the hole and shatter the rock, they'd come up with boat anchors, an old outboard motor, and iron barbells. Those had done the trick, fracturing the stone a little at a time.

Back in the hole, Doug and Brad hacked at the broken rock with their steel rods and sledgehammers, then dropped the shards into the bucket. Its rope was wound around a pulley at the top of the well where Brad's boys, Jeremy and Drew, dumped it out. Mark and Zach worked outside the hole again, preparing the bricks for the walls.

As they waited for the bucket to be lowered back down, Brad stopped digging and took a long swig from his jug of water. "I thought of a way to make some money after the disbursements are given out. Something we could sell, once people have money they can spend."

The bucket came back down, and Doug grabbed it. "What's that?"

"I thought we could make washboards. Judith and the boys and I could probably come up with a way to build them and sell them for some change. Everybody needs them."

Doug grinned and shook his head. "From Maytag to washboards. We've come a long way, haven't we, pal? Full speed in reverse."

"You got that right." Brad rammed his steel rod into a crack, trying to break it further. "So you're sure Kay is up to washing clothes and cooking and cleaning for four extra people?"

"She'll have to get a lot of help from the kids. Two of them are too little to be much help, but the older two are tough. They can pull their weight. Frankly, I don't know how they've made it this far. You would think they'd have starved to death or died of thirst, but they're relatively healthy." Doug positioned his rod again, then whacked it with the sledgehammer once, twice, three times ...

"Hey, man! Hold up! It's wet!"

Doug stopped whacking and turned to where Brad stood. The slightest bit of water had seeped up under his feet. Doug looked up at Drew, wondering if someone was playing a practical joke. "Hey, did anybody spill something down here?"

"No, sir," the boys called.

Doug looked back at the rock. Already, more water was seeping up, forming a small puddle beneath his feet. His heart jolted. "Oh, man! Is that what I think it is?"

Brad stooped down and began to laugh. "I think it is."

"Get back." Doug straightened and took Brad's pick, raised it over his head, and hacked with all his might. This time the water sprayed upward.

"We hit an aquifer!" he shouted. "We have water!" Brad sent up a whoop and high-fived him. They hugged, their sweaty flesh sticking together. Above them, he heard cheers as the other workers leaned in to see.

"We've struck gold!" Brad shouted up.

A flurry of activity began above them as people in neighboring homes ran out. They had much to celebrate.

EIGHTEEN

THERE WAS TOO MUCH NEWS TO KEEP QUIET, AND DENI decided there was no better day to start her newspaper than today. While her siblings and the Gatlin kids did their chores, she sat down at the patio table and began working on her first story—the one about Jessie's disappearance.

Her mother had written a letter to the grandparents earlier that day, and Jeff had taken it to the post office to mail. It might take weeks for it to get to them, and then they'd have to wait for a reply to work its way back. Either way, they'd have the children for a while.

Unless they found their mother. And her article might help with that.

Twenty-five-year-old Jessie Gatlin of Crockett disappeared about two weeks after the Pulses began. She left behind four children, ages three to nine, who've been fending for themselves in the Sandwood Place Apartments since that time. The children have managed to survive but are now living with another family until their mother or suitable relatives are found. Jessie Gatlin, who attended Crockett High School, is purported to have had a drug problem, according to her friend, Lacy Frye, who hasn't seen the woman since before the outage. She suspects that Jessie's disappearance had to do with drugs. Sheriff Scarbrough, who took the children into custody and placed them in foster care, has started an investigation to find Jessie Gatlin. If you have any information about her or have seen her at any point since the outage, please contact Sheriff Scarbrough's office immediately. Authorities are also trying to find the children's grandparents or other relatives who may not be aware of their situation.

The handwriting was pitiful, and it was written on a yellow legal pad, but she supposed she could copy it by hand and staple several copies to the message boards around town. It wasn't perfect, but it was a start.

She heard yelling and looked through the yard toward the sound of the voices. Her mother, who was hanging a wet shirt on the clothesline, ducked under it. "What's going on?"

"I don't know," Deni said, rising from the table.

Her mother rounded up the kids, and they all ran out the back gate toward the sound. They found the crowd celebrating around the well where Deni's father had been digging.

"They hit water!" someone yelled.

Giving a shout of victory, Deni hugged her mother. Little Sarah and Luke jumped up and down like long-time residents of Oak Hollow, while Joey stood back, hands in pockets, watching with detached interest.

There was still much work to do to get the well ready to use, but all of the men who had helped with the shifts began to make plans for finishing it off. Everyone was jubilant. The women began feverishly planning a party, a huge blowout that would provide a welcome relief from all the hard work—and from the drudgery their lives had become.

NINETEEN

DOUG AND DENI FOUND MOE JENKINS THE NEXT DAY, sitting on the steps of another apartment building, digging through a bag of garbage. An unlit cigarette butt hung from his mouth. His dark curly hair was greasy and tangled, and his beard was scraggly and unkempt.

Doug was about to introduce himself when, to his surprise, Deni stepped in front of him, brandishing her legal pad. "Hi, are you Moe Jenkins?"

He stopped digging and took the butt out. "Who wants to know?"

She thrust out her hand. "I'm Deni Branning, and I'm writing a story about Jessie Gatlin for the *Crockett Community Journal*."

Doug shot her a look. It was the first time he'd heard the name of the newspaper. He wondered if the name had just come to her.

"This is Doug Branning," she said, failing to mention that he was her father. "We were told that you used to be involved with Jessie."

Moe's eyes narrowed. "I told the sheriff I ain't seen Jessie in a long time. She got everything she wanted out of me and moved on."

Doug leaned on the stairwell. "Did you know Jessie's missing?"

He shook the garbage bag and resumed his digging. "Sheriff told me."

"Did he tell you she hasn't been seen in weeks?"

Moe put the cigarette butt back in his mouth. "She's probably holed up in a crank house somewhere."

"How long were you involved with her?" Deni asked.

"Three, four months. She was like a leech, hard to shake off once she settled in. Her and those bratty kids."

"If she was so awful, why did you take her in?" Doug asked.

"She was hot, that's why. I'm a sucker for a pretty face. But it got old fast. She started stealing from me. That was it. I threw her out."

"How long ago was that?"

"After she got pregnant the last time. She was a real drag then. Cranky and dope-sick, 'cause of the baby."

"Dope-sick?" Doug asked.

"Yeah. She didn't do as much dope when she was pregnant, and she was a nightmare to live with."

Doug met Deni's eyes. So she *had* used some. According to Moe, at least. Hard to tell who was a less reliable source—Moe or Lacy. Poor kids. It was a miracle they were all right. "Which child of hers is yours?" Doug asked.

"None of 'em." He kept rummaging through the garbage bag. He pulled out the heads of a couple of eaten carrots, their long leaves wilted and brown. He set them aside on the steps. Doug wondered if he was going to eat them. "She lied and said that fourth one was mine, but she was just trying to get money out of me."

Deni set her hand on her hip. "She looks kind of like you. The same eyes, curly brown hair. Have you ever seen Sarah?"

He spat the butt onto the ground. "Sarah who?"

Deni glanced at Doug.

"Your daughter," he said.

Moe started to laugh then. "I told you, she ain't mine. There's not a bit of proof."

Doug could see Deni's disgust flaring up, and he touched her arm to quiet her. "So do you have any idea where Jessie could be?" he asked.

Moe shook his head. "I haven't given her a thought in years. She's probably dead in a gutter somewhere."

Pursing her lips, Deni wrote that down. "Do you know if she had any relatives in town?"

"She didn't get along too well with her folks. Whole time I was with her, she didn't talk to them at all. They were always giving her a hard time, you know, treating her like trash, trying to take her kids. She kept moving so they wouldn't find her."

Was that why the parents hadn't been able to get the children yet?

Doug leaned on the rail of the stairwell, watching the man pull out some chicken bones. "Moe, what would a drug addict do after the outage? Were there still places to buy drugs?"

He discarded the bones. "It got real interesting. Most people had a little cash on them when the lights went out. Dealers sold it 'til they ran out. Couldn't get it here without transportation. Some's just now starting to work its way to town."

Deni might have known. They couldn't get food shipments in, but they'd found a way to get dope.

"Could Jessie have been selling?" Doug asked. "Could a drug deal have gone wrong or something?"

He shrugged. "Anything's possible with that girl. She wasn't above it, I can tell you that. Lot of folks turn to dealing to pay for their habits." He finished sorting through the garbage, then got to his feet. He was almost as tall as Doug. "So where are them kids, anyway?"

"They're staying with our family," Doug said.

"So you'll get their disbursements?"

Deni looked at her father and he froze for a moment. She could almost see the wheels turning in his mind. "We haven't worked that out yet. Hopefully we'll find their family before then."

As they rode their bikes away, Deni ranted. "What a jerk. Jessie sure knew how to pick 'em."

Doug just shook his head. "Those poor kids."

"You got a little pale when Moe asked you about the disbursements. Why was that?"

He sighed. "I just don't trust him. Didn't want him to start changing his tune about paternity, just for the almighty buck."

Deni considered it. Surely he wouldn't go to all that trouble. The man didn't look that resourceful. She studied her dad as he rode a little in front of her. "Dad, do you think she's alive?"

"Probably," Doug said. "From what we've heard about her, I'd say she's alive and taking care of number one, and she's forgotten all about her children. I think they may be better off without her."

TWENTY

KAY WAS PACING IN THE GARAGE WHEN DENI AND DOUG GOT home. "Thank goodness you're back! I have to show you something."

Doug braced himself as he got off his bike. "Uh-oh. What now?"

"Come upstairs and you'll see."

He left Deni to close the garage, then followed Kay up the stairs and into Logan's room. It looked like a tornado had hit it. The Gatlin kids' things were everywhere. She reached into a grocery sack stuffed with toys.

"I was going through their stuff to wash their clothes, and I found this." She pulled out a small revolver.

Doug caught his breath and took the .38 Special from her. "But the sheriff *took* their gun."

"Apparently they had another one."

Doug moaned and checked to see if it was loaded. Thank goodness, it wasn't. "Did you look through the rest of their things for the ammo?"

"Yes, I went through everything. But if we missed the gun, maybe we're missing the bullets too. We helped them pack—you'd think we would have seen it."

Doug took the bag and pulled out the battered Barbie, the baseball cap, and the Superman cape. "He brought this one home yesterday. My fault. I should have searched it."

Kay rubbed her temples and sat down on the bed. "What should we do?"

"Confiscate it, of course. I'll tell the sheriff."

"Doug, do you think they're dangerous?"

He thought of telling her that he'd warned her, but that wouldn't be fair. Taking them in had been the right thing. If he'd gotten nothing else from Moe Jenkins, he'd seen a glimpse of what the lives of these kids had been like. "Not dangerous. Just desperate. Aaron has been in survival mode for a long time. In his mind, this is part of his survival."

She stood up and looked around at the mess. "I want to help them," she said. "And we gave them our word that we'd keep them until we found their grandparents. But I admit, I'm a little nervous. A nine-year-old kid who packs a pistol is not someone I should have in my house. But what else can we do?"

He'd wrestled with these same thoughts. "Let's not panic. Yesterday, you had some really good arguments about God leading us to them. I don't think we should change our course now."

Her eyes were hopeful as she looked up at him. "Do you think I was right about that? That God really brought them here?"

He searched his heart and found confidence there. Slowly, he lowered himself to the bed and patted her leg. "Yes, I think you were. When you look at Aaron and his behavior, it seems all about the other kids. I'm not suggesting he's a saint, but he does seem to have their best interests at heart. How bad could a kid like that be?"

"I hope we find his mother alive so I can wring her neck."

"Yeah, me too. Why don't we just talk to him, tell him we found it? Let him know we're not going to tolerate this kind of thing."

She nodded. "I'll go get him."

He waited, sitting on the bed, turning the gun over in his hand. Where in the world had they gotten two guns? Did they both belong to Jessie, or had they stolen them? Their next-door neighbor had been aware of their weapon, and she claimed others were, as well. Why hadn't even one of the neighbors reported it?

Kay came back a few minutes later, with Aaron and Joey shuffling behind her.

Aaron saw the gun in Doug's hand as he entered the room, and he stopped cold.

"Aaron, Kay was just getting ready to wash your clothes," he said, "and she found this."

The boy crossed his arms. "Yeah? So?"

"Where'd you get it, Aaron? Is it your mother's?"

His face was hard. "No, it's mine."

"They don't sell guns to kids." Doug got up and stood over the boys. "Now tell me where you got it."

"I found it, okay?"

"Found it where?"

Aaron hesitated. "In a Dumpster."

"Which Dumpster?"

"I don't know. I dug through lots of them looking for food. I can't remember which one."

Not likely. But Doug doubted he'd get anything else out of him. He turned to Joey. "How long have you had it?"

"A long time," Joey said.

Aaron gave him a look that told him to shut up.

"Joey, where are the bullets?"

Joey shrugged and looked at his brother.

Color crept up Aaron's cheeks. "I did have some, but they're all gone now."

That sent a chill through Doug. "What did you use them on?"

Aaron turned away then and went to put his stuff back in the bags. "I used the gun for protection," he said. "A time or two I had to shoot at the ground or at the sky to keep somebody away. It kept people from taking everything we had."

Joey's face was distraught as he said, "Every time we came back with food, some of the neighbors tried to steal it."

Doug threw a glance to Kay, then fixed his eyes on the boys. "Is that why the neighbors didn't call the police on you?"

"Why would they?" Aaron asked. "Sometimes I just gave them stuff, so they'd leave us alone. They liked what I brought them."

So the kid was also a politician.

"But when I didn't have enough, some of them would get rough. Sometimes just waving the gun got the message across."

Doug could imagine. Anger rose to his throat. Maybe those neighbors deserved to live the way they did.

But then Aaron shot that thought down. "It wasn't all of them. Some of them were nice and helped us. We traded off. Sometimes they'd give us their water, if I found food. And when Joey and I weren't home, they'd look in on Sarah and Luke."

"But they let you live there alone!" Kay said. "How could they do that?"

Aaron and Joey exchanged looks again. "We didn't tell them Mama wasn't home. She was always gone a lot anyway. Sometimes she didn't come home at night. They just figured nothing had changed."

Doug looked at his wife, saw the tears in her eyes. He swallowed. "I understand why you needed this, Aaron, but we're going to take it and put it up for now, okay? You're not going to need it here."

They could see the hesitation and fear on the boy's face. "Where are you gonna put it?"

"I'm locking it up with our other guns."

"Will I get it back?"

"I doubt it. But let's hope you never need it again."

Rage twisted the boy's face. "It's ours! You can't have it!"

"This isn't negotiable, Aaron. You can't stay here with a gun."

"Then let us go. We didn't ask to be here!"

Joey spoke up. "They don't trust us, Aaron."

"Joey, it has nothing to do with trust," Kay said. "It's against the law for children to own guns. Period."

The boys stood staring up at them, clearly unhappy at the turn of events. Doug wished he could make them understand that they were safe here. But only time would do that.

He started to the door. "Now let's go down to the well and see if the chemist has tested the water yet. If it's clean, we can get our first drink of it. It's nice and cool. Perfect for drinking."

Life returned to Joey's eyes, and he smiled. But Aaron wasn't moved.

As they led the children down the stairs, Doug realized he would need to report this to the sheriff. Then he'd need something more secure to keep his guns in.

What a way to live.

TWENTY-ONE

THE PLIGHT OF THE PEOPLE AT THE SANDWOOD PLACE Apartments haunted Doug for the next few days. As he worked on his sermon on Proverbs for the following Sunday, God's Word convicted him: "Do not withhold good from those who deserve it, when it is in your power to act," Solomon had written.

It *was* in his power to act. He knew things they needed— how to sort the garbage taking over their land, how to dig a well, how to invest their disbursement dollars so they could survive the winter. Though there was still work to be done on the Oak Hollow well, he felt so blessed to have hit the water table. The chemist who'd tested it confirmed that the water was pure, perfect for drinking, washing, bathing. And there was plenty of it. They had almost finished building the housing over it with a stronger pulley for lifting water. And the walls around it had to be high enough to keep out children and animals. It needed a top to keep out debris. But it would all be finished tomorrow.

He had the skill now—the power to act, as Solomon described it—so how could he withhold it from the people of Sandwood Place?

Doug took Jeff and Deni with him to the Sandwood Place Apartments after supper that night. Kay had wanted to come herself, but since Deni begged to accompany him so she could interview some of the residents about the missing woman, Kay stayed home with the children. They didn't think Beth could handle Aaron and his brothers.

Doug rode with his rifle slung on his back in case of trouble. As they grew closer to the apartments, he tried to plan what he would say.

I've come to show you how to sort your garbage and handle your finances.

What was he? An expert on everything? Why would they even want to listen to him?

No, he needed a more humble approach.

He glanced at Jeff and Deni, riding beside him. "Guys, I'm coming to help these people if I can, but I don't want to put them on the defensive. Let's just start out talking to them about Jessie, and then maybe I can ease into the stuff we've done to make life easier in Oak Hollow. If they're interested, I'll go on with my ideas about investing their money and digging a well."

"Okay," Deni said. "Why don't you let me lead? I'll do the journalist bit and interview them."

"I don't know ..."

"No, really, Dad. In college, when I did stories for GUTV, I was the one they sent on the toughest interviews."

"What's GUTV?" Jeff's voice dripped with contempt.

"The student-run television station at Georgetown."

"And they put *you* on it?"

"Yes, smart guy. I happen to be very good at what I do. That's why NBC hired me."

Doug knew Jeff was just trying to rile her. He'd been as proud as they were of his sister when she'd sent videos home.

As they rode into the parking lot, Deni said, "Seriously, Dad. I'll take out my notepad and tell them it's for the newspaper, and you'll be surprised who'll talk to me."

"If you let her do it, Dad, you'll never get a word in."

Doug laughed. "I think it'll be okay. Jeff, I want you to stay with the bikes, all right?"

Jeff sighed. "Story of my life."

Deni's eyes shone with purpose as they parked their bikes. She pulled out her pad and headed into a cluster of families congregated around the grill, her dad following. "Hi, I'm Deni Branning with the *Crockett Community Journal*. I'm doing a story on Jessie Gatlin—the missing woman in 4B—and I wonder if any of you would answer a few questions for me."

Doug watched as the families perked up with a respect he hadn't expected. Her sudden credentials seemed to give her the perfect entree.

She introduced him as Doug, as if he were her sidekick instead of her father, and before he knew it the neighbors were telling stories of Jessie and her druggie friends, her all-night escapades, and her screaming fights with her children. Most of them swore they hadn't known the children were living there alone, but Doug had trouble believing that.

As Deni finished her interviews and moved on to other groups, Doug would remain behind and engage them in conversation about their plight. They told him that they got their water from a pond over a mile away—and when they washed clothes, they had to haul them there and back. A lady in 6A, a retired schoolteacher, babysat for several of the families when they trekked there for water. Some of them listened as he shared ideas with them; all seemed interested when he mentioned digging a well.

A cluster began to form around him as he talked. He noticed that Deni had stopped her interviewing and was listening as he explained how they'd dug the well—and told them how important it was that they process their garbage first. The crowd got bigger, and by the time he'd finished, two dozen or more people were hanging on every word.

But most of them were female heads of their households, and as malnourished as many of them were, they didn't appear to have the strength to dig a well. They needed to get more men involved. But looking around, Doug didn't see that many able-bodied men. They would need outside help.

When they'd finished talking, he and Deni walked around the building to look for a place to dig a well.

"Deni, I want you to do a story on the plight of the apartments in town," he said. "The community needs to get involved. These people need our help. And as surprised as I am to say this, it looks like people are actually reading your paper."

She laughed. "I know. It's weird, huh? Handwritten legal pads tacked to a wooden board. But people are hungry for communication. Maybe we could set a date for people to show up here to work, and I could post it around town. Do you think anyone would come, with so much of their own work to do?"

"I'll try to get the church involved," Doug said. "We have twenty families now. Surely I can get several of them to come."

The stench grew more intense as they made their way around the building and encountered the mountains of garbage festering there. Deni covered her nose and started to choke. "This place is gross. I'm gonna throw up."

"You can go back and wait with Jeff if you want. I'm going to walk into the woods here and see if I can find a clearing big enough to dig a well."

"No, I'll go with you, but can we please hurry? We're probably breathing bacteria as we speak. This can't be good."

He led her around the garbage and into the thick stand of trees at the back of the property. "The people can't even open their windows to let the air circulate, because if they do they'll smell this. But if we start showing them how to process the garbage, we'll have to teach them how to compost, and we'll need water to wash everything that can be reused. This could be mission impossible."

She stepped over a fallen tree. "I thought you didn't believe in impossibilities. If I remember, you call those God-sized tasks."

The stench was growing stronger the farther they went into the trees. He pulled his shirt up over his nose.

Deni had both hands over her face. "Dad, this is seriously disgusting."

He had to agree. "There must be something dead back in here. If we find it, we can bury it or burn it. That'll help."

"I'm not touching it!" Deni said. "I'll go back and watch the bikes and you and Jeff can do it. I have a weak stomach."

Since she didn't turn back, he supposed her curiosity was stronger than her revulsion.

He pushed through the brush, following the stench, and saw a clearing between the trees. Other than some bushes and a sapling or two, there were about fifteen feet open where they could dig the well without hitting significant root systems. "This is it," he told Deni. "This is where we could dig the well."

"It's perfect," she agreed. "You wouldn't have to cut down any trees. But the smell is rancid. Do you think the water would even be clean? It smells like a toxic waste dump. I'm gagging."

They must be getting closer to whatever it was.

For all her gagging, Deni didn't stop talking. "It's worse right here than it was standing over the garbage. This place reeks."

He pushed through the brush, stepped over some dead limbs, waved back the leaves of a mimosa tree. A squirrel dashed in front of him, startling a big black bird he hadn't seen before. Its wings flapped noisily and clumsily as it lifted off.

Deni caught her breath. "Dad, it's a vulture."

He looked where it had been. There was nothing there. Only a pile of leaves covering a filthy blue blanket. He stepped closer and picked up a corner of the cloth. Slowly, he lifted it.

And then he saw the source of the stench—the decaying body of a dead girl.

TWENTY-TWO

DENI SCREAMED. STUMBLING BACK, SHE SHIELDED HER EYES from the sight of the decaying body, covering her nose from the stench. She tripped over a fallen branch, caught herself, then crashed back through the woods the way she had come, pushing through brush and thorns and branches, snagging her clothes and skin as she ran.

When she got to the edge of the woods, to the piles of garbage, she bent over and threw up. She was vaguely aware that some of the residents from the apartments were wandering toward her to see what the commotion was.

And then her father was there, panting hard, bending over with her, holding her hair back as she retched into the refuse. "It's okay, honey. Calm down."

She retched again.

As more and more people gathered, asking what the screaming was about, Deni straightened and tried to pull herself together. She looked back toward the trees, where that dead body had lain for days ... weeks ...

Someone had to go for the police.

Drawing in a deep breath, she looked at her father. "Dad," she said. "I'm going to send Jeff for the sheriff."

He looked at the inquisitive crowd forming around them. "Tell him to hurry."

TWENTY-THREE

THE SHERIFF AND HIS DEPUTIES WERE THERE WITHIN A FEW minutes after Jeff alerted them. Two of the neighbors in the apartments came with them into the woods to identify the body. They both thought it was Jessie Gatlin, but since she'd been shot in the face, it was difficult to be sure. The girl had a tattoo of a butterfly on her ankle. If Aaron could confirm that Jessie had one, then maybe they wouldn't have to find anyone to identify the body. Asking the child to do it was out of the question.

The sheriff and his men roped off a perimeter around the body and began to work the crime scene.

Doug sat with Deni and Jeff on the steps of the apartments, waiting to talk to Scarbrough again before they went home.

"Those poor kids," Jeff said. "Dad, you're not gonna tell them she was murdered, are you? No kid should have to hear that about his mom."

"If it's her, I don't see how we can avoid telling Aaron. He'll hear about it. It's a homicide investigation now. That'll get a lot more attention than a missing-persons case."

It was getting dark, but most of the neighbors had come out of their apartments and stood in the parking lot or sat on dusty, rusting cars, waiting to hear whatever evidence the sheriff was able to find.

"What if it wasn't a homicide?" Deni asked. "What if it was suicide?"

Doug hadn't considered that. "I guess it could be. I just assumed it was murder when I saw the gunshot."

The sheriff came around the building, scanned the parking lot, then started toward them. "Would you mind stepping into Jessie's apartment with me? I'd like to talk to you."

They followed him up the stairs and into the sweltering, sewer-stench apartment.

"Sheriff, do you think it could have been suicide?" Doug asked as he closed the door.

The sheriff shook his head. "No. She was shot twice," he said, "and neither bullet was at close range. It was clearly a homicide. And we found some shell casings. They look like they're .38 caliber."

Doug's eyebrows shot up. "One of the guns Aaron had was a .38."

"That's what I thought." Scarbrough set his foot on a box. "Where did he say he got it?"

"He said he found it. Do you think it belonged to the killer?"

"Could very well be. The kid may have stolen it from the guy who killed his mother."

Jeff came further into the room. "But Aaron didn't know his mom was dead. How could he know who killed her?"

"I'm not saying he knew," Scarbrough said. "I'm saying that maybe it was someone familiar to the family. Someone around here, even."

"Are you sure it was the same gun?" Doug asked.

"No, and we won't know for sure until we get the ballistics report, which could take some time. My department doesn't have the capability to handle ballistics, but Birmingham does. They have their own specialists who analyze firearms. Problem is, we have to wait in line. With the boost in crime, there aren't enough specialists to get it all done."

"Even when there's a killer on the loose? Seems like they'd move it to the top of the list."

"Unfortunately there are a lot of killers on the loose and they don't have the resources they used to have to work with. We'll have to wait our turn. But if I'm right, then Aaron is the key to finding his mom's killer. All we have to do is get him to admit where he got that gun."

"Then we'd better get home and break it to him," Deni said.

Scarbrough reached for the doorknob. "I'll take you all home. And after we tell him, maybe he'll have some idea who the killer is."

TWENTY-FOUR

HEARING THE SHERIFF'S VAN PULLING INTO HER DRIVEWAY,
Kay dashed outside.

Doug, Deni, and Jeff were in the van with Sheriff
Scarbrough. Something was wrong.

"What happened?" she asked Doug as he got out.

He looked past her, making sure no one could hear.
"Where are the kids?"

"Out back," she said. "Doug, tell me what's wrong. Why
is the sheriff here?"

Deni and Jeff unloaded their bikes and rolled them into
the garage. Deni looked pale and shaken, and Jeff seemed
somber.

"We found a dead girl in the woods behind the apartments. We think it may be Jessie Gatlin."

She sucked in a breath. "Oh no."

"She'd been there for weeks. She was shot twice."

"Murdered?"

"Apparently."

She turned to Sheriff Scarbrough. "Do you know who
did it?"

"Not yet," Scarbrough said. "Kay, I'm going to have to
talk to Aaron. We need to break the news and ask him some
questions."

"Of course." She led them into the house and looked out
the back window. The kids were washing their recyclables in
a rubber bin. They were laughing and splashing each other.

Even Aaron had joined the fun. She hated to interrupt, especially for this.

Kay went to the back door. "Aaron, can you come in for a minute?"

He stopped splashing. "Okay, but I'm all wet."

"It's okay. I'll get you a towel." Her gentle voice must have alerted him, for his smile faded. He came inside and saw the sheriff, and the color drained from his face.

"Hi, Aaron," Scarbrough said. "Could I talk to you for a minute?"

Aaron froze. "What do you want?"

"Sit down, Aaron," Kay said. "Please ..."

Fury flashed across the child's face. "If you came to take us out of here and split us up, we'll run away." The corners of his mouth pulled down as he got the words out.

"That's not why I'm here, Aaron."

Doug stepped toward the boy, touched his arm. "Come on, son, sit down."

Aaron jerked away from him. "I don't want to. And I ain't your *son.*"

Doug sighed and pulled out his own chair, sitting slowly down. The others followed, but Kay kept standing. She moved closer to the boy, wishing she could hold and comfort him ...

The sheriff cleared his throat. "Aaron, it's about your mother. Could you tell us if she had a tattoo?"

Aaron's face tightened even more. "You found her, didn't you?"

"We're not sure. *Does* she have a tattoo?"

"Yes," he said. "She got one on her ankle. A stupid butterfly."

Kay turned to Scarbrough to see if that confirmed it. He nodded.

Aaron seemed to sense it too. His face crumpled, and his lips trembled. "You'd think if she was gonna go through all the money and pain to get a freakin' tattoo she'd get something important like an eagle or a spider or something. But no, she had to go and get a butterfly so Sarah would want one too."

Doug's voice was raspy. "Aaron, we need you to sit down. We have to tell you something."

He stood there a moment, staring at his shoes.

"We found your mother," Doug said. "Aaron, she's dead."

The boy didn't look up. He didn't move at all. Finally, he asked, "Where?"

"In the woods behind your apartments."

For a moment, Kay watched his jaw muscle popping in and out, but he kept his eyes on the floor. Finally, he spoke. "She prob'ly deserved it. Stinking junkie."

Kay caught her breath. "Aaron!"

His face twisted and he started backing away. Kay reached out to hug him, but he jerked out of her reach.

"We'll have a funeral, Aaron." Deni's voice was soft. "We'll give her a proper burial."

His ears turned red and his mouth trembled. "I don't want to see her."

"You don't have to," Kay said.

The sheriff gave him a moment, and Kay watched Aaron's valiant struggle to hold back his tears. She wished he'd just let them go.

Scarbrough cleared his throat. "Aaron, I need to know where you got that gun the Brannings found. The .38."

"I already told you I found it."

"Found it where?"

"I don't remember."

Doug got up and went toward him. "Son, whoever owns that gun might be the one who killed your mother."

Aaron's expression changed, and he looked up, surprised. Kay realized they hadn't explained that she'd been murdered. Was that shock on his face, or rage?

"She was shot, Aaron. We need to find the gun's owner."

"I don't know who it was," he said again. "I found it in the garbage."

"The garbage behind your apartments?" the sheriff asked.

He shook his head. "No. Some other garbage. I don't remember where."

For some reason, the kid was lying. Kay wondered who he was trying to cover for ... and why.

Scarbrough turned to Doug. "I'll need that weapon. We need to log it as evidence."

Doug went to get it out of the gun cabinet. He brought it back in a towel to keep from smudging any prints that might be on it. Carefully, he handed it to the sheriff.

Scarbrough dropped it into an evidence bag and took another look at the boy. "I have to go now, Aaron. But if you think of who might have killed your mother—or who owned this gun—I need you to tell me immediately. It's real important. We need to get the killer off the street before he kills anybody else."

Aaron just nodded.

Kay and Doug walked the sheriff out.

"He's lying about the gun," Scarbrough said in a low voice. "Maybe he just needs time to think it over. Keep working on him, will you? And when he's willing to talk, send for me, any time of day or night."

"I will," Doug said. "But right now I have to break it to the rest of the children, and find a way to notify the relatives."

"We'll have to schedule an autopsy," the sheriff said. "But you might want to go ahead and have a funeral service without the body, just to give those kids some closure. By the time you get word to her relatives, maybe the body will be ready for burial."

TWENTY-FIVE

"THEY FOUND MAMA, AND SHE'S DEAD."

Aaron's words were not the ones Deni would have chosen to tell the other three Gatlin children of their mother's demise, but now that they were out, she couldn't snatch them back.

But the children didn't react. They only stared at their brother.

"Where was she?" Joey asked finally.

"Laying in the woods." Aaron's tone was cold, belying the tears still glistening in his eyes. "Somebody shot her."

Joey was silent then. Finally, little Luke spoke up. "Then she ain't coming back?"

Sarah's thumb went to her mouth. Clutching her baby doll against her stomach, she turned her big eyes to Aaron.

"No, she's not coming back," he said. "I told you, she's dead."

Kay took Luke's hand. "She would come back if she could, Luke. But the important thing is that she didn't just leave you all to fend for yourselves. She would have been there for you if she could. I'm sure her heart would have been broken to know what you guys have had to do to survive."

"Yeah, right." Aaron's words were hard, sharp.

"We need to have a memorial service for her," Kay said in a soft voice.

"What's that?" Joey sat slumped on the couch, staring at her.

"It's a time to remember the good things about her. To lay her to rest."

"Like a funeral?" Joey asked.

"Yeah, like a funeral. But we can't do a burial. Not yet."

"Why not?"

Kay didn't want to tell them that they had to wait for the autopsy to be done. "We'll wait until we get in touch with your grandparents for that. But it would just be a nice way to say good-bye to your mom."

Luke and Sarah weren't crying, which surprised Deni, but she supposed they'd been away from Jessie for so many weeks now that they felt detached from her. Joey looked like he needed to crawl under a bed somewhere, where no one would see, and cry his little eyes out. But she didn't know what Aaron needed.

"We'll have the service after supper," she said quietly. "Is that okay with everybody?"

The children just looked at her.

"Okay, then. Be thinking of some nice memories. Good things to say about her. That would be a nice way to say good-bye, wouldn't it?"

Tears escaped from Joey's eyes, and he nodded his head and slid his knuckles through the tears.

Sarah looked at him, fascinated. "Why are you cryin', Joey?"

Luke patted his hand.

"No reason." His face reddened with the effort to stop.

Sarah moved to sit beside her brother. Putting her arms around his shoulders, she laid her head against his. "Don't cry, Joey. It's okay. You'll see. Everything's gonna be just fine."

Deni smiled at the comfort the child was offering. Someone in her life had said those words to her many times. Despite Jessie's problems, she apparently had had some maternal instincts. Deni tried to picture her holding a crying Sarah, petting her and whispering assurances into her ear. Now Sarah was passing that on to her brother.

Maybe Jessie had left a bit of a legacy, after all.

THAT EVENING AFTER SUPPER, DOUG ASSEMBLED THE CHILDREN on the back patio, pulling their chairs into a circle, for the memorial ceremony that Kay hoped would bring closure to these children.

Joey had stopped crying hours ago and now wore a hard mask of indifference. Sarah and Luke seemed excited about the ritual, and Aaron still brooded.

Doug wanted the children to participate. "I'd like to start this with a song," he said. "But I'm not sure what song you all know."

"How about 'Jesus Loves Me'?" Beth suggested. "Do you know that?"

Sarah's hand shot up. "I know it!"

"Me too," Luke said with a grin. "We learned it at vacation Bible school."

Kay's eyes widened. "You guys went to church?"

"Just Bible school," Aaron muttered. "They had a bus from one of the churches that came to get us. We learned stuff there."

Good, Doug thought. That gave them a starting place. "Okay, then let's sing 'Jesus Loves Me.'"

It had been years since Doug had sung the words to that song, but as they sang, he realized the message bore an eternal truth. One he desperately wanted these children to learn. Aaron, arms crossed and head hanging, didn't sing. Joey followed suit, but Luke and Sarah sang their hearts out, delighted that the others knew their song.

When they finished singing, they all sat down.

"Guys, I didn't know your mom. But you did. Why don't you tell us some of the good things you remember about her?"

Luke raised his hand. "I know something."

Aaron frowned at him.

"Go ahead, Luke," Kay said.

He gave them a self-conscious grin. "She was pretty, and her hair was soft. And she was always nice."

Kay stroked his hair. "Good, Luke. That's a nice memory. Anything else?"

He thought for a moment. "Yeah. She told me a story one time."

One time? Kay glanced at Doug.

"It was about a turtle and a rabbit."

The Tortoise and the Hare, Doug thought. "I think I know that story."

"And she never hit us or nothin'."

The last phrase stopped Doug cold. Why would a kid remember that as a happy memory?

Sarah popped her thumb out of her mouth, and gave him an indignant look. "Yes, she did, Luke."

Luke frowned and shook his head, as if to silence her. "No, she didn't. She was nice. And her hair was soft."

"Did too hit us," Sarah said again.

Aaron spoke up then, as if to draw attention off his sister. "Sometimes she was fun. She would take us to the park and play Frisbee with us."

Joey shot him a confused look. A signal seemed to pass between them, and finally Joey jumped in. "Yeah. And she liked to decorate for Christmas. She'd bring home a Christmas tree and have all these presents under it. We always got more than anybody else at Christmas."

Doug looked at his wife. Were they making it up?

Sarah looked confused. "When?"

"Last Christmas," Aaron said. "Remember when you got your baby?"

Sarah looked down at her dirty baby doll, as if trying to remember when she'd gotten it. It looked much older than eight months old. That doll had been dragged around for years, probably by someone even before Sarah was born.

But she slowly put her thumb back into her mouth and accepted that.

Anger roiled up inside Doug at the woman who had been such a poor mother that her own children couldn't think of anything honest and good to say about her. He wondered why Jessie hadn't just given the children over to her parents, if she cared so little about them.

When there was clearly nothing more to say, Kay got the potted rosebush she had dug up from the Caldwells' yard, after Brad and Judith decided to dig up the flower garden so they could plant vegetables.

"Now we're going to dig a hole at the back of the yard," she said, "and we'll plant this little rosebush in your mother's memory. As it grows, you can remember her."

They went to the back of the lawn and dug the hole, then Kay gave the plant to Joey to put into the ground. He set it gently down, then pushed the mound of dirt on top of it and patted it down.

"The best thing your mother ever gave you was each other," Kay said softly. "And for that, you can be thankful. If you'd like to say good-bye to your mom, why don't each of you take a handful of dirt and sprinkle it at the base of the rosebush?"

When none of the children stepped forward to do it, Deni did, then Beth, then Logan and Jeff. Finally, Luke came forward, that self-conscious five-year-old grin on his face again. He swept up some dirt into his hand and sprinkled it carefully over the fresh soil around the plant.

Then Sarah stepped up and took some dirt into her hand. Sprinkling it, she said, "Asha to asha, dirt to dirt ..."

Kay stooped next to her. "What did you say?"

Sarah was happy to repeat it. "Asha to asha, dirt to dirt ..."

Deni frowned. "Did she mean 'ashes to ashes, dust to dust'?"

Luke's grin grew bigger. "Yeah, that's it!"

"Where did she learn that?" Doug asked Aaron.

He shrugged. "Who knows? TV prob'ly." He picked up his own handful and tossed it onto the dirt.

Doug talked a little about heaven, careful not to give assurances that Jessie was there. As he spoke, Joey, Luke, and Sarah hung onto every word.

But Aaron wasn't buying a word of it.

TWENTY-SIX

DENI'S EYES WERE TIRED, AND THE YELLOW GLOW OF THE oil lamp in her father's study didn't provide quite enough light. But Jessie Gatlin's little memorial service had started her thinking, and as night fell, melancholy had set in. Jessie had probably had no idea that she would die young and leave her children without even one parent. Would she have done things differently, if she'd known the legacy she would leave behind?

Life was short. Too short to waste on fruitless things.

And the depression Deni had been fighting over Craig was fruitless.

Yes, she was disappointed in the letter he'd sent her. She had brooded long enough, nursing her wounds, trying to see it in a different light. She'd tried to latch onto Mark's take on the letter, but somehow, deep inside, she couldn't make herself believe that Craig's unspoken love had been hidden between the lines.

But if they ever hoped for their impending marriage to work, she needed to be honest with him about how the letter had hurt her. So she started a new letter.

> *Dear Craig,*
>
> *It was so good to finally get a letter from you, after eleven weeks with no word. I was disappointed in its tone, though. Maybe you didn't mean to sound uncaring. I had just hoped for a little more.*

She paused for a moment, hoping she didn't sound like a love-sick teenager.

A high-pitched scream cracked through the night, startling her, and she got up and stood behind the door, listening for the source.

It was Sarah.

Deni ran up the stairs in the dark, feeling her way to the landing. She followed the sound of the crying to the room Sarah had been sleeping in.

Moonlight came in through the window, and against it, she saw the silhouette of someone in the rocking chair, holding the child. She stepped closer, listening to the words of comfort.

"Don't cry, Sarah. It's okay. You'll see. Everything's gonna be just fine."

They were the same words Sarah had used to comfort Joey earlier. Sarah hadn't gotten them from her mother, but from Aaron.

She might have known.

She stooped in front of them. "Everything okay?" she asked, stroking Sarah's curls.

"Yeah," he said in a soft voice. "She just had another bad dream. But she's okay. I've got her."

Deni knelt there for a moment, watching as Sarah's eyes drifted closed in the safety of Aaron's arms.

"You're a good brother, Aaron," Deni whispered.

He didn't say anything. She wished she could see the expression on his face in the darkness.

Finally, she left them alone and went back to her letter.

TWENTY-SEVEN

THE NEXT DAY, AARON BEGAN PACKING. TOMORROW THEY would leave here, he had decided. Now that the sheriff knew his mother was dead, there was no telling what would happen to them. Either they'd find the grandparents who'd spent years trying to break up their family, or they'd be separated out to foster families. Either way, it wasn't likely that anyone would want to take in all four hungry children.

Joey came into the room. "What are you doing?"

"Packing. We're leaving this place tomorrow."

Joey looked at him like he was crazy. "Why?"

"Because Mama's dead, and we're orphans now. Do you know what they do to orphans?"

Joey sat on the bed. "No, what?"

"They lock them up, that's what. In some horrible orphanage with bars on the windows. Or they split up families and give each one to some fat slob who gets money for taking foster kids, and he uses the money to get drunk every night and slap the kids around."

"He won't slap me around," Joey said. "I'll slap him back."

"You and me might, but what about Luke and Sarah? They're not old enough to defend theirselves. They need us to fight for them, Joey."

Joey watched him throw all of his things into an old crumpled grocery sack. "But what about the Brannings? I like them. They're nice. They said they'd keep us till they found our grandma and pop."

"Yeah, that's what they said. But use your head, Joey. They're in it for money too. The disbursement is in just a few days. They want to take us through that line so they can get our money."

"No, they won't. They're not like that, Aaron!"

Joey could be so dumb. "Everybody's like that, Joey. They all want something."

"But if we leave, we don't get that money, anyway. We have to go with grown-ups or they won't give it to us."

"Then I'll find somebody else to take us through. Somebody at the apartments."

"What about Sarah?"

Aaron stopped packing and looked at his brother. "What about her?"

"She's happy here. She likes having a lady taking care of her. She's not gonna want to go. Besides, Beth promised her the part of a princess in that play she wrote. It's about this dude who kills this big giant. And it's got songs and stuff, and Sarah's all excited."

"You sure it's her you're talking about? Not yourself?"

Joey didn't deny it. "She said I could be a soldier and have a uniform. It might be fun."

"We can't stay that long," Aaron said.

"We have food here, Aaron. We don't have to break into people's houses. We have as much water as we can drink. And Doug and Jeff keep us safe."

"*I* can keep us safe. I don't need them."

"You don't even have the gun anymore. I'm just saying, Sarah's gonna cry. She's had enough happen to her, Aaron. Let her stay here and be happy for a while. What's so bad about that?"

"She might get to feeling like they're *her* family, that's what. But they're not. And as soon as they get what they want, they'll dump us. Then how will she feel?"

"What if I don't want to go?" Joey asked.

Aaron's eyes flashed. "*I* decide what we're gonna do, Joey. Haven't I always decided what's best? Haven't I always took care of all of us? Don't you think I can do it again?"

"But it was nice to be in a family with a mom and dad."

Aaron turned on him. "They're not our family, you little twerp! We're all the family we got. We have to stick together and do what's right for all of us. So I don't want to hear you whining no more. Got it?"

Joey didn't answer.

"Joey, answer me."

Finally, his brother crossed his arms, pouting. Aaron hated it when Joey acted like some stupid little kid. Being seven was no excuse.

"I got it," he bit out.

"Good," Aaron said. "We're going tomorrow, and that's that. We'll have our own play. I'll make you a general, and Sarah can be a queen."

Joey kept brooding. "We don't got a stage or costumes or music. You think you're so smart, but you can't do everything."

But Aaron didn't feel smart at all.

TWENTY-EIGHT

TORRENTIAL RAINS CAME JUST AFTER SUPPER, TURNING THE tilled part of the Brannings' yard into a mud pit. Aaron hid his packed bag under the bed in Logan's room, then went downstairs and out to the patio. He sat down, pulling his feet up onto the chair. He rested his chin on his knees and looked out at the rain, wishing tomorrow would hurry and come.

Most of the family was in the kitchen, watching the rain out of the bay window.

The rain had cooled the summer heat, and a breeze blew a fine mist into Aaron's face. He wished he could walk out into the middle of it and let the warm water pour down over him, pool at his feet, then rise to his knees, his waist, his shoulders, his face. He wished he could drown in the clean warmth of it, leaving all his cares behind.

It would be so cool if there really was a heaven, if he could just close his eyes and drift up to some beautiful place, where the lights were on and there was food hanging from trees, where his sister and brothers could be safe, where a nice God welcomed him and loved him.

But if a God like that existed in a real heaven, he wouldn't want the likes of Aaron Gatlin there. Not after all he'd done.

You made your bed, now sleep in it. His mother had said that so many times, as if her own bed wasn't a filthy mess.

No, a real God wouldn't have a bunch of snot-nosed orphans dirtying up his heaven. He'd be scared they'd steal some of those fancy pearls off the gate.

A tear rolled down his face, and he roughly smeared it away. He wasn't going to cry. He wasn't. He couldn't be weak like some whiny little baby. Sarah, Luke, and Joey depended on him.

He heard distant thunder, and the rain came harder.

Doug and Kay came out, their arms full of recycled containers, bowls, and buckets, and they set them out in the rain to catch the water. Doug glanced at him. "Might save us a trip to the well."

Aaron doubted they'd catch enough to make much difference.

"Hard rain, huh?" Doug said over the roar of rain hitting the patio roof. "We needed it."

Aaron didn't turn around. He didn't want them to see his stupid tears. Pulling up his shirt, he dried his face.

He heard someone else come out, then Kay said, "Beth, what are you doing?"

"Taking a shower," she said, shooting past him out into the yard. She was wearing her bathing suit and held a bottle of shampoo and a bar of soap. She walked out to a place in the yard that hadn't been tilled and stood in the grass with her face turned up to the rain.

"What is she doing?" It was Deni's voice behind him, and Aaron turned and saw the rest of the family spilling out onto the patio.

Sarah giggled wildly and jumped up and down. "I want to get wet too!"

"Aaaah," Beth cried. She let the rain roll through her hair, then poured out a handful of shampoo and lathered up.

"You're really gonna regret that when it stops raining before you can rinse," Logan said.

Beth just laughed. "It's not gonna stop. Look at it! It's pouring." She rinsed the shampoo out, then started soaping her arms, her neck, her legs.

"That's it," Deni said. "I'm getting into my bathing suit. Come on, Sarah. We'll change you into something and we'll both play in the rain. I've been dying for a shower."

Logan and Jeff pulled off their shirts and ran into the storm. Aaron dropped his feet, and a slow grin tugged at his lips. Luke was next to strip down to his shorts, then Joey. But the kicker was when Doug tore off his shirt and went sliding across the grass. "Give me that soap!" He shouted.

Soon all six Brannings and Aaron's brothers and sister were dancing and playing in the rain, lathering up with soap and shampoo, fighting with the suds, laughing their heads off.

And the rain kept coming.

"Come on, Aaron. It feels great!" Logan said.

"Yeah, Aaron," Kay shouted. "Don't make us come get you."

He couldn't help smiling now. He pulled off his sweaty shirt and slowly sloshed out to the grass. Before he knew it, Jeff and Logan and Doug had descended on him, soaping him up like a greased pig, tickling him and making him laugh even if he didn't want to. Suds went flying, hitting Kay in the face like a pie, Doug in the back of his head, and Deni right between the shoulder blades.

They looked like the opening theme song of some TV sitcom. The perfect family, having fun and acting silly. Even the parents.

For a good hour, it all seemed like reality.

TWENTY-NINE

DOUG'S SERMON SUNDAY MORNING SEEMED TO STRIKE a chord with the flock he had accumulated over the past month. The group that had started in his living room had now outgrown his home, and they'd had to start setting up church at the lake. The bring-your-own-lawn-chair service had become a little more popular. Twenty families were coming now, and more joined each week. He hoped that the sound of their praise music would rise on the wind and waft across the neighborhood, luring others who needed time to worship during this dark time of their lives.

He had never planned to be a preacher. Just ten weeks ago he'd been a jet-setting stockbroker, working the economy to his advantage. But when the lights went out and he realized how little control he really had over his life, he had felt a yearning in his soul to worship the God who did have control. And since their home church was twenty miles away, too far to make it by bike every Sunday morning, he'd felt the need to start a church of his own.

Since then, he'd embarked on a serious study of God's Word—a study that had sustained him through this trial and enabled him to lead his small congregation.

He'd carefully prepared today's sermon about helping others in need, and the group had listened earnestly, many of them glancing at the Gatlin children sitting on the front row, lined up like object lessons of the sermon itself.

He paced as he spoke, his voice rising on the breeze. "I've realized after all these weeks that I can't make the electricity come back on. I can't make my generator come to life. I can't make my car crank up. My cell phone will probably never work again, and my computer may be a thing of the past. The Pulses could last years. My whole career is down the tubes, since the stock market hasn't been open in months and the banks are still closed and the economy has tanked."

He had their attention. They all knew of that out-of-control pain he spoke of.

"And as I prayed about that and cried out to God, he brought some children into my life."

He glanced down at the Gatlin kids, thankful they were still here. Kay had found their packed bags under the bed this morning, and they'd had to do another song-and-dance to keep them from leaving. Sarah was coloring on a piece of paper on the front row, and Luke was almost asleep. Joey and Aaron sat side by side, mirror images of one another, arms crossed like sentinels guarding their deepest secrets. Their faces were red in the hot sun.

"And these children led me to a place I needed to see. It was an apartment complex called Sandwood Place, not far from this neighborhood, and what I saw there made me realize that we in Oak Hollow, who before the outage, were the haves who towered above the have-nots, had not changed our status. This was a surprise to me, because I believed that we were in poverty.

"But then I went to Sandwood Place, and I saw people starving because they can't grow food. I saw children stealing just so they could eat. I saw people having to walk over a mile to get water. I saw sewage backed up and garbage stacked on itself, festering and breeding rodents and insects. And I started to understand how rich I truly am, even without electricity, even without computers and cell phones and cars. Even without a running refrigerator or a telephone. I'm rich because I live in a beautiful home with lots of rooms and lots of comfortable beds. I'm rich because my family is intact and they're all here with me. I'm rich because Oak Hollow just finished working together to dig a well, and now we have clean water. And I'm rich because, before that, I had a lake that was meeting my needs."

His eyes grew intense as he stepped closer to the crowd and leaned in. "And I'm rich because I know the God who holds all of this in the palm of his hand, the one who provides for me and guides me. And this morning when I was reading the Psalms, I came across Psalm 105, verse 19. It said, 'Until the time that his word came to pass, the word of the Lord tested him.'"

Doug looked up at the congregation. "You see, God made it clear to me weeks ago when my own daughter was missing—" he glanced at Deni—"that he had created the Pulses for a purpose. He's doing a mighty work with all the suffering and all the inconvenience, and it's going to have the results that he wants. But in the meantime, he's testing us, and as we've all found out, God doesn't work on our timetable.

"And so I started really asking what my test was in this. And I realized that it had to do with loving my neighbors as myself. So today, I'm asking each of you for your help. I know of one apartment complex in town where people are suffering, and I have to believe there are many more. In Oak Hollow, we figured out a way to dig a well, and some of us are growing food, and we can do even more if we co-op. Digging up our front and backyards will give us acres of property that we could till and cultivate and grow food on. I'm going to present it to the neighborhood and see if we can't arrange a co-op. But I think while we're doing that, we—as the church—need to reach out and give a helping hand to those people who don't have those resources. And it might mean getting our hands dirty, and it might mean extra sweat, and it might mean that we take time away from our work for our own survival to help them. That's what the Lord is showing me."

He paused as a low mumble started up, people whispering to each other, some frowning as if they didn't want to be asked to do anything else.

But he went on. "Now we have twenty families here. About half of us are kids, but that leaves thirty adults. I'm suggesting that we get together, and as a church, go to that apartment complex.

We start with that one area and try to clean up the garbage, try to educate residents on how to dispose of their garbage when there aren't any garbage trucks running. Heaven knows, if Eloise hadn't educated my family, we'd still be piling the garbage up in our back-yard. Educate them on composting, teach them to recycle, help them clean up the backed-up sewage in their bathrooms. Show them ways around their problems. It can be done. We can change their quality of life with a little muscle and a lot of sweat."

He couldn't tell from their faces whether they were with him or not. He sure hoped he'd gotten through to some of them.

"My family has already agreed that we're in. Who will go with us?" He waited, hoping for everyone there to raise a hand. But there was a long pause.

Finally, Stella Huckabee spoke up. "Doug, there's just not enough time. Already, we're doing everything we can to survive ourselves. We don't have time to go digging up somebody else's garbage. And if we're going to survive winter, we have a lot of hard work to do now."

"I'm not suggesting we spend hours and hours a day there. Maybe one day a week, or maybe just a couple of hours a day. We were able to take time out to dig a well. Why can't we do this?"

"Because," Hank said, "you're talking about people who don't want to help themselves."

"How do you know they don't want to, Hank?"

Doug saw Aaron look over his shoulder at the man. His face grew harder.

"If they wanted to, they would have done it by now."

"Hank, what do you suggest they do? If they have no place to grow food, if they have no place to get jobs, if they have no place to get water, what else can they do? Yes, some of them are stealing to get by, and there are people looting and stealing things that have nothing to do with survival. But let's not paint the whole group with that brush. I don't think any of us should provoke God by saying we would never do the same things."

Andy Honeycutt looked troubled. "Doug, I want to do what God wants us to do, but this is something new to me, and I want to make sure before we do this that we're not just throwing our labor down the drain. I mean, what if we go and clean up all their garbage, and then a week later it's all right back where it was?"

"It's going to take some patience and some time," Doug said. "There may be some people there who *don't* want to do for themselves, but there are others who are seriously trying to survive and doing everything they know how to do—but it's not enough. There are a lot of people in that apartment complex who worked hard for a day's pay before the outage. They don't have any place to go now to get a paycheck. The Bible commands us to help our brothers."

"They're not our brothers," someone said. "That place is full of drugs and crime. It was that way before the outage, and it's got to be worse now."

"Not all of them are dopeheads," Aaron muttered. "They're not all losers. Some of them are good."

Doug heard the defensive edge to his tone. His voice was gentler as he answered. "They've had the same wake-up call we've had. Maybe God has gotten their attention just like he got ours."

"He hasn't even gotten the attention of everybody in Oak Hollow," someone shouted. "There are only twenty families here, Doug. If he'd got their attention, this whole lot would be full."

Sweat dripped down his temple, despite the breeze sweeping across the water. Looking across the lake, he saw people working out in their gardens. Someone nearby was hammering. A horse-drawn wagon full of produce for sale was circling the neighborhood, the clop of the horses' hooves gentle in the quiet morning.

Doug opened his Bible. "In 1 John 3:17, we're told: 'If anyone has material possessions and sees his brother in need but has no pity on him, how can the love of God be in him?' We're commanded to show mercy, as God has shown us mercy. And that means we have to put our faith into action. If Jesus were still walking the earth and saw those people struggling, do you think he would turn his back on them? They're not going to find God when they're struggling so hard they have to look up to see the bottom. I'm just telling you, if Christian people go and show them how to live and teach them what to do, and help them find food and water,

then maybe they'll see something different in us, and want what
we have. What difference does Christ make in our lives if we're not
willing to do that?"

There was silence as his congregation stared back at him. He
met Aaron's pensive eyes, and hoped the kid knew how hard he was
trying. But Aaron looked like he was waiting for the punch line.

"Maybe after the disbursement," Hank said, " when we've each
got a little cash in our hands and we can buy some of the things we
need, maybe when they have some cash in their hands, that would
be the best time for us to start helping them. Maybe we can just
work toward that."

Doug didn't like it. He was ready to help them now. But the
disbursement was just a few days away.

"All right," he said. "Meanwhile, I'm going to be doing what
I can to lay the groundwork, but I'm going to need commitments
from you people. I want you to go home and seriously examine
your hearts and ask God what his will for you is in this. He's provided for us, and now we need to help him provide for someone
else."

"God is the creator of the universe," Max Keegan said. "He
doesn't need our help."

"No, but he wants to bless us," Doug said, "and this may be the
way he's going to do it."

THIRTY

THE WOMAN STANDING AT THE DOOR LOOKED FAMILIAR, but Kay couldn't place her. "Can I help you?"

"Yeah. I was looking for the Gatlin kids. Somebody said they were at this address."

"And who are you?"

"I'm Edith, their next-door neighbor over at the apartments. I heard about what happened to their mom and stuff, and I wanted to make sure they're all right."

Now she remembered. Edith was the woman who'd told them in the apartments' parking lot about the kids being alone—the neighbor who had done nothing to help them all those weeks after their mother vanished. "Oh ... how are you?"

"Okay, considering I had to hitchhike and got a ride with some sweaty old man with a horse and wagon. I woulda been better off walking."

"Maybe so," Kay said. "It's not that far if you cut through the woods."

"Whatever. It was worth it, because I was just so worried about those sweet kids." Something about her description of them didn't ring true. The woman Jeff had met at the apartments that first day had shown no love for them.

"Well, they're fine." Edith tried to come inside, but Kay blocked her.

"Can I see them?"

Kay searched for an out, but realized she didn't have one. The children were in the backyard helping Doug build a coop for the chickens they hoped to buy on Disbursement Day. The Gatlin boys had tried to get out of it, but Doug had managed to get them to anyway. It had turned into quite a task, requiring them to tear down their own wooden fence for the lumber.

The belligerence of the Gatlin children had been something Kay and Doug had struggled to tolerate for the last few days. It was difficult getting them to do anything, and because of their reluctance, Logan had been dragging his feet on every task he'd been assigned to. Their youngest child had been complaining more than ever that there was nothing to do that was fun, how he needed his video games and television. He and Aaron had formed a bond when they discovered each other's love for movie heroes, from Rambo to the Terminator to the X-Men. Kay and Doug tried to allow them time to play each night—the Gatlin boys had probably not had the chance to do that in a very long time. But tonight Doug needed more help.

"I've missed those little tykes," Edith said in a saccharine-sweet voice. "I just want to see their cute little faces and let them know I'm thinking about them. That little Sarah is as cute as they come."

Kay refrained from rolling her eyes. "They're out back building something." She led her through the house and to the open back door.

"Aaron, Joey, Luke, Sarah, you've got a visitor!"

Aaron looked out from around the coop and saw Edith in the doorway. "What are *you* doing here?"

"Aaron!" She crossed the patio and hugged him. Aaron stood stiffly in that hug, a troubled look on his face as if he didn't trust her. Kay's antennae went back up.

Doug dropped the fence boards he was carrying across the yard and set his hands on his hips, as if bracing himself.

Kay looked at him. "Doug, this is Edith, from the apartments. The next-door neighbor."

He nodded.

Sarah sat a few feet away, clutching her baby doll and sucking on her thumb. Edith reached out for her, and slowly Sarah slipped out of her chair and came toward her.

The woman hugged the child. "Poor little thing. I heard about what happened to your mama and my heart just broke. All this time, her laying out there, and there we were, looking all over for her. I've been crying since I heard."

She let Sarah go and didn't bother to hug the other two. It was just as well. They hung back, just out of her reach, frowning. Kay pulled out a chair at the patio table. "Would you like to sit down?"

The woman ignored her. "I don't want you four to worry now," she told them. "I plan to do everything I can to help you. That's why I came here. I woke up this morning thinking what I could do to help you, and all of a sudden it just hit me. I thought, I can let them come live with me!"

Doug crossed the yard then. "Can we talk inside?"

Edith stood her ground. "I came to talk to them, not you."

Aaron just stared at her. "You don't even like us. You used to cuss us out fifty times a day. You didn't even get along with our mom."

"Okay, so I'm not perfect. But I've changed, you know? I'm trying to do better with my life. And I just got to thinking that you and me, we're so much alike, and we could help each other. And this preacher guy I've been going to, who's helping me to learn to do better, he told me I need something to be responsible for."

Kay almost laughed. She wanted to tell this woman to get a cat—that the "preacher guy" certainly hadn't meant that she needed to take in four children.

Doug cleared his throat and glanced at Kay, as if asking her why she'd allowed this woman back here. "That's nice. But it won't be necessary. We've offered them a home here until we can locate their relatives, and so far, we've been able to provide for them pretty well."

"No offense, but they don't even know you," Edith said. "You just kind of came in and swept them off without giving them a choice. I just want them to know that they do have a choice, and if they want to come back to the place they're used to, they're more than welcome to come and live with me."

Kay set her teeth. "The judge has given us temporary custody of them, but thanks anyway."

Edith's face hardened, and she didn't look like she was going to budge. Kay's eyes met Doug's, and she wondered if he was going to have to bodily remove this woman—who weighed all of ninety pounds. Kay could probably take her herself.

As quickly as she had that thought, Kay mentally kicked herself. What was she doing? Planning to fight the woman? Had she gone insane?

Yes, she felt like she had. The stress was so great, and her fatigue so heavy, and the emotional distance so great between her and Doug because they were so busy ...

Edith hadn't finished with her spiel. "Now you kids know you don't have to stay where you don't want to stay. You have options."

Kay's lips stiffened. "Edith, I think it's time for you to leave."

"Not yet, lady." Her tone was defiant. She turned back to Aaron. "You know, you probably have a lot of rules and stuff here, kid. But if you come live with me, I'm not into rules. I just feel like people should get along with each other, you know? Besides, Aaron, you're almost grown up. Shoot, you're more mature than half the guys I've gone out with. You don't need anybody telling you what to do."

Now she'd gotten Aaron's attention. Kay saw the change on Aaron's face, the lifted chin, the heavy lids as he peered up at the woman.

"That's enough." Doug took the woman's arm, urged her toward the street. "It was nice of you to come by and say hi, but the kids are busy right now."

The woman shook free of him, and turned back to Aaron. "What do you say, Aaron?"

"I'll think about it," he said.

Kay wanted to throttle her. "No, he won't think about it! They're staying here. The judge put them in our custody and we're going to take care of them until their family is found."

"Their family doesn't care about them," Edith said. "If they did, they'd be here. They wouldn't have let them starve like they have. Besides, these kids know me better than anybody else. I've been their next-door neighbor for the past year."

Kay grabbed her arm, taking over the physical removal herself. She pulled the woman back through the house and to the front door.

"You can't make them stay in this prison," Edith said, her voice getting louder. "Those kids have never done anything they didn't want to do. They'll be out of here before you know it!"

Kay opened the front door and put her out.

"At least they know now they have a place to go!"

Doug reached around Kay and slammed the door. Kay watched out the peephole as the woman descended the front steps, still shouting over her shoulder. Kay turned back to Doug. "Can you believe that?"

"You shouldn't have let her in. What were you thinking?"

She might have known he would blame her. "What would you have done? She acted all worried about them after hearing about Jessie." She looked down at the children who had followed them into the house. "Aaron, I want you to forget all about her invitation. She didn't take care of you when she had the chance. She could have helped you anytime after your mother disappeared, but she didn't."

"We took care of *her*," Joey said bitterly. "She was always taking our water and our food. No wonder she wants us back."

"That's what I figured," Kay said. "Don't you worry. We'll keep her away if I have to have her arrested."

Aaron just kept staring at the door. "She wasn't that bad, Joey."

Kay wanted to scream. "Aaron, you're fine here, okay? Everybody's fine. You have plenty to eat, all the water you need, a clean place to live. You don't have to steal to get by. And you don't have to go back to that place for freedom. *That* was a prison, not *this*!"

Aaron didn't say anything. He just went back outside and resumed his work. The boys followed him, but Sarah stayed behind, her dirty little thumb still in her mouth.

Kay picked her up. "Let's wash your hands, sweetie," she said, taking her to the water bowl.

Sarah took her thumb out of her mouth. "Do we have to go back home?"

Kay looked into her big, round eyes and pushed her curls back from her face. "No, honey. You never have to go back there again."

She hoped the child would take her at her word, but as she washed her hands, she saw the worry on Sarah's little face. And Kay determined right then that Edith would take them over her dead body.

Doug came into the kitchen and stood watching the children through the bay window. He was angry at her, and that was fine with her. She was angry at him too. He had no right to accuse her when he might have done the same thing.

Then he sat down at the kitchen table, set his elbows there, and lowered his face into his hands.

Suddenly her heart melted. She dried off the child's hands and lifted her down to the floor. "Go back and help the boys, honey."

Sarah nodded and went back outside.

Kay went to the table, pulled out a chair, and sat down next to him. Gently, she touched the back of his head.

He looked up at her, his eyes glistening. "What's happening to us?"

She shook her head. "I don't know."

He reached out and took her hand. "We're both so tired, so preoccupied. If you're like me, you feel like the whole world is on your shoulders. It was heavy enough a week ago. Now it's twice as heavy."

She nodded. "Guess I'm like you, then. That's exactly how I feel."

He drew in a deep breath. "Jesus said, 'Come to me, all you who are weary and burdened, and I will give you rest.' I could sure use some rest right now."

"Me too. I haven't slept well since they got here. I'm afraid if I sleep I won't hear them sneaking out or robbing us blind."

"Maybe that's what we're doing wrong. Maybe we're trying to carry it ourselves and not taking Christ's yoke. He says it's easy and his burden is light."

"It's hard to do, when there are constant fires that need putting out." She brought his hand to her lips. "I miss you, you know. I miss spending time alone with you. I miss watching a movie with you. I miss just relaxing and reading a book with your head in my lap, while you watch football."

He nodded. "I miss that too. Maybe we need to find a way to take some time for ourselves."

"Even with eight children?"

"Especially with eight children. If you and I fall apart, what can we offer them?"

He stroked her hair and brought her face to his. Gently, he kissed her, and all the tension that had crusted over in her heart began to soften and melt slowly away.

THIRTY-ONE

DENI TRIED TO CONCENTRATE ON HER CHORES ON Monday, but all day long, she could think of nothing but getting to the post office to see if there'd been a letter from Craig. Now that the trains were running, the postal deliveries were expected to come more frequently, but Deni couldn't wait for the latest bundle to make its way to Oak Hollow. Surely by now Craig had gotten her stack of letters describing what she'd been through trying to get to him. By now, he'd probably written back, something more than that one short page with all his dry, cold facts.

As soon as she finished her work, she hopped on her bicycle and rode to the post office. The doors and windows were all open and the air in the moldy place was stifling. The door to the offices was locked, so she went to the slot that said Metered Mail and called through the hole. "Is anybody here?"

On the other side of the wall, someone yelled, "Yeah, I'm coming."

She waited for a moment, then saw the postmaster coming toward her beyond the glass doors. The woman looked close to retirement age, and she was wearing a baseball cap and a pair of smudged reading glasses. She unlocked the door and pushed it open.

"Everybody who slows me down is getting their mail a little bit later. What do you want?"

Deni tried to look contrite. "I'm sorry. Really, I am. I'm just expecting some real important mail. It's very important. Life-or-death stuff."

The woman shook her head. "I'm not through sorting it. I'm the only one working. And I can't pay any employees, so as postmaster, it's left to me to sort out thousands and thousands of pieces of mail, and it's taking me a while to get it delivered. Every interruption costs me time."

"I don't want to do that," Deni said, "but could I come in and just look through Oak Hollow's mail and see if there's anything for me?"

The woman took off her baseball cap and mopped her forehead with the sleeve of her T-shirt. "You got to be kidding. There are twenty thousand people in Crockett and weeks' worth of mail. I've got them sorted by neighborhood, but that's the best I've been able to accomplish so far."

"But you must have a system. Don't you even have bags from different places that I could go through? I'm looking for something from Washington, D.C."

"The mail doesn't come straight here from Washington, D.C.," she said. "It all goes to a distribution center, and then it's sorted out and sent here."

"Okay, the distribution center then. If I could go through that bag, I'm sure I could find my letter."

"You're insane," the woman said. "That would take days."

Deni breathed out a sigh. It was hopeless. She was going to have to wait.

But then the woman's face softened. "Aw, come on in. I'll let you go through the Oak Hollow mail. I've already sorted some of it. If it's there already, you can take it. But don't bother me."

"Yes, ma'am." Deni rushed behind her into the hot office. She thought it must be over one hundred degrees in the moldy place, and there were mountains of mail that the woman had been sorting through. "This is ridiculous. You should have help doing this."

"Well, I can't get anybody to come in for no pay. You want to come help, be my guest."

Deni didn't think she wanted to volunteer for that, but she sat on the floor in front of the Oak Hollow box and began sifting through pieces.

An hour later, drenched with sweat and drained of every ounce of energy, she finished looking through it. There was nothing there. Craig hadn't written her again.

She had tears in her eyes as she got back to her feet, dusted herself off, and peered around a mountain of mail at the postmaster. "Ma'am, I'm leaving now."

The woman didn't look up. "Didn't find it, huh?"

"No. I guess he didn't write."

The postmaster stopped sorting, took off her glasses, and cleaned them on her shirt. Glancing up at Deni, she said, "Don't give up on him. It may just not have gotten here yet."

Deni looked at the woman and realized she wasn't as hardened as she'd seemed. She swallowed. "Thanks for letting me look. My name's Deni Branning, by the way."

The woman stuck out her hand. "Nice to meet you, Deni. I'm Annie Lipscomb."

Deni forced a weak smile and shook Mrs. Lipscomb's sweaty hand. "I hope you get some help with all this soon."

"Yeah, me too."

Deni pushed back through the glass door and out into the fresh air where it was only eighty-seven degrees. Her bike was hot as she got back on it, but she rode toward home, wanting to deal with her disappointment in the privacy of her room.

MARK GREEN WAS WALKING UP HER DRIVEWAY WHEN SHE GOT home, carrying a big box. She didn't feel like talking, but she saw no way around it. "Hey, Mark," she said, getting off her bike. "What have you got?"

He grinned. "Something for you."

She pulled her bike into the shade of the garage. "What is it?"

He set it down on the concrete floor. Opening the flaps, he said, "Take a look."

She looked inside. "A typewriter?"

He grinned. "Yeah, isn't it great? I was going through my attic looking for something else, and my mom had it. It's manual, so it still works. She even had an unopened ribbon in a box nearby. You can have it, if you want it."

Deni took it out, marveling at its lightness. She pushed one of the keys. It took a lot more effort than a computer keyboard to make it strike the page, but she could get used to it.

"It'll make your newspaper look a little more professional."

Her depression slowly lifted. "Mark, this is great. Thank you."

"There's something else." He reached to the bottom of the box and pulled out a big manila envelope. "I found some carbon paper. My mom never throws anything away, and she had some in the back of a drawer in her desk at the house. I mean, it's so old and brittle that it'll probably fall apart, but hey, you might find a way to make it work."

"Carbon paper? Like that purple paper they put in credit card slips? They have that in big sheets?"

"Uh-huh. It won't save you a lot of time, and you'll only be able to make as many copies as there are carbons, plus my mom said to tell you that you're going to have to press really hard on those keys to make it go through very many copies. But it'll save you a little time."

"It's wonderful," she said. "I can do a lot with this, Mark." She sighed and pulled her sweat-dampened hair into a ponytail. "I needed something good to happen today. I've been at the post office for the last couple of hours digging through the letters, hoping to find something from Craig. Nothing."

"He'll write. You'll see. Hey, maybe he's even on his way here."

She wished that were true, but she didn't think it was. "No, I doubt he would do that when the trains are going to be transporting passengers soon. If he's going to come, he'll come then. I just don't think he will."

"Don't lose faith in him," Mark said. "If he's worth his salt, he'll come. Count on it."

She wished she could.

"And if he doesn't come, I might have to go to D.C. myself and beat him up."

Warmth surged through her. Mark was a good friend.

She wished Craig was more like him.

THIRTY-TWO

ABOUT TWENTY SANDWOOD PLACE RESIDENTS CAME TO Doug's meeting the next evening, after the Brannings passed out handwritten invitations to all of the families there. They sat on the hoods of the useless cars as Doug paced across the hot pavement. The thick humidity of the afternoon had lifted, and a cool breeze gave some relief. The doors to almost every apartment in the place were standing open. Upstairs, neighbors stood in their doorways or leaned on the rails overlooking the parking lot, curious enough to listen from a distance, but not committed enough to come all the way down.

But that was okay. Doug would take what he could get. "In Oak Hollow, we found a place to dig a well, and it took us weeks, but we finally hit water. You could do the same. I found a clearing in the woods that would be a good place to dig if we clean out the garbage that's back there on the edge of those woods. But it's going to take a lot of work. We would need every person who'll volunteer, and they would need to work through all the daylight hours in one- or two-hour shifts."

"Sounds good to me," one of the women said, "but there ain't that many men here. The ones who are here don't want to work. They're lazy whelps."

"Excuse me, but I take exception to that," a big burly man with a long beard said. "I'm not lazy and I'm not a whelp. Count me in. I'll work on that well."

"Me too," another man said. "If this thing's going on as long as they say, we're going to need a water source."

"But how do you know we'll hit water?" one asked. "I mean, isn't it possible just to dig and dig and dig and never get to the end?"

"No," Doug said. "If we dig deep enough, through all the different levels of earth and rock, we'll hit the water table eventually. And if we pick the right place to dig, the water will be clean."

Some of them listened skeptically as he described how he and the others had built the walls around the well as they went, but others followed him closely, eyes riveted.

"Of course, first things first. We've got to clean up the garbage. Besides the stench, it could pollute the groundwater. I know what it's like to have garbage piling up and not know how to get rid of it. We were doing the same thing in Oak Hollow until some of the older residents explained to us what would work better. First you have to separate it by category, find the things that can be washed and recycled, start a compost pile for anything that will biodegrade. And then you've got to find a place to burn or bury the rest of it. I'm willing to help with that work. Does anyone want to volunteer to join me?"

No one stepped up.

He tried again. "I know it seems like a big task, but you won't be doing it alone. My family and I are going to be out here tomorrow starting that process," he said, "and I'm trying to get as many people in my church and my neighborhood to help as possible."

"Last thing we need is a bunch of church people comin' over here and lookin' down on us," someone shouted from upstairs.

He looked up and found the source. A woman sat beside the rail, two toddlers on her lap. "We're not judging you," he shouted. "We all started out doing the same things you're doing. It's only been a few weeks since the outage. There's a learning curve, and if we're to be good neighbors, we need to share what we've learned. We can get you started on the well, and we can get you started on the cleanup, and those of you with apartments that have sewage backups, we'll figure out something to do with that, as well.

"And there's something else I can help you with. In a week, we're all going to have some cash. I'm not getting any more than any of you. But if you'll come down here and listen, I'm about to tell you some ways to make money with what you're given."

A few of those from upstairs came down to get closer. Among them was Edith. She sidled up to Aaron and the kids and stroked little Sarah's curls. Kay moved between them.

Kay and Doug had seriously considered leaving the Gatlin kids at home when they came here today to avoid exposing them to Edith. But then they decided that it might help to bring the kids along. Maybe seeing that the kids had been well cared for would make the neighbors trust Doug more. Besides, Aaron had been insistent on checking on his apartment. He was certain the neighbors were going to break in and clean it out with his family gone.

When everyone who wanted to hear had come down and found a place in front of him, Doug resumed his talk. "As you know, prices are falling pretty drastically. Supply and demand will be what drives the prices. Wise people will start now looking around town to figure out what people need and what they're willing to spend their disbursements on. Those wise people will purchase a few key items with which they can make things that they can sell or barter. If you're smart, you won't squander your twenty-five dollars on spontaneous purchases, because we're not going to get another disbursement for another three months. My background is in finance, though I'm unemployed now, just like you. But I'll give private consultations for free if any of you want to talk."

"What's in it for you?" Edith asked.

He turned to her, meeting her defiant eyes. "Believe it or not, nothing. I'm doing this because Jesus Christ told us to help each other. I'm a follower of his, so I'm doing what he commanded."

"We don't need your kind coming in here and treating us like trash. We can help ourselves without you."

He felt the blood rushing to his face. "Sometimes we need ideas. I sure did, when garbage was piling up at my house. If someone hadn't shown me what to do, I'd have had a mountain of it behind my house just like you do now. And if someone hadn't known about digging wells and how it could be done, I'd still be hauling dirty lake water to my house several times a day."

There was silence for a moment, and he looked around at the faces of the residents, wondering if this was going to end badly. But finally, the big burly man spoke up. "We appreciate you, Doug. We can use a little guidance. I'll be here tomorrow night."

"I'll be here, too," someone else said.

Slowly, some of the others joined in. But most of the residents just stared at him belligerently. Maybe between tonight and tomorrow, the recruits would persuade them. It only took a few people to change a community.

"I'll be here tomorrow night at six," he said. "I'll have as many people with me as I can get to come. Together, we'll start to work on the garbage cleanup, then we can look more closely at the clearing where I think a well might work. I'm not promising you it'll be easy, but I am promising that it will make your life better, one day at a time."

As the crowd broke up, he prayed that some of the residents would actually show up to help.

THIRTY-THREE

THE NEXT DAY DENI AND BETH AND THEIR BROTHERS worked on digging up the sod in their front yard, preparing to till the ground for planting. Sarah and Luke played on the front porch with some of Beth's old Barbie dolls and Logan's army men. Aaron and Joey had volunteered to go to the well, but they'd been gone way too long. Deni imagined they were lingering to keep from having to do any work. Logan would have been right there with them if their father had let him go too.

With every dig of the shovel, Deni hated more the situation they were in. Though she'd come to accept their plight, she still had moments when she longed to be with Craig in Washington, D.C., playing her iPod through the car stereo, heading to one of his important parties where she could be his trophy wife-to-be and revel in his position and influence. By now, she should have been in her third month as an intern at the NBC affiliate. Maybe by now they would have promoted her to a full-fledged employee and given her field-reporting jobs. Maybe, if she was really lucky, they would have recognized her talent and put her behind the news desk.

But no. Instead, she was here, digging up grass and baring her yard in the early steps of a laborious job that would hopefully feed them through the winter. She never would have dreamed she'd be in this position.

"Who's *this* guy?"

Deni followed Jeff's gaze to a man walking up the street toward their house. She caught her breath. "That's Moe Jenkins. He's one of Jessie's old boyfriends. Dad and I talked to him the other day. We're pretty sure he's Sarah's father, even though he denies it." She squinted in the sunlight. "Is he coming here?"

Jeff jabbed his shovel into the ground as the man swaggered closer. "Looks like it."

The man gave them a cursory wave as he reached the yard. "How y'all doing?"

Deni muttered that she was fine. Moe was dressed in filthy jeans that looked like he'd rolled in the dirt. He wore a threadbare T-shirt, its hem coming loose, and a backward baseball cap on greasy hair. His skin looked dry and brittle, and the leathery wrinkles around his eyes made him look middle-aged. She suspected he was younger than he looked.

Spotting the two children on the porch, he started to cross the yard.

"Excuse me," Jeff said, blocking his way. "Can I help you?"

The man smelled of alcohol. "I came to see my little girl."

Deni glanced up at the porch. Sarah looked up at him without recognition.

"That's funny," she said. "When my dad and I came to talk to you, you denied *having* a little girl. You said nobody'd ever been able to prove it."

"Yeah, well, I got to thinking after you left. Started feeling a little guilty about that, and then I found out about Jessie's death."

He pushed past Jeff and started up the porch steps. Luke started to cry. Gripping his army men in his hands, he stood up and backed away.

"What's the matter, Luke?" Moe said. "It's me, Moe. Don't you remember me?"

Luke nodded, but the fear remained on his face.

That was it! Deni wouldn't allow this man to torment these children. She stepped on to the porch and sat down in the rocker, and pulled Luke onto her lap. He buried his face in her neck and clung to her, trembling.

"Moe, the sight of you doesn't give these kids warm fuzzies. I don't think Luke wants to see you."

"That's okay. I mainly came to see my daughter." He bent over and stroked Sarah's hair. "Hey, sweetie. How are you?"

She took her thumb out of her mouth and looked up at him skeptically. "Fine."

He reached out as if to pick her up, but Jeff grabbed his arm. "Don't touch her."

Moe turned back, eye to eye with the sixteen-year-old. Jeff's hard glare was intimidating. "I'm not gonna hurt her!"

"Then what do you want?" Jeff demanded.

For a moment, Deni feared a fight would break out, but she was confident Jeff could take him. She reached out for Sarah, and the little girl came quickly.

Moe's voice softened. "The truth is, after I saw you and your dad, I got to feeling like I was shirking my responsibility. And now that Jessie's dead, I decided I need to step up to the plate. Be a man."

Deni's stomach tightened. Surely he didn't mean . . .

"I thought it was time I came and got these kids. I'm Sarah's daddy, and the boys are her brothers. So I guess I'll take all four of them."

Deni caught her breath. "No way. My parents won't let you take them!" She set Luke down. "Honey, go find my dad and tell him to come out."

Luke scurried into the house. Deni got to her feet, still holding Sarah's hand.

"You must be crazy," Jeff said. "A few days ago you didn't want anything to do with them. Now you want to herd them up and take them home?"

Moe held up a hand to calm him. "No need to get upset, now. I can explain. See, those kids were Jessie's heart and soul. And I loved her. So what else can I do?"

"You *loved* her?" Deni repeated. "The other day you acted like you hated her guts!"

Doug came out of the house, Luke cowering behind his legs. Kay followed.

"What's going on?" Doug asked.

"He thinks he's going to take the kids," Deni said. "All four of them."

Kay gasped, and Doug's mouth fell open. "This wouldn't have anything to do with their disbursements, would it? The hundred bucks you could pad your pockets with if you had four extra kids around?"

Deni couldn't believe she hadn't realized it. Of course that was what he wanted.

The man looked indignant. "Are you accusing me of exploiting these kids?"

"Yeah, I think so," Doug said. "That's what it sounds like to me. You weren't that interested in them when I talked to you a few days ago. You even denied paternity."

"I told your son, I got to thinking."

"Yeah, you got to thinking about the money," Doug said. "Look, we have custody of these kids. We're trying to find their family."

"Hey, I *am* Sarah's family."

"But as you said, nobody's been able to prove that yet."

"Look on her birth certificate," Moe insisted. "My name is listed as her father."

Deni doubted he'd even shown up at the hospital when Jessie had given birth. "Do you have a copy?"

Moe threw her a look. "No. Jessie had that."

"Then there's no proof at all, is there?"

Moe was getting angry. "Man, if I have to get a lawyer, I will. But I'm getting those kids."

"Fine," Doug said. "Why don't you go straight to the sheriff right now and talk to him? He's the one who put them in our care."

"Hey, I don't need the sheriff. All I need is a judge."

"The judge knows us. He gave us a court order."

"That was before somebody who was blood kin came to claim them."

Doug's teeth came together. "It's time for you to get off my property."

The man backed away, lifting his hands in the air like he didn't mean any harm. "Fine. If that's the way you want it, that's the way you got it. Expect papers to be delivered in the next day or two. Mark my word, I'm getting those kids."

As he turned to walk off the porch, Aaron and Joey walked up carrying a bucket of water from the well. When he saw Moe, Aaron stopped and set the bucket down. "What's he doing here?"

"I came to see you, Aaron."

Aaron's chin shot up. "Get lost. You don't belong here."

Moe crossed the yard to the boy and kicked his bucket over. Leaning down, he looked into the kid's face. "Nice to see you too, buddy."

Doug seethed as the man sauntered away. He stared at him until he was off their property.

As he went away, Deni saw that Luke was still sobbing. She bent down and looked into his frightened, tear-stained face. "What's the matter, Luke? Has that man hurt you before?"

"Not me," he said, sniffing. "He hurt my mommy."

"What'd he do? How did he hurt her?"

"He hit her."

"It's true," Joey said. "He broke her nose once and knocked out some of her teeth."

Aaron went up to comfort his brother. "Don't worry, Luke. Moe's not gonna touch us. We're not going anywhere with him!"

Sarah pulled her thumb out of her mouth and looked in the direction the man had gone. Deni hoped her father had a means of keeping him from getting her. If that man got custody, it would be the biggest disaster of Sarah's life.

Even worse than her murdered mother.

THIRTY-FOUR

THAT NIGHT THE BRANNING FAMILY ASSEMBLED THEIR
little team of workers—the whole family and a few church
members. Of the fifty families represented in the Sandwood
Place Apartments, only fourteen people showed up to help
with the garbage cleanup. Aaron didn't know why Doug
wouldn't listen to him—the whole thing was just a great
big waste of time.

The whole process made him sick, and he couldn't stop
thinking about his mom lying in those woods for all those
weeks, just behind all that garbage.

He wondered where her body was now. Lying on a table
somewhere? In a coffin? The police had taken her off to do
some tests or something, but he didn't know when they'd
give her back. It troubled him to think that she hadn't been
buried yet. But if they gave her to him, what would he do?
Where would he dig the hole to bury her? Planting a rosebush in her honor was one thing, but putting his mother in
the ground was another.

He started to feel sick, so he wandered back toward the
building.

"Aaron, where are you going?" Kay asked.

"To my apartment," he said. "I need to get something."

Kay's eyes were concerned as she gazed at him. "Okay,
but let Deni go with you."

Earlier they'd made plans for him and Joey, Luke, and
Sarah to stay home, but he'd convinced them that if anyone

was going to Sandwood Place, he was. It was his home, and he had things to check on. They'd finally given in, but they insisted that he keep someone with him at all times.

What did they think he'd do? Get lost? They were his apartments, and he knew his way around. He sure didn't need a babysitter.

Deni followed him up the stairs. There was crime scene tape on the door, and the sheriff had lectured the residents about leaving the apartment alone. According to one of the neighbors, the sheriff had told them that if he found so much as a hair or fingerprint that didn't belong, that person would be considered a suspect. So far it had worked. Aaron and the Brannings had permission to go inside, though.

Deni wouldn't give him the key, so he waited as she opened the door. He stepped into the sweltering, rancid air that smelled of sewage. The smell almost knocked him back.

Deni covered her mouth and nose. "Man, how'd you ever live here? This place is gross."

"Toilet's backed up," he said.

Deni choked.

What a drama queen.

"We're going to have to get in here and clean this up," Deni said, "but it's not a job I'm volunteering for. Mom and Dad can do it. They're used to cleaning up stuff that makes them nauseous. Just hurry up and get what you need so we can get out of this place."

Aaron resented her disgust. This place was his home. It was where he'd lived with his mother, and all things considered, they'd had a few happy memories here. Like that time after she got out of jail and she was clean for a few days. She'd made spaghetti and a birthday cake for Joey. They'd watched some lame Disney movie on TV. *The Little Mermaid* or something like that. Things had been good those days.

There were times when his mother had been a nice person, though not many people knew it. They only knew her as a doper. Half the time she couldn't walk straight. But every now and then, she had been like a real person, with a personality and everything.

And during those times, he'd clung to hope that things would change.

They just never had.

He walked into her bedroom, looked around at her things. There was nothing here that he needed, not right away. But there was a picture of her tacked to a bulletin board on the wall. He took it down and looked at it, and that old knot swelled up in his throat.

She'd been a terrible mother. He should be glad she was dead.

Then guilt, strong and stark as the apartment's smell, pulsed through him. She was his mother. He had always taken care of her. But things had gone so wrong.

"Hurry up, Aaron," Deni called from the other room. "I'm gonna throw up if we don't get out of here."

He shook himself free of her memory. He grabbed a Wal-Mart bag from the floor. She had bought some thread, of all things, and some polka-dot material, like she was going to make Sarah a dress or something. She must have bought it during one of her I'm-sorry-I'm-a-lousy-mother-and-I'll-do-better episodes. He dumped out the bag's contents, then grabbed a few things that he wanted and dropped them in.

Then he granted Deni's wish and got out of there.

The truth was, he was glad to be out of there too. Even to him, the stink was awful. He couldn't believe he had lived there all that time. He should have cared more about his brothers and sister and forced himself to clean it up. But the sewage backup wasn't his fault. How many other apartments here had the same problem and were living with that smell?

Deni locked the door behind them and took a deep breath of air. "Thank goodness," she said. "They need to just burn that apartment out and start over with it."

"No, they don't. They need to leave it alone."

"I'm just saying they'll never be able to rent it out again. The bathroom's probably ruined."

He felt his ears burning. "Everything's ruined, or haven't you heard? Nothing works in this stupid town."

She seemed surprised she'd insulted him. "Sorry, I didn't mean to upset you."

"I don't go around talking about the mess in *your* lousy room," he said.

"Don't be so sensitive."

He wasn't sensitive, but he didn't feel like going on with this lame conversation. He stormed back to the stairs as if anxious to get back to digging up the garbage. Behind him, a door opened.

"Hey, Aaron, you're back!"

He turned and saw his next-door neighbor Edith leaning out of her doorway. "Yeah," he bit out. "I came to dig through your garbage. Why aren't you down there doing it?"

Before, if he'd said a thing like that, she would have cussed him a blue streak and threatened to hit him. Instead, she smiled like he was the cutest thing. "Garbage isn't my thing," she said. "I'm, like, allergic to refuse."

Allergic to refuse? Where did she get this stuff?

She strolled toward him. "So, Aaron, have you thought about my offer?"

He shrugged. "Not really."

"Well, you should. I thought it all out. We'll put a door between our apartments—"

"Stop it," Deni cut in. "He's not coming to live with you, so give it up."

Whoa.

Edith challenged Deni with a look, and he almost expected his neighbor to lunge. He'd seen her lose her temper before.

"I don't believe I was talking to you." She turned from Deni back to Aaron, her tone all sweetness. "As I was saying, Aaron, we can put in a door and you can stay in your own apartment, and I can stay in mine, but we can go between and I can look after you. Wouldn't you like that?"

"My apartment needs a plumber," he said. "It smells bad."

"Well, we can clean it up. Didn't your warden say he was getting some plumbers to come help us?"

Warden. That was a good word for Doug Branning. He gave her a smirk. "I thought you were allergic to refuse."

"Hey, for you I'd do anything."

He tried to think of one thing she'd ever done for him before.

"Come on," Deni said. "Give me a break."

Edith ignored her. She was really piling it on. "Think about it, Aaron. I know you're mature enough to do what you want. You've been surviving just fine for the last couple of months and taking good care of your brothers and sister. It's not like you need constant supervision."

Deni took Aaron's hand and started to pull him toward the stairs. "I told you to leave him alone."

"Yeah?" Edith thrust her chin up. "And who made you queen? I'll talk to him if I want."

Aaron jerked free. "They won't let me live here," he told Edith. "They don't trust you."

"Well, if you tell the judge that you really want to live with me, he'll listen. They care what you think."

"No, they don't. Nobody cares what I think. You get a judge involved with us and we'll be in four different foster homes before you know it."

"Just think about it," Edith said. "You know you want to live with me, Aaron. I can give you your freedom."

Aaron let Deni pull him toward the stairs, but he looked over his shoulder at Edith. He'd never associate the word *freedom* with her. Instead, she seemed like a slave. To what, he wasn't sure. She was so skinny that it looked like her bones would break. Her skin was pale, her hair stringy.

Something wasn't right about her offer, but it was tempting.

They reached the stairs, and he followed Deni down.

"Do you believe her?" Deni asked. "Like she really wants to help you? After all those months when she didn't care a thing about you?"

The not-caring might be a good thing. If someone didn't care, they wouldn't watch you that closely. If there was anything he wanted right now, it was his freedom. Chances were, she'd be like his mother, hardly paying attention at all. The judge and the sheriff would *think* he was supervised, but really, he could do whatever he wanted, take care of his brothers and sister the way he needed to without any outside help. Maybe it would work.

He couldn't see her going in there and cleaning out the toilet, though. He'd have to do that himself. But since being at the Brannings, he'd kind of gotten used to work. Maybe if he came back here and cleaned it up, the sheriff would look and see that it wasn't such a bad place after all. Maybe he would agree to let them come back.

As he followed Deni back around to the garbage dump, he began making a plan.

THIRTY-FIVE

THE SHERIFF CAME BY SANDWOOD PLACE THAT EVENING TO interview some more of the apartment dwellers about Jessie's life and death. When he was finished, he came around back to talk to Doug.

"I've been trying to investigate Jessie's current boyfriend," he said. "The guy has a rough past. It looks like he's cleaned up his act. He's living with his parents, working hard. I don't really think he was involved with the murder, but he's helping me piece together the timeline leading up to her death. Oh, and by the way, Moe Jenkins actually managed to get a lawyer to file papers today to get immediate custody of the kids. Probably paid him with stolen goods."

Doug couldn't believe it. "You know why he's doing this. The same reason that Edith woman wants them. The disbursement is next week and they want the kids' money."

"Don't worry, Doug. I've already talked to the judge, and he's keeping them with you. It'll take months to get it to court, especially with the outage and so few lawyers and judges working. By that time, some things will have shaken out, and hopefully you will have found their grandparents."

"But won't a biological father have more rights than the grandparents? Couldn't he get Sarah if he wanted to?"

"I would say yes, if he were a fit father. But Jessie had him in court twice for failing to pay child support, and we have it on record that he denied being her father. That ought to play against him. Besides that, the court will want to keep the kids together. If the grandparents come forward to take them together, I think it'll work out."

"Let's just hope the grandparents are decent people."

Doug glanced toward the woods and saw Aaron peering into the trees with a dull, vacant look in his eyes. Was he thinking of his mother? Maybe bringing him here hadn't been such a good idea.

He went toward him. "Aaron? You all right, son?"

Aaron jumped, as if he'd been caught in his thoughts. "Yeah, I'm fine."

"Ready to go home?"

The boy turned back to the building and looked up at the window that had been his home. Was he longing to go back to that rancid apartment? Or was he simply longing for his mother?

Whatever the longing, Doug's heart swelled with compassion. The child was in pain, and he didn't know how to help him.

Only God and time could undo the damage now.

THIRTY-SIX

MARK RODE HIS BIKE BY THE HOUSE FRIDAY AFTERNOON AS Deni was working in the yard. "Hey, Deni. I was just at the post office, and Mrs. Lipscomb said to tell you that you got what you were waiting for."

Deni dropped her shovel and almost leapt into his arms. "Really? A letter from Craig? Did you bring it?"

He laughed. "No, she wouldn't let me. But she said to tell you that she was delivering to Oak Hollow sometime late this afternoon."

"I can't wait until then!" She dropped her shovel and started for the garage. "I'm going there now."

"Don't bother," he said. "She's not there. She's out delivering mail."

DENI FIDGETED ALL AFTERNOON, WAITING FOR THE MAIL TO come. It still hadn't come by the time her parents were ready to go to Sandwood Place, so she convinced them to let her stay home. She waited on the front porch for the old Dodge pickup to turn into the neighborhood.

At ten after seven, she heard it coming. She leaped off the porch as the old rattletrap rumbled into the neighborhood. She tried to wave it down, but Mrs. Lipscomb just kept driving.

Fighting the urge to run behind the truck, Deni instead took a shortcut through the yards and got to the neighborhood gazebo before the truck pulled in.

By the time the postmaster climbed out, there were thirty or forty people crowded around. Still wearing her baseball cap and baggy T-shirt, Mrs. Lipscomb grumbled. "Wait your turn, everybody. Never thought I'd be so popular."

She pulled out the first pack of letters. "Branning!"

Deni lunged forward and took them. The woman winked. Obviously, she had put her letters on top so she would be the first to get them. Deni wanted to kiss her. "Thank you, Mrs. Lipscomb! You rock!"

Quickly she pulled the rubber band off the stack of letters and flipped through. And there she saw it—Craig's return address. She pulled out the letter and practically danced as she waved it in the air.

"I got it," she cried to anyone who would listen. "He wrote!"

A few people applauded. Then she saw Mark leaning against the gazebo, a piece of straw in his mouth. Amusement twinkled in his eyes. "How many did you get?" he asked.

She flipped through the rest of their mail, but there were no more. "Just one," she said, "but I'm sure this one's all I need."

She hurried home, then went into her house and ran up to her room to read by the evening light at her window. Carefully she opened the envelope and pulled out the letter.

Dear Deni,

I got all your letters. It's taken me almost a week to read them all. Glad to know you've been keeping up your journalistic skills while everything's been down. Sorry you had so many problems at first, what with the airplane crashes and all, and I'm shocked that you had so much trouble trying to get to Washington. Too bad you didn't make it all the way.

She stopped reading and stared at those words again. After she'd told him of almost dying at the hands of a mad killer, could he really be this dispassionate?

She read back over that first paragraph, trying to imagine the tone of his voice if he were talking. Was there compassion in those words? Love? Longing?

She told herself she was being too critical. He loved her; she knew that.

I was a little surprised you got religion on me. I thought we were of the same mind about those kinds of things. Not that I have anything against religion. It always just seemed like another crutch to me, and you know how I hate crutches. But I guess if that's what you need to get through the outage, so be it.

Now that I think about it, it's probably a good thing that you didn't make it all the way to Washington. It's not the best time to start a marriage, if you know what I mean. Too much stress, and everything's just too hard right now. I can't imagine trying to set up housekeeping with no electricity and no food or water. We'd be at each other's throats. I guess the best thing to do is postpone until things are a little better. But you're still my fiancée, and I do still look forward to a future with you. I honestly don't think I can do better.

She paused and stared at the offhanded compliment, looking for the romance in that statement. But there wasn't any. Was that why he was with her? Because he thought she was the best he could do?

I'm really busy at work. We've got our hands full trying to put out fires ... literally. Last week a group of people got up in arms about the food being brought in for the government workers, and they started a riot. Somehow they managed to set a fire at the Capitol Building, and it was a nightmare getting it put out. The fire department is voluntary now, and we all had to line up in a bucket brigade, dumping water and using fire extinguishers until the fire was out. Thankfully no one was hurt. Now we have security all over the place.

She stopped reading and tried to imagine the scene. Desperate people screaming outside the building, fighting over food. Craig and the others holed up inside, fighting a fire with little more than squirt guns.

No wonder he didn't have time for romance. She sat down on her bed, feeling selfish and ungrateful.

Important people are coming to depend on me because I'm competent and reliable. Others have thrown in the towel and gone home. If Daniel Jacobs would just leave, I might be considered for Crawford's chief of staff. His wife is freaking out over all the violence here, and she's begging him to take her to Ohio to be with her family. I'm egging him on. Might turn out that those crazy citizens shaking the place down will help me to climb the ladder. All of this can't do anything but help my career when things get back to normal.

She stopped and took that in, wondering if he meant that as coldly as it sounded. Surely not. He couldn't interpret the suffering of desperate people and the social and economic upheaval of the Pulses as nothing but a career boost. Could he?

Sighing, she read on.

I'd better go for now. Hope all is well with you.

And it was signed simply, "Craig."

She read it again, searching for the words *I love you*, but he hadn't written them. Didn't he know how hungry she was for them?

Had his feelings for her changed or had he never cared that much? Maybe he'd been cold all along. Maybe she'd just been too blind to see it.

She wadded up the letter and tossed it into the trash. Then she got it back out, unwadded it, and read it again. She couldn't throw it away, but it wasn't worthy of folding neatly and putting back into its envelope. So she crushed it into a ball and shoved it into her pocket.

She sat on the patio and stewed for over an hour, anger roiling up inside her. She deserved better than this. God had a plan and a future for her, and he certainly wouldn't have chosen someone who was godless and mocked religion. He certainly wouldn't have matched her with someone who placed so little value on her. There must be something more for her.

Maybe that was why all this had happened, so she would see the error of her ways and back out of this marriage to Craig.

Oh, right. God had rearranged the universe and changed civilization just to work in her life. How selfish of her, to think it was all about her.

She knew it wasn't. But could *some* of it be about her? Maybe God—with all the millions of things he had to do—really did care about the details of her life, the big things and the small things, the love and the losses. Maybe in her corner of the universe, she was being taken through this trial for this very thing, so that she would break up with Craig and stop dreaming about something that was not God's best for her.

Letting her fury drive her, she went back into the house and up the stairs and got out a piece of paper. She sat down at her desk and started writing. Then she realized that he didn't deserve a hand-written letter. She'd type it.

She rolled the paper into the typewriter and started hitting the keys.

Dear Craig,

I just got your letter and I have to say I'm disappointed at how cold it sounded. You probably don't even realize it. You probably think it was fine. But a girl who hasn't seen her fiancé in months needs a few reassurances. I'm not asking for poetry, just an "I love you and I miss you," and I guess if you felt that way, you would have included that. Instead, you told me that you figured you'd hang on to me since you were pretty sure I was the best you could do. Those words didn't exactly sweep me off my feet, Craig.

I couldn't be more disappointed in you. It's been almost three months since the Pulses started and you've had ample time to get to me if you really cared. I've told you of my harrowing journey across the country to get to you and all you could say was, "Too bad you didn't make it." I told you that I could have died in the airplane that very first day, but that didn't faze you, either. I guess someone of your importance doesn't want to be bothered with details.

I agree that our wedding shouldn't happen in October, but things are a little clearer in my mind than they obviously are in yours. I don't think the marriage should happen at all, and I don't want to keep wearing your ring in the hope that no one else better comes along for you.

So, consider me a part of your past along with electricity and cell phones and cars and computers. Just another one of those things that isn't working for you anymore. It was fun while it lasted, Craig. Sorry it had to end this way.

Deni

Before she could change her mind, she ran downstairs to her father's study, got an envelope, stuffed the letter inside, and sealed it. Affixing a thirty-nine cent stamp—since that was all she found—she got on her bike and rode to the post office. She took it inside and threw it down the hole before she could change her mind.

Then she rode home on pure anger, her heart breaking over what she had just done.

THIRTY-SEVEN

"I BEEN THINKING, AND I DON'T THINK IT'S RIGHT FOR YOU to take our money." The Brannings had been making their plans for getting to the football field early for the disbursement the next day, but Aaron's blunt statement stopped them cold.

Doug just looked at the boy. He'd been up since before dawn working on daily chores, then hunting for enough food to feed ten people. Then he'd spent three hours working on the garbage mounds at Sandwood Place. He was too tired to deal with this again. "Aaron, stop acting like I'm robbing you. The disbursement money is to help people survive. And since we're feeding and caring for you, we need that money to help pay for expenses."

"But you said yourself you're gonna buy stuff with it."

"I said I was going to invest some of it to make it grow. For instance, I'm going to invest it in the seeds we need to plant in our garden so we can grow more food. I'm going to buy some chickens so we'll have eggs to eat and sell. And we're going to figure out something that the family can make and sell to earn even more money. That's not so we can bask in luxury. It's so we won't have to struggle quite so hard during the winter months."

"So you *are* gonna take our money?" Joey asked. "All hundred dollars of it?"

"Yes," Doug said. "We've been all through this. You can't get the disbursement without an adult, and that's because it's the adult who is taking care of you."

"What if you find our grandparents? Are you gonna give *them* the money?"

Kay spoke up. "Of course. We won't spend it for a month after we get it. If we don't find them by then, we will start using it, but we'll give them what we haven't used to take care of you."

Doug knew he'd never make the kids understand. To them, he was exploiting them just like the others wanted to. A hundred bucks seemed like a lot to them, when they hadn't had a handful of pennies since May.

But like it or not, he wasn't going to back down. He needed the money to feed them, and that was the end of that.

BEFORE BED THAT NIGHT, AARON ROUNDED UP HIS BROTHERS AND sister. "Sarah," he said quietly, "I want you to say you don't want to sleep with Deni tonight. I want you to sleep in here with us."

"But why? I like sleeping with Deni and Beth."

"Because after everybody goes to sleep, we're gonna sneak out and go home."

Sarah's eyebrows shot up. "Home? I don't want to go. I like it here."

"Listen to me," he whispered harshly. "They only want our money. If we stay, tomorrow we'll go through that line with them and they're gonna give us our twenty-five dollars each. And what do you think's gonna happen to it? Mr. Doug is gonna snatch it right out of our hands and use it for what he wants."

"But he said he was gonna use it to buy us food," Joey said. "Maybe we should let him have it. This is a good place, Aaron."

"A good place? It's like a prison. We work like slaves."

"But he does too. And we have good water to drink. And Luke and Sarah are happy."

"Yeah," Luke said. "I don't want to go, either."

Aaron couldn't believe they were turning on him this way. "What is wrong with you? Don't you see? They don't care about us. It's been about money from the very beginning. From the first day, they were probably looking for a bunch of kids to keep so they could get all their money. They're practically doubling their cash if we're with them."

Joey wasn't buying. "They found us because we robbed their house. They weren't looking for extra kids."

"That's what they *want* you to think." He could feel the heat blotching his cheeks. Somehow he had to convince them. Time was running out. If they were going to leave, they had to do it tonight ... *before* the disbursement. "Have I ever let you down before?" He looked from Joey to Luke, then to Sarah, demanding an answer. "Any of you?"

One by one, they shook their heads.

"Haven't I always took care of you?"

"But I like Miss Kay," Sarah said. "And Deni and Beth. We're gonna be in a play. Beth is making me a costume."

"I'll make you a stupid costume, and we can have our own play."

"But how will we get our money?" Joey asked.

Aaron didn't know what had gotten into him. He'd usually gone along with whatever Aaron said. He'd never given him this much trouble before.

"They make us have a grown-up with us," Joey said.

"We'll go with Edith. She said she wouldn't hassle us and try to run our lives. We can live in our own apartment."

"Our apartment stinks," Joey said. "It's even grosser than when we left it."

"Edith promised to have some buckets handy and some garbage bags if she can find them. She said she would help us clean out the commode. She said bleach would help kill the smell, so tomorrow, when we have money, I'll buy some."

"But what if they find Grandma and Pop?" Joey asked.

All these stupid questions. He didn't have the time to answer them all. "It's better if we're gone when they find them. Mama always warned us about them. But for now, we're gonna do this. And if the sheriff comes and tries to force us to go back to the Brannings, we'll throw a huge fit and tell them that we love Edith and want to stay with her."

"But I *don't* love her," Sarah said. "I hate her. She's mean."

"Not lately, she's not. She's been real nice lately."

Joey breathed a laugh. "That's only because she wants our money too."

"No, she doesn't. She told me she would let them put it directly into our hands."

"She's never helped us before."

Aaron was getting tired of Joey's mouth. "Look, Joey, everybody's in this for something. You think the Brannings are all perfect and everything, but they're not, okay? And once they get our money, they're not gonna be all that nice, either. So this is how it's gonna be. I'm gonna get all of you up after the Brannings are asleep, and we'll steal two of their bikes and ride home. Edith will be waiting, and she said we could sleep in her apartment tonight."

All three of his siblings just stared at him with dull eyes.

"Look, I'm doing what's best for us, okay? I'm not letting anybody steal our money. Now we're going to get out of here while we can, and then first thing in the morning, we'll get up and go with Edith to collect our money. After that we'll have our freedom and some money to buy some good stuff. Sarah, I'll buy you a princess crown, and Luke and Joey, we'll buy a basketball hoop to put up in the kitchen. We'll move out that worthless refrigerator and make a basketball court out of the whole room."

Luke grinned then and looked over at Joey. Sarah took her thumb out of her mouth and smiled, as if trying to picture it. But Joey still wasn't moved.

"Can we buy stuff to make our TV work?" Luke asked.

"No, Luke. Don't you know that even if we had a million dollars, we couldn't make our TV work? Those stupid Pulses are still going, messing everything up for all of us." He looked at Joey then. "Joey, are you in or out?"

Joey thought for a long moment, and Aaron began to fear that he was going to revolt. Finally, he answered. "Okay, Aaron, but you better be right about this. Because the Brannings'll be so mad that they'll never take us back. And the sheriff might come and split us up for sure."

"Would I let that happen?" Aaron demanded. When Joey looked away, he got in his face. "Answer me, Joey. Would I let that happen?"

Joey snapped. "Yeah, you might let that happen! You're not the king, you know. You don't get to decide everything!"

The door opened, and Kay stuck her head in. She looked from one to the other. "Everything all right in here, guys?"

Joey let out a breath and sat back on the bed. "Yeah, fine."

"You're not fighting, are you?"

There was a long beat of silence. Aaron turned back to her. "No, we're not fighting. But Sarah wants to sleep in here with us tonight. I guess we'll let her."

He held his breath as Kay looked at Sarah. "Why, Sarah? There's not much room in here."

"I'll sleep on the floor," Aaron cut in.

Sarah's thumb went back into her mouth.

Kay hesitated. "Well, okay, if that's what Sarah wants. But Sarah, if you change your mind, you can go get in bed with Deni."

Sarah just nodded, and Aaron breathed again. She was going to go along with it.

Tonight, they would all be free.

LATER THAT NIGHT, AARON LAY ON THE FLOOR, STARING AT THE ceiling, fighting sleep until he was sure everyone was asleep. Then he tiptoed to the stairs and went halfway down, peered across the house toward the master bedroom. He didn't see the flicker of an oil lamp through their door, so they must be in bed.

It was time.

He hurried back up into the bedroom where they all slept and woke Joey up. Joey didn't fight it this time. He just got up, pulled on his clothes, and grabbed his bag out from under the bed.

Aaron woke up Luke and Sarah. It wasn't easy. The children were groggy and didn't want to wake up, but finally he got them out of bed and reminded them what they were doing.

"Now get dressed. Hurry."

Sarah's hair was in her sleepy face, and he pushed it back and helped her get dressed. "Now listen," he whispered. "When we go out, we have to be really quiet. You got that, Sarah? We can't let nobody hear us."

"I will," she muttered.

"No sounds, okay, Luke? Joey?"

They all nodded and got the stuff he'd packed for them.

They crept downstairs, their feet creaking slightly on the stairs, but no one woke. Since he didn't want to raise the garage to get the bikes out for fear of alerting Doug and Kay, he got the flashlight they always kept on the kitchen counter and went into the dark garage. Joey helped him roll two bikes through the house and out the back door.

Quietly, they stole around the house and piled on the bikes—Luke on back of Joey's bike, Sarah on back of his. The moonlight was bright, guiding them home.

And the cool air smelled like freedom.

THIRTY-EIGHT

THE MORNING BROUGHT REGRETS.

Deni sat up in bed as dawn intruded on her sleep, bringing with it recriminations about the letter she'd sent to Craig. Had she really mailed it?

She wondered if it was too late to find Mrs. Lipscomb and get it back. The postmaster already suspected she was crazy. Now she'd have no doubts.

She got out of bed and got dressed. Today was Disbursement Day, and they had to get to the football field early. Even if she wanted to get the letter back, there was no time now.

She pulled open the drawer where she'd put Craig's letter. Unwrinkling it, she read over it again. As she did, anger pulsed through her. Yes, she had done the right thing. She wouldn't let herself think of it again. She balled the letter up and shoved it into her pocket.

She heard footsteps on the stairs outside her room. "Anybody awake?" Her mother sounded too perky.

"I am, Mom."

"Good. Get everybody up, Deni. We have to get moving."

Beth stirred, then sat up.

"Get dressed, Beth. It's Money Day."

While Beth got out of bed, Deni went down the hall to the room where the Gatlin kids slept.

No one was there. The bed was rumpled, and the pallet they'd made for Aaron on the floor was twisted and pushed to the side. But there was no clutter—no shoes lying around, no toys, no discarded clothes.

Something wasn't right.

She woke up Logan and Jeff, then hurried downstairs. Her mother was in the kitchen, slicing a loaf of bread Amber Rowe had made for them yesterday.

"This is it for breakfast," Kay said. "I'm trying to slice it ten ways. It may have to last us all day, depending on how fast the line moves." She sighed. "We're not getting the disbursement a minute too soon. I can't wait to buy some chickens. I wasn't this excited when I got my Expedition. Imagine eggs for breakfast!"

Deni took her slice and bit into the dry, tasteless bread. "Mom, where are the Gatlin kids?"

Kay glanced back at her. "They slept together last night, remember?"

"I know, but they're not there."

Kay stopped slicing. "Did you check the bathroom?"

"Yes. They're not there."

"Don't tell me—" She abandoned the bread and ran to her bedroom door. "Doug!"

He came out of their bedroom, dressed but barefoot, tennis shoes hanging from his fingers. "What is it?"

"The Gatlin kids. They're gone."

"No way!" Doug dropped his shoes and ran up the stairs; Deni was right behind him. Jeff stood in the hallway. "Where are they?" Doug demanded. "Did anybody hear them leave?"

"I didn't," Jeff said.

Logan came out of the bathroom. "You mean they took off?"

Doug looked under the bed. "Looks like it. They took all their stuff."

Beth joined her brothers in the hall. "But Dad, it's Money Day!"

Kay, who'd just come up, pushed through her children. "Doug, you've got to go after them. We've got to get there early and they won't get theirs if they're not with an adult!"

"Tell me about it." He ran downstairs and into the garage. When he came back into the kitchen, he said, "They stole two bikes."

That was serious. They'd only had four bikes as it was, since they'd given two away to neighbors who didn't have any. Deni watched him pull on his shoes, then go back into the garage and open the door.

"Where are you going?" Kay shouted.

"To their apartment." He mounted one of the bikes. "I'm going to get them back."

"Hurry," she said. "I don't want us to be late."

"Kay and Beth, you take the other bike and ride ahead so you can get in line. Jeff, Deni and Logan, you start walking. I'll find you all when I get there."

"How come *she* gets to ride?" Logan demanded.

"Because I said so." That would have to be good enough for now.

THE KNOCK ON EDITH'S DOOR WAS URGENT AND ANGRY.

Even though it was barely past dawn, Aaron knew it was Doug Branning.

His brothers and sister were still asleep on Edith's living room floor, but Joey stirred to life and sat up.

Edith grabbed her gun from the top of a bookcase, and ran through and looked out the window. "It's him!" she said. "Aaron, get everybody into the bedroom. Hide till I tell you to come out."

Quickly, Aaron woke Luke up, and Joey led him back. He didn't even try to wake Sarah. Instead, he picked her up, carried her to Edith's room, and laid her on the dirty sheets. "Get between the bed and the wall," he told his brothers. "Wake up, Sarah, and don't make a sound."

His sister woke up, and he pulled her down with her brothers. Doug pounded again.

Edith's bedroom was right next to her tiny living room, its window looking out to the landing outside the front door. He pulled down one of the miniblinds and peered out. Mr. Doug looked ready to bust an artery.

He heard Edith opening it. "What do you want?" she yelled.

"I want the Gatlin kids. I know they're here." He looked like he was coming in, so Aaron hit the floor.

"The Gatlin kids?" he heard Edith say. "Why would they be here?"

"Because I've already checked their apartment and they're not there. Let me in. I'll find them myself."

"You can't come in here! I told you they're not here!"

"Where else would they go?" His voice boomed over the apartment. "You're the one peddling freedom ... putting ideas in their heads."

He was at the bedroom door now. Aaron put his hand over Sarah's head, keeping her down.

"You're out of your mind," Edith shouted. "What do you think I am? Some kind of fool? Now get out! I don't let strange men into my apartment!"

Aaron couldn't count the number of strange men she'd had in her apartment. He heard heavier footsteps bounding across the floor.

"What's going on?"

It was Horace, one of the biggest, angriest men on the floor, and Aaron heard a scuffle as Doug tried to come into the bedroom.

"Aaron, if you're in here, you need to know that you're making a big mistake!" Doug shouted. "It's not too late. You can still come with me."

"They can't hear you," Edith said, "because they're not here! I'm warning you!"

Doug's voice was brittle. "Put the gun down, Edith! You know I'm not here to hurt anybody."

Horace's raspy voice intervened. "Come on now, Branning," he said. "Don't make her shoot you!"

"Aaron, I'm telling you, you're going to get into trouble if you trust this woman! She's going to take your money!"

"*You're* the one who wants their money, not me!" Edith said. "Now get out of here or I'll call the police!"

"How? You gonna try the telephone?"

"That's enough, bud." Horace again. "Come on, let's go."

Aaron heard the footsteps retreating. He raised up enough to peer out the window again.

Horace hovered over Doug on the landing, threatening him with his very presence. "Look, Branning. I don't want to hurt you. You've done a lot to help us here, but if the kids ain't here, they ain't here, and there's nothing you can do about it."

Undaunted, Doug turned back to Edith and pointed a finger in her face. "You hurt those kids in any way—emotionally, physically, or financially—and so help me; I'll make you regret it."

Aaron stood there listening; amazed that Mr. Doug would get this upset. He must really want that money.

"I want to go with him, Aaron." Sarah's little voice was muffled against the floor.

"Hush," he whispered. "You're not gonna. I'll take care of you."

Finally, Doug stormed away.

Aaron heard Edith slam the door and lock it.

Edith ran in, smiling and flashing those smoker's teeth. "We did it," she said. "Come on, everybody. Get ready. We've got to get down to the football field."

This was going to be a good day.

THIRTY-NINE

THE CROCKETT HIGH SCHOOL FOOTBALL FIELD TEEMED
with Crockett residents waiting for the twenty-five dollars
that would have to sustain them for the next three months.
It had taken Deni and her brothers an hour and a half to
walk to the football field, and then another forty-five minutes to find their mom and Beth. By now her father had
already returned from the apartments and joined them in
line, but it was clear they would all be there for hours.

FEMA's plans had seemed like a good idea when she'd
first heard the announcement, but now Deni wondered
about the wisdom of it. There had to be a better way than
lining up twenty thousand people on the same stretch of
land all at once. But she supposed she should have expected
as much. FEMA's performance in past disasters had proved
flawed, at best.

She had hoped that her parents would find the Gatlin
kids, but the volunteers who were working the crowd had
lined them all up in a maze that snaked back and forth
across the field — Disney World style — moving ever so
slowly toward the front of the stadium where the tables were
set up. In all the thousands of people, it was difficult to find
anyone.

Government employees sat behind the tables, exam-
ining documents and giving out the cash. There was no

breeze, and the crush of people made the sun's rays hotter and more oppressive.

Deni had worn her baseball cap with her ponytail pulled through the back to keep the sun off her face. She wondered if Craig had had to wait in a line somewhere in Washington, or if the senators and their staffs had gotten the first disbursements. Somehow, she couldn't picture him waiting in a line like everyone else hour after hour, but then she couldn't picture him scrounging for food or living in virtual poverty, either.

A toddler in the family in front of them cried miserably as they passed him from one family member to another, trying to bounce him and keep him quiet. The field sounded like a day-care center just before lunch, as miserable children cried out to go home or be fed or just to run free instead of standing next to their parents. The place was too crowded to let children run and play, and since everyone—young and old, sick and healthy—had to be present to receive their share, no one wanted to risk losing a family member for even a little while. Some had ropes attaching children to their parents. Others kept their kids bound in strollers that they pushed through the line.

Logan had whined nonstop since they'd left home. "This is retarded. Why can't they move faster?"

"They're moving as fast as they can," his father said. "This isn't easy. They have to verify the documents to cut down on fraud and make sure everyone who gets money actually lives here. Without computers, it's tedious."

"So we walk up there and hand them our documents," Beth said. "What's so hard about that?"

"It will probably be pretty cut and dried for our family," Doug said, "since I have a deed to our house to show them. But some of the others—like renters—they may not have those kinds of documents. They'll take longer."

"So how do they know no one's coming through twice?"

"They're stamping hands with indelible ink. It won't wash off for days."

Jeff sat on the grass where he would have been playing football this fall, if school had been able to open. "How are the Gatlin kids going to get disbursements if they don't have all that paperwork?"

Doug's face tightened again and he looked at Kay. She'd been teary-eyed all morning as she'd stood in line.

"I don't know what they'll do. I guess whoever brings them will need proof of residency."

"We should have made them understand that we weren't money-hungry," Kay said. "We could have let them keep their money. Then we'd at least know they were safe, and they would have stayed."

"No, they wouldn't," Doug said. "They wouldn't have believed us. They have it in their heads that we're up to something. They don't have much experience with people doing good for them without an ulterior motive."

"We have to tell the sheriff," Kay said.

Doug wiped his forehead. "I already did. He was at the gate when I came in. He's keeping an eye out. I also told him about Edith's gun. She may even be holding the kids against their will. If he sees her, he'll arrest her."

The line moved forward a few feet, and Jeff got up and moved, then plopped down again.

"Deni got a letter from Craig last night." Beth's announcement turned all eyes to Deni. She had hoped no one would ask her about it. She didn't want to discuss it.

Kay turned to her. "Oh, Deni, we were so busy last night when we got home, I didn't think to ask you about it."

"That's okay. There wasn't much to tell."

"What do you mean?"

"I mean, it was just like the other letter. Cold and unfeeling. Just the way he is." She didn't miss the exchanged looks between her mother and father.

"Well, honey, it's like I told you before. He's a guy."

"Don't make excuses for him, Mom. You don't have to do that anymore. I broke up with him."

"You what?" Beth swung around, gaping up at her. "Are you kidding?"

"No, I'm not kidding. I wrote him a letter last night and took it to the post office. It's probably on its way to him as we speak."

"You *broke up*?" Jeff asked. "I thought he was supposed to be the dream guy, the one you'd waited your whole life for ..."

His tone was so mocking she wanted to slap him. "I don't want to talk about it anymore, okay?"

"All right," Kay said, "everybody leave Deni alone. She doesn't have to explain it."

Deni kept looking straight ahead, knowing it wasn't over. She was right.

"Are you sure you did the right thing, honey?" Kay said quietly after a pause. "I mean, maybe you should have thought about it for a few days. Prayed over it."

"I didn't need to pray over it, Mom. It was becoming clearer and clearer that he's not the man God chose for me." She spoke the words bitterly, but when she saw a flicker of satisfaction in her dad's eyes, she wasn't surprised. He hadn't liked Craig from the start. She should have listened to him.

Kay stroked her sweat-drenched back. "I know this must be a hard day for you then," Kay said.

"So the wedding's off?" Logan asked.

She breathed in a deep sigh and let it out in a huff. "Yeah, it's off. Not that it would have happened anyway, even if I hadn't broken up." She blinked back the tears in her eyes. If it hadn't been for the Pulses, in just a few weeks she would have walked down the aisle, her designer gown trailing behind her. She didn't even have the gown now—she'd lost it as she ran from the killer a couple of months ago.

She had planned so long for that wedding day. She'd looked forward to seeing Beth—her maid of honor—nervous as she faced the prospect of straightening the gown's train and taking the bouquet in her trembling hands as she handed the ring to Deni. Her brothers would have been fidgeting and sweating in their rented tuxes. Her father would have been all emotional at her side as he passed her hand to her groom, and her mother would have been smiling and crying on the front row. Lately she'd even been thinking of the Gatlin kids lining up at the front, and little Sarah acting as her flower girl. Her sorority sisters, none of whom she'd heard from since she graduated, would have been standing to the side, tears in their eyes as they longed to be in her shoes.

They'd bought tickets to Maui for their honeymoon — but now they were as useless as her engagement. The irony of her standing among twenty thousand people on a football field waiting for twenty-five measly bucks did not escape her.

Man, how things changed.

Would Craig even care when he got her letter?

The line moved up, and she and her family followed like robots. The child in front of them screamed louder. It was giving her a headache. Her feet were aching, so she sat down on the turf and pulled out Craig's letter. It was still wadded in a ball, so she carefully unfolded it and looked down at Craig's sad handwriting. He should have been a doctor instead of a lawyer with an illegible scrawl like this. He probably hadn't had to write much in years, since he'd done everything on his BlackBerry before. He was a whiz on the keyboard, but he and his Bic had only had a passing acquaintance.

The line moved again. She told herself to get over it. She'd shed enough tears, and she didn't intend to cry in front of all these people. She glanced at her mom and saw that Kay had been trying to see what the letter said.

"Honey, do you mind if I read it?"

Deni shrugged. She handed it to her mother.

She watched as her mother scanned the page. The compassion on her face faded into anger. "You did the right thing, honey. You do deserve better."

She nodded. Her head knew it was true.

She just had to get the message to her heart.

FORTY

"Two more families and we're up." Deni had waited all day to say those words. They had been in line for almost seven hours, with nothing to eat and only a couple of bottled waters each that FEMA had given out. People had been passing out all day, losing their places in line as they were taken to a medical tent set up in the parking lot.

Their proximity to the front had revived Logan. He jumped up and down as they moved closer. Deni looked at the long table in front of the line. There were several government employees disbursing cash, so about six families at a time were being helped. Right now all the slots were filled, but there were only two families ahead of them. Finally this debacle would come to an end.

The man standing at the table nearest them looked upset, and he began to raise his voice. "I told you, she had a baby this morning! She wasn't able to come!"

"Sir, we were very clear that everyone had to be present to get paid. Now we'll give you fifty dollars for you and your son, but your wife and baby will have to be here before—"

The man bent over the table. "Do you have children? Have you ever given birth?"

"Yes," the woman said.

"Tell me, were you able to walk six miles or ride a bike that day?"

The woman looked around, as if searching for security.

"Sir, I know that in your case this seems unreasonable, but I'm not authorized to give any cash to anyone who's not here. Now, please, either settle for your fifty dollars or step aside."

"Even if I can get them here, she's in no shape to wait for hours to get to the front of the line. It's barbaric not to have provisions for people with special needs! This is so typical of FEMA!"

The woman turned to a coworker. "Bob, find security for me, please!" She looked around the angry man and called, "Next!"

The family in front of the Brannings shot forward.

"I'm not finished!" the new father shouted. He pushed the father of the new family out of the way. "Get back, pal. It's my turn."

The woman pursed her lips. "Sir, you just lost your turn."

"No way! I get fifty dollars at least for standing here for seven hours!"

"Get to the back of the line," she said through her teeth.

Deni could feel his fury rippling in the air. There was going to be a fight, and she couldn't blame him.

"Oh no, you don't." Letting go of his little boy's hand, he lunged over the table and grabbed the woman's throat. "Give me my money now!"

Deni screamed, along with several others. Two national guardsmen came running.

Doug shot forward and tried to wrestle him off the woman.

The guardsmen descended on them and pulled the man away from the woman. Handcuffing him, they jerked him away.

"She wouldn't give me my money!" the man shouted. His preschool son cried as he followed behind them, calling for his daddy.

Doug turned back to his family, his lip bleeding from the tussle. "You all right, Dad?"

He wiped his lip and looked back at the injured woman. "Yeah, but I'm not sure if she is."

A crowd formed around the injured woman, who was coughing, crying, rubbing at the reddened fingerprints on her throat.

"Great," Jeff said. "Now they're down one and it'll take longer for us to get our money."

Deni speared her brother with a look. "The woman was hurt, Jeff. Have a little compassion."

"Sorry about that," he said, "but come on, I don't blame the guy. You don't jerk around with people when they've been standing in line for most of the day, especially when he was up all night helping his wife have a baby."

"He didn't have a right to attack her, son," Doug said.

"Admit it, Dad. You'd have attacked her too if she refused to give you your money after all this. I've seen you lose your temper."

Doug didn't answer that.

The woman took a break, leaving her spot empty. The family who'd been called a moment before had to come back to the line.

"Stupid jerk," the man muttered. "He messed it up for all of us."

"Someone will take her place," Kay said. "You're still next."

But everyone at the table now had some sort of problem. One lady with about nine children didn't have the right documentation, and one of the other workers had found the imprint of the "indelible" stamp on two children who were being brought through — someone had tried to wash it off so they could collect a second disbursement for these children.

Finally, a space cleared. The Brannings were now next in line. They waited at attention, all six of them ready to dash forward as soon as the next space cleared.

Deni saw the guardsmen escorting the angry man to one of the sheriff's vehicles.

She felt sorry for the man who was on his way to jail. She couldn't imagine what his poor wife would think as she lay in bed with her newborn, waiting for her husband to come home. Would anyone tell her he was in police custody? She wished she knew where they lived so she could go and lend a hand.

Their time came, and they all rushed forward. Her father handed the worker the deed to their house and the birth certificates of all six of them. The woman studied them carefully, as if she wasn't aware that fifteen thousand more residents waited their turn.

Finally she said, "Okay, 150 dollars." She counted out the bills to Doug, then stamped each of their hands. "Next."

Deni wanted to dance with relief. Doug rolled the bills up and shoved them into his pocket. "We did it, guys. We have some cash. Let's go."

They elbowed their way through the sweating crowd and off the football field. The parking lot and streets around the football field were full of vendors—wagons full of produce, baked bread, flour, batteries, matches, oil lamps, candles. Farmers had pulled in flatbed trailers on which chickens and goats cackled and bleated. One farmer even had some cows lined up, their smell wafting through the air. Merchants lined up selling camping stoves and lanterns, guns, hunting traps, fishing poles, farming tools, carriages, and bicycles. Logan and Beth wanted some of everything, but Deni's parents stuck to their plans and refused to part with a nickel.

Chris's family had one of the wagons, selling the apples from their orchard. Deni envied them. They'd probably triple their disbursement by the end of the day. "Dad, can I have an apple?" Logan begged.

"No, Logan. We talked about this. We have plans for every penny we've got."

"But just one. They're only a nickel apiece. I have twenty-five whole dollars."

"No, you don't," Kay said. "That's our family's money, Logan. Not yours."

"Man!" He stomped his foot. "Not fair."

Today they would have to buy seed and farming tools and stuff for canning, since they had run out of jars. Deni had come up with the idea of making aprons and tool belts out of some of the old clothes in their closets. Now that everyone was a manual laborer, they all needed something to cover their clothes. Her father thought her idea was a good one, so she planned to start on making the items tonight after her parents bought some of the supplies she needed.

Her mother planned to use part of the money to buy flour and baking goods so they could sell loaves of bread to the other families in the neighborhood. Not that her mother was that good at making homemade bread—but at least she was better than Amber. But

Deni supposed that her mother would improve. It would become a family effort.

Getting to the chickens proved impossible. The lines for them were hundreds of people long, and it was clear they were running out. They would have to wait and find a place from which to order them. They pushed their way through the crushing crowds to the chain-link fence around the field, where hundreds of bicycles were chained. They found the two bikes they had chained there, but her mother wasn't ready to leave.

"I don't want to go until we find those kids," Kay said. "They're here somewhere. I want to look for them a little longer. What if they're hurt? What if somebody's done something to them?"

Doug wiped the sweat off of his forehead. "All right. But then we've got to get moving. We've got a lot of stuff we need to buy today and supplies are low. I don't want the few merchants open to run out of goods before we get what we need."

"Mom, can the rest of us go home?" Jeff asked. "I'm dying."

Kay nodded. "Okay, you kids can walk home. Your dad and I will need the two bikes to carry back our supplies. Everybody be careful now. If the looting was bad before, it's going to be worse now that people actually have cash."

Deni knew that was true, but since the cash was on her parents, she figured they'd be safe. As she started walking away from the crowd, she longed for the days of McDonald's and Wendy's. She'd kill for a cold Diet Coke right about now. The kind from a fountain ... in a Styrofoam cup that would keep it cold. Air-conditioning to cool off in. A nice long bath.

But those days seemed gone forever.

FORTY-ONE

IT WAS ALL AARON COULD DO TO KEEP HIS BROTHERS AND
sister from running off to play as they stood in the line that
slowly wormed its way through the football field and up
toward the tables. Edith was being real sweet to them today,
sweeter than she ever had before, and she hadn't yelled at
them once.

She had dressed Sarah up in a baseball cap and Luke's
clothes. When Edith had put Sarah's hair in a ponytail and
shoved it into the cap, Sarah had cried and tried to pull it
out because she didn't want to look like a boy. But she didn't
have a choice. Her curls made her too easy to spot, and they
couldn't take the chance of having the Brannings find them.
But he doubted they would in this crowd.

They'd stood in line for hours, the hot sun beating down
on them, but Aaron knew it was worth it. Once he got the
hundred dollars due to him and his siblings, he'd be home
free. A hundred dollars was a lot even *before* the outage.
He'd be able to do a ton with it now.

They finally reached the front, and he noticed Edith jit-
tering, nervous and impatient as they waited for their turn.
"Okay, kids, remember what I told you. You let me do the
talking."

Aaron stiffened and watched the woman working at the
spot they would soon occupy. He hoped she would be nice,
since they didn't have their birth certificates. They had torn
the apartment up last night trying to find them, but it was

191

no surprise that they hadn't—his mother couldn't keep up with her driver's license, much less documents she rarely needed. They had, however, found some welfare paperwork in a box under the bed, and it listed all their names.

Edith had thought about trying to use Jessie's identity so that she wouldn't have to explain how she'd gotten the kids, but she decided there had been too much publicity about Jessie's murder. She couldn't take the chance. Instead, she had forged a letter supposedly written by Jessie herself, asking Edith to take care of her children if anything ever happened to her. Edith was good at forging signatures, and she'd nailed Jessie's easily.

The space at the front of the line cleared and Edith grabbed Luke and Sarah's hands and hurried them to the table. Her hands were shaking as she put the documents down.

"These are not my kids, but their mama's dead. I'm raising them for her."

The woman studied the paperwork, then looked at the forged document. Sweat dripped from her face down onto the paper, smearing some of the ink. She must have been sitting here for hours and hours, doling out money left and right. Aaron hoped that it hadn't put her in a bad mood.

"Well, these aren't the right documents, but I guess they'll do," she said. "Give me your hands." They each held out a fist, and she stamped the back of their hands. Aaron's heart soared as she got a handful of cash and started counting it out. "That'll be 125 dollars for five people."

She counted it into Edith's hand.

Aaron's heart jolted. "A hundred of it goes to me," he said.

The woman laughed at him. "Sorry, kiddo. We only give it to the adults."

"But it's mine."

Edith ground her thumb into his shoulder, telling him to be quiet. "Hold on, Aaron. We have to follow the rules."

He supposed she was right. They'd have to go through the motions, and then he'd get his share. He stood quietly, watching her count out the money in twenties. She finished with a five dollar bill.

They stepped away from the table, and he thought he was going to burst. He wanted to celebrate, but first he wanted the cash.

Edith waited till they'd left the stadium and entered the parking lot before crying, "We did it!" and fanning the bills in her hands. Sarah clapped her hands, and Luke looked like he'd just won a prize.

Aaron stuck his hand out. "Thanks, Edith. I'll take ours now."

Her laugh was high-pitched and brittle. "You *wish*."

He felt the blood rushing to the tips of his ears. Surely, she wasn't going to back out on him now. "Edith, you promised."

"Do you think I'm a fool?" she asked. "I can't give little kids a hundred dollars. You'd blow it on something stupid. I'll hang onto it, don't you worry." She started to sashay away.

"That wasn't the deal! You told us you would take us through and help us get our money!"

"I know what I told you," she said, "but forget it. I'm not giving you the money. It's mine now."

Aaron's heart beat in his throat. He tried to grab it, but she jerked it back. "It's mine, you greedy witch! Give it back!"

"What are you gonna do about it, you little creep? Go whine to the Brannings?"

Joey kicked her in the shins. She bent double and screamed a string of curses at him. Grabbing him by his hair, she threw him to the ground. "Get away from me, you little jerk, or I'll scream that you're robbing me. They'll throw you in a dark jail cell and throw away the key."

"Yeah?" Joey cried. "Maybe I'll go find the sheriff and tell him what you did, then *you* can rot in jail!"

"The sheriff won't let you have this money, you fool. Even the Brannings were gonna take it from you. He'll just put you back with some other foster family. Go tell him, I don't care. I don't need you anymore."

Something exploded in Aaron's heart, bursting out in rage. No way! Edith was not gonna pull this on him! She took off into the thickest part of the crowd, but Aaron wasn't going to let her get away. "Catch her, Joey!" he cried as he ran after her, pushing people out of his way.

"Aaron!" Sarah screamed.

He looked back at his little sister. She had fallen, and the crowd was so thick that he feared she'd be trampled. He stopped. "Get her, Joey!"

Joey ran after Edith, fighting his way through the crowd.

Aaron picked Sarah up, keeping his eyes on Edith. Then the worst thing Aaron could think of happened. A big guy who looked like Magic Johnson came barreling through the parking lot, grabbed the money out of Edith's hand, and ran off so fast that no one would ever catch him.

Edith's scream pierced through the noise. "He took my money! I've been robbed! Stop him! Somebody stop him!"

But the man's long legs carried him out of the area and to the road faster than anyone could react. Joey froze. Aaron came up behind him, his eyes wide as he watched their money disappearing down the highway.

"It's gone," Joey said in a raspy voice. "He took our money."

Edith was screaming, grabbing people, trying to get them to help her. It served her right. He supposed it might serve *them* right too, but there was nothing he could do about it now. The rage that had been beating through his throat suddenly turned to sorrow. For the first time in his life he felt helpless.

Tears ran down Joey's dirty face. "She double-crossed us. She lied. We shoulda known." He shoved Aaron, knocking him back. "I *told* you, Aaron. But no, you were so smart."

Aaron didn't fight back.

"We shoulda stayed with the Brannings. At least they were gonna take care of us with the money. But now they'll never take us back. You think you know everything, Aaron, but you don't, you stupid idiot!"

Aaron hated himself for crying, but he couldn't stop the tears. He just stood there, letting his brother's words hammer him. Sarah's wounded cries only made it worse.

"You told us to trust you," Joey ranted. "You said you knew what you were doing. But you don't, Aaron!"

Aaron slapped the tears rolling down his face. "I'll get it back. I'll find out who that man is, and we'll steal it back from him and more."

"How? We don't have a gun any more. We don't have *anything*!"

"Aaron!" Aaron heard his name and turned. Doug and Kay Branning were rushing toward them.

But being found didn't even matter anymore. Even the Brannings would leave them alone as soon as they knew they'd lost the money.

They were of no use to anyone now.

FORTY-TWO

KAY RAN TOWARD THE GATLIN KIDS. LITTLE SARAH STOOD crying with bleeding, skinned knees, her hair stuffed up in a baseball cap. Joey and Aaron were crying too. Luke just watched them all with horror in his eyes.

She fell to her knees in front of the little girl. "Sarah, are you all right? Did you fall?"

"Uh-huh."

Kay picked her up and pulled the cap off her head. Her curls were soaked with sweat. She pulled Sarah into a hard hug, then kissed Luke on the cheek and stooped down in front of Aaron and Joey.

"We thought we'd never find you," she cried. "Where have you been?"

Aaron couldn't answer.

"We've been listening to this idiot," Joey said, pointing to his brother. "Doing everything he said. He had this great idea that Edith was gonna help us get our money. But she stole it from us, and then some guy stole it from *her*!"

Kay closed her eyes as the news sank in. She looked up at Doug.

He mopped his forehead with the sleeve of his shirt. "Did you know the guy? Can you describe him?"

"He was tall and fast," Aaron bit out. "That's all I know."

Doug looked down at them, his eyes full of so much frustration that Aaron expected him to spit on them and walk away. But he didn't. "Aaron, we'll go report it to the sheriff,"

Doug said. "Maybe someone around here saw it and knows who he was."

Kay's heart sank. These poor kids. They'd been lured and double-crossed, tricked and deceived far too often. It made her sick. She wanted to find Edith and slap her face. How dare people treat children this way? She was glad Edith's money had been stolen. She didn't deserve any.

"It's okay," Aaron snarled. "We don't need the stinking money. I took good care of my sister and brothers before today and I can do it again. I don't need no adults. I don't need nothing!"

Doug's face softened, and he looked at Kay. She brought her fingertips to her lips as tears rolled down her face. Doug ruffled Aaron's hair. "Son, I know this is bad. But it's not the end of the world. I want you to come home with us. It'll be all right."

Aaron gaped at him. "Don't you get it? We don't have the money. We don't know the guy who took it. You're not gonna get anything out of us."

"I don't care about the money," Doug said. "We got our disbursement, and it'll have to be enough."

"But you *said* you couldn't take care of us if we didn't have the money," Aaron said. "You *said* you needed it to feed us."

Doug bent down and looked into his eyes. "Listen to me. God will provide. We're not letting you go back on the street just because we can't get your money. I told you in the beginning we weren't in it for the money. It would have helped, sure. But we'll manage."

Kay touched his shoulder. "He's right, Aaron. We'll be fine."

Aaron shook his head. "Why would you *do* that?"

"Because God loves you," she said, "and he put that love for you in our hearts."

Aaron looked at Doug, searching his eyes.

"It's true, Aaron. We want to help you find your family, people who will love you and take care of you even without getting something out of it."

Kay lifted Sarah onto her hip, and the little girl looked down at her brother. "Please, Aaron," she said, hiccupping her sobs. "Can't we go back?"

Kay saw the confusion on his face. "People aren't nice for nothing," he bit out.

Joey spoke up. "But they haven't been mean to us, Aaron, and they don't make us work any harder than their own kids. We got a nice comfortable bed to sleep in at night and food and clean water." He lifted his chin, brooking no debate. "I'm going back."

Aaron looked from Kay to Doug, as if giving them one final assessment.

"What are you waiting for?" Joey cried. "Maybe they're telling the truth. Maybe they're just good people!"

"Please, Aaron." Kay reached down and touched his face, wiped the tears from his cheek. "We want to help you, son. Come home with us."

Aaron couldn't seem to speak, but slowly he nodded his head, clearly too tired to fight anymore.

FORTY-THREE

"WHAT A DAY!" KAY FELL INTO BED THAT NIGHT SO exhausted that she'd almost been too tired to change clothes. "Ten weeks ago, who would have dreamed that we would stand in line for six hours to get 150 dollars and then beg four orphaned children to come live with us?"

"These are the times we live in." Doug pulled the sheet back and got in.

"At least we've convinced them to stay."

"Don't bet on it."

She propped herself on an elbow and looked down at him. "What do you mean?"

"I mean, they still may be planning an escape."

"Why? They don't have any money, and they know now that no one at the apartments is going to help them."

"They may try to get *our* money and take off again. That's why I'm sleeping with the money on me tonight." He reached into the pocket of the jogging shorts he slept in and pulled out the roll of bills.

She sighed and collapsed on her pillow. "You're right."

"Tomorrow I'm going to the apartments to confront that Edith woman," he said. "Maybe she knows who robbed her. At least we can tell the sheriff. It's a long shot, but maybe he can get the money back."

"I feel sorry for her," Kay said. "Now she's without anything."

Doug just gaped at her. "Sorry for her? Are you kidding? That conniving woman exploited and abused these children. She deserves everything that happened ... and jail too."

Kay stared at the darkness. "I know. But think of how she feels right now. She's got to be devastated. She'll need help."

"Well, she'll benefit from our work at the apartments. But that's all I'll do for her."

A moment of silence followed. Then Doug kicked off his sheet and turned on his side, facing her. He braced his elbow on his pillow and propped his head up. "You've changed, you know," he said softly.

She looked up at him. His eyes were soft in the moonlight coming through the window. "What do you mean?"

He ran his knuckle along her cheekbone, outlining the shape of her face. "I mean, you're more caring now. More selfless. You're willing to do hard things even when it costs you."

She smiled and turned her face to kiss his hand. "I just took the lead from you."

"Really? Because I don't feel all that giving right now. Sometimes I feel like I'm just going through the motions."

She turned on her side and stroked the stubble on his jaw. "I think that's okay. Love is more about what we do than how we feel."

He grinned and moved closer to her. "I don't know. Sometimes it's about how we feel."

He kissed her then, a long, slow, stirring kiss that reminded her of all the reasons she'd fallen in love with him. She needed that reminder.

LATER, WHEN THOSE BARRIERS OF WEARINESS AND DUTY HAD melted away and they felt once again like beloved partners, they lay snuggled together, waiting for sleep to come.

"Doug?"

"Yeah?"

"I have a bad feeling that instead of making things better for us, the disbursement is going to make things more evil. I'm afraid there will be more robberies and murders."

"That's what I was thinking, too," he said. "We'll just have to be alert. We can't let our guard down. But God has brought us this far."

"I feel safe with you," she whispered.

He reached down beside the bed and felt the rifle lying there, once again resolving to use it if he needed to.

FORTY-FOUR

THE INFUSION OF CASH INTO THE ECONOMY HAD ALLOWED some of the stores to open in Crockett, and when the first passenger locomotive came through town the day after the disbursement, Deni went to the station and covered the story for her little newspaper.

The sight of travelers getting off the train and running into the arms of loved ones broke her heart. Craig could have come—or she could have gone to him. But that was all over now. She wondered how soon he'd get her breakup letter. When he got it, would it faze him, or would he just toss it on his desk and get back to business? It had taken him a week to read her letters before. Would he read that one in one sitting?

Things would soon get a little easier at home; her parents had bought some kerosene and made some lamps, so that they had light in more of the rooms at night. Now she could work on her paper in the quiet of her room without having to sit at the kitchen table while everyone hovered around. With four extra people in the house, it was getting a little crowded. She wished they'd been as successful with buying the chickens, though. It might be weeks before their order was filled.

To celebrate the disbursement and the striking of water in the well, Oak Hollow planned a celebration for Friday night. There wouldn't be food there, since no one could spare any, but they had lined up every musician in the neighborhood and some outside Oak Hollow to come and play. They could dance and mingle and find some relief from the labor that had occupied every waking hour these last few weeks. Deni looked forward to the reprieve. She needed a break from her melancholy.

In the meantime, her father was bent on making Edith pay for her greed. When he went to confront the woman at Sandwood Place, Deni went with him. The conniving woman met them at the door with swollen eyes, wearing a hollow look of desperation. "What do *you* want?"

Her father's voice was steady, though a current of anger drifted on his tone. "We understand you took the Gatlin children's disbursements."

"So? Not like I have anything to show for it." She thrust out her arm. "Here, take it out of a vein if you want."

If her father had any plans of reaming the woman, her pitiful look stopped him. "Who took it, Edith?"

"If I knew, don't you think I'd have gotten it back by now? If I ever see that man's face again, I'll claw his eyes out."

Deni grunted at Edith's righteous indignation. "When you stole it from the kids, did you really think you'd get away with it?"

"Look, I got mine, okay? Is that what you wanted? I don't have the money. I can't give it back. But my life has been pure misery since then. My neighbor three doors down is dead 'cause somebody broke into her apartment the night of the disbursement and stole her money. The man in 16D got in a fight over his. Now he's dead too. That money was supposed to help! It was supposed to make things better!"

Deni's anger shattered, and she looked at her father. His face changed, and that hard glint in his eyes softened.

"It's so easy for you to come telling me how to live!" Edith spat out. "I saw that house you live in! You have well water, you have food growing—"

"That's because we work hard, Edith," Doug cut in. "So can you. That's why I've been trying to help. If you would quit trying to figure out shortcuts and get used to the idea of hard work, you'd be able to make it."

She tried to close the door. "I have nothing to say to you."

Doug stopped her from closing it. "Give me their things and we'll leave. They need their clothes, and I want the bikes they stole from us that night."

She left them at the door and came back with the kids' bags. Thrusting them at Doug, she said, "I put the bikes in their apartment. I should've sold them. Have a nice life. Someday you'll get yours."

The door slammed.

Doug stared at the wood grain for a moment, his jaw clenching. Deni waited, expecting her father to let out a rare curse or kick the door, like she wanted to do. But he didn't.

"Hard to feel sorry for her, huh?" Deni asked.

Her father's lips stretched tight over his teeth.

"She's kind of like that Haman guy in Esther," Deni said, "with her wicked scheme coming back to bite her. She deserves what happened to her."

He sighed then and turned away from the door. "Come on, let's get the bikes."

She followed him to the Gatlins' door. He opened it with Aaron's key and rolled the bikes out.

"We shouldn't help her with all the others who live here, Dad. We should let her clean up her own garbage and walk five miles for water."

"We can't do that, Deni. Whatever we do for the others, we'll do for her too."

Deni blew out her frustration. "I knew you'd say that. But anybody would understand if we didn't include her."

"It's not anyone I'm trying to please, Deni. It's God. And I have my marching orders."

FORTY-FIVE

THE PARTY DIDN'T START UNTIL EIGHT O'CLOCK FRIDAY
night, after the sun went down and the temperature cooled.
Citronella candles, every one the neighbors could gather,
cast a sweet glow around the place. Several of the musicians in Crockett had gotten a band together and were playing from a truck bed in the street. Jeff had been invited to
join them on his guitar. Someone had lifted a piano into
the truck bed, and musicians with fiddles, guitars, trum-
pets, saxophones, and drums accompanied it as they played
everything from bluegrass to rock and roll. The road had
become a dance floor, and everyone from ages two to eighty-
five was making use of it.

Determined to feel festive, Deni had made herself put on
makeup tonight and had washed her hair before she'd come.
Instead of the T-shirts and shorts she'd been wearing every day
for the last two months, she'd pulled on a pair of her jeans and
a red silk blouse. The jeans were now so big on her that they
threatened to fall off, but she laced a belt through the loops
to hold them up. She supposed everybody's clothes were loose
these days.

A few months ago, she'd have killed for the body she had
today. She'd have paid big bucks and worked out for hours
a day, stepping and cycling, to get into this kind of shape.
Now it came naturally. She wasn't complaining. It was just
too bad Craig would never see it.

She sat in a lawn chair sipping the cool water from their well, watching the neighbors they'd gotten to know so well over the last few weeks. Eloise, the dear lady who lived across the street, had been too weak to walk over, so Kay had brought her in a borrowed wheelchair. Deni watched her mom serving the cancer victim, who seemed to be having a wonderful time.

On the street, Judith and Brad, her next-door neighbors, danced and laughed. It had been a long time since there had been so much laughter in this neighborhood.

On the grass near the lake, Beth had rounded up most of the neighborhood children and was working on the play she had written. It was an ambitious undertaking—a musical about David and Goliath—but it was a nice diversion for the children.

Mark sat next to Deni and Chris, his chair tilted back on two legs. He was still something of an outcast here, so he stuck close to the two who accepted him. There were others who sat quietly like outcasts, their faces soft and longing. Amber Rowe seemed that way as she sat nearby, watching her children spin and play. Her husband had left her and moved in with some woman just before the outage; since then, he'd been around only once or twice to see the kids and had done little to help her survive. Amber was clearly still mourning.

And Cathy Morton, the doctor's pregnant young wife, sat by herself, watching her husband with jealous eyes. Deni couldn't blame her. He'd been known to wander, and he hadn't quite grasped the fact that his wife needed security at this vulnerable time in her life.

Deni followed Cathy's gaze to the doctor and saw him coming toward them. She hoped he wasn't coming to talk to her.

The doctor, who had the look of a California surfer dude, had Chris as his target. "Hey, Chris. Want to dance?"

Chris glanced uncomfortably across at Cathy. "Doc, I think it would be better if you danced with your wife."

"Hey, I'm just being friendly," he said, "trying to bond with my nurse, that's all."

She forced a smile. "I just don't feel like dancing right now. It's too hot."

He moseyed off into the crowd, and Deni gave Chris a look. "What's up with that?"

Chris rolled her eyes. "I like working for him. I mean, it's the only place I can get a job right now. But sometimes I feel like he's coming on to me, you know? I just don't trust him. I mean, maybe his intentions are good, maybe he *is* just trying to be friendly, but I know his history."

A lot of people in the neighborhood knew his history, ever since his wife had almost thrown him out of the house because he'd been sneaking around at night, visiting a girlfriend on the other side of the neighborhood. Cathy had been so hurt. She had been five months pregnant at the time, and as her stomach had swollen ever bigger, her paranoia and distrust of her husband had also grown. If not for the outage and the fact that they had no place else to go, Deni wondered whether the marriage would be over by now.

"I've tried to make friends with Cathy," Chris whispered. "She's there all the time, watching him like a hawk. It almost makes me think I should quit the job, but I really need it and I'm helping a lot of people. I don't want to quit."

"Maybe you need to try to be less cute when you go to work," Deni said on a giggle.

"Yeah," Mark said. "Blacken out a tooth, pull back your hair, wear some coke-bottle glasses."

Chris laughed. "I don't think you have to be particularly attractive for Derek Morton to hit on you. He's just that way."

"So—is he hitting on Judith?"

Chris sought out the black nurse dancing with her husband. "No, she's a little old for him. He doesn't seem interested. I think Cathy feels safe with her too. I feel like I should tell Cathy she doesn't have to fear anything from me. I'm not after her husband. I think he needs to straighten up and take care of his wife. But I can't really say that to her. Hopefully when the baby comes, it'll change his attitude and he'll start taking a little more responsibility for his family."

"He's a good doctor, though," Mark said. "Most of the neighbors don't know what they'd do without him. My mom had strep throat, and he helped her a lot. Could have gotten really bad if we hadn't had him here. And poor Eloise might have died by now."

"And that's why I haven't quit my job. That, and the fact that it's helping my family survive."

"Your family's already rich," Mark said. "How much did you make off those apples you sold at the football field?"

"Enough to buy a horse and a goat."

Deni's eyebrows shot up. "You got a goat? Does it give milk?"

"You bet it does."

Deni sighed. "You're so lucky. Who knew investing in apple orchards would have such a payoff?"

The music moved from a country theme to slower love songs, and that sad feeling started to creep over Deni again. Chris got up to talk to some of the neighbors, and Deni was left with Mark, who noticed the change in her mood. Leaning back on two legs again, he asked, "You okay?"

She nodded. "Yeah, just a little sad."

"About Craig?"

"Isn't it always about Craig?"

He gazed at her. "Am I going to have to read your letter and interpret it again?"

"It would take a lot more imagination than you have, Mark, and it would be pure fiction."

"I doubt that."

She forced a smile. "I think it's really sweet of you to try to make me feel better about him, but you don't have to do that anymore. I wrote him the other night and broke up with him. He's probably gotten the letter by now, so I guess it's official."

His chair fell to all fours, and all humor drained from his face. "Oh, Deni. I'm sorry."

She swallowed the knot in her throat. "It's okay. It just wasn't meant to be."

"How do you know?"

She combed her fingers through her hair and pulled it off her damp neck. "The outage has clarified a lot of things for me. This is just one of them."

"Wow. I don't know what to say."

He looked so shaken, she almost felt sorry for him. "Come on, Mark. Surely you have an empty platitude or two."

He smiled then. "Let's see. It's better to have loved and lost ... If you love them, let them go."

"Yeah, love that one," she said. "How about, absence makes the heart grow fonder? That's a real winner."

He thought for a moment. "A bird in the hand is worth two in the bush."

She laughed. "Can we stay on the subject of love and leave the poor birds out of it?"

She loved the way his laughter transformed his eyes. "See there?" he said. "You're gonna be all right."

Her smile settled softly on her lips. "So are you gonna dance with me or what?"

Still grinning, he took her hand and pulled her to her feet.

The band was playing "Unchained Melody," drawing dozens more dancers to the street. Zach Emory, Jeff's friend, stood like Elvis on the edge of the truck bed, belting out the lyrics.

Mark's hand was rough and big as he pulled her among the dancers. Hers felt small inside it.

Craig's hands had been soft.

He turned and pulled her close, and for the first time she was aware of the height difference between them. He stood a good eight or nine inches taller than she. He held her right hand out and put his other hand on her waist, and danced the way their grandparents had danced at the USO in pictures she'd seen years ago. There was something charming about that.

They swayed to the rhythm of the music, and she enjoyed the pleasure on his face. He didn't gaze into her eyes or make her feel uncomfortable. Instead, he spoke softly, which made her move closer to hear.

"Look at the Huckabees dancing," he said. "Did you know they'd been married thirty years? They celebrated their anniversary last week."

"Is that right?" she asked. "I didn't know that. You know, my parents have been married twenty-five this year."

"It must be nice, having parents that have stayed together."

She knew he was thinking of his own parents' divorce. "How long has your mom been married to your stepfather?"

"Thirteen years," he said. "They have a great marriage. I'm proud of that."

They danced for a while, and she realized that they had gotten even closer. She moved her hand up to his shoulder and felt his breath on the side of her face.

"You look really pretty tonight," he said against her ear.

The words sent a jolt through her heart, and she felt her cheeks blushing pink. This was crazy. She used to be the biggest flirt in town. If a guy had said that to her before, she would have had a ready comeback ... She would have tossed her hair back and said something bordering on suggestive. But her heart felt so fragile ...

"Thank you," she whispered. "You don't look so bad yourself."

They were quiet for the rest of the song, and she found herself feeling at home in his arms. That surprised her. They'd been such close friends in high school, buddies who hung around at football games and went out to eat after youth group. He had dated some of her friends, but there had never been any chemistry between the two of them.

Not until now.

As they danced, her depression over her breakup began to lift, and joy fluttered like a butterfly breaking free of its cocoon. When the song ended, they stayed on the street. She didn't want to sit down.

As the band launched into an acoustic rendition of "When a Man Loves a Woman," Mark pulled her toward him again. The crowd pressed in around them, dozens of others cheek to cheek. She felt his breath in her hair, his hand on her back.

Something was happening in her heart, and she didn't know quite how to feel about it.

When the song came to an end, Mark took her hand in his and led her back to their chairs.

"I'll get you a drink," he said.

She nodded and watched him walk toward the table where the water pitchers sat. A slow smile curled across her lips.

Chris came and sat down beside her. "Well, well."

Deni tried to banish her grin. "Well, well, *what?*"

"Is something going on with you and Mark?"

"I don't know. But it's over with Craig. It's time for me to move on."

Chris couldn't hide her smile. "I never would have pictured you and Mark together a few months ago, but now it seems like the perfect match."

"Well, don't jump the gun," Deni said. "I don't really know how I feel."

He turned back toward her, one of the lanterns lighting his face as his eyes caught hers. She looked away. "All I know is he's a good dancer. And a good friend."

He came back toward them, carrying three cups.

"Here you go, ladies," he said in his best Rhett Butler voice.

Deni accepted the cup—and the reprieve from her broken heart. Things were beginning to look up.

DENI STAYED LATE TO HELP CLEAN UP AFTER THE PARTY WHILE Mark helped the musicians break down. Perhaps the neighbors were beginning to warm up to Mark a little. She hadn't noticed as many whispers tonight.

It was hard not to notice how hard he worked for the good of the community, but he kept a low profile, humbling himself and not trying to force the issue.

When he'd finished helping the musicians, Deni folded up the last of her own family's lawn chairs and started to carry them home. He jumped down from the truck bed and came to rescue her. "Here, let me help."

"Thanks, Mark."

He took all six chairs and walked with her on the dark street around the block to her house. "That was really fun tonight," he said.

She slid her hands into her pockets and watched the street in front of her. "Yes, it was. I'm glad we did it. We had a lot to celebrate."

"Did you hear that Tate Osbourne got drafted? He had to register today, and he's waiting to find out where he'll be assigned."

"He's a mechanic? I thought he went to college."

"No, he worked for the Toyota dealership before the outage. He's hoping they'll let him stay in the area, since he's got a girlfriend here. Man, I wish I knew more about fixing cars. I'd love to help with the effort."

She smiled as they turned up her driveway. "You do help. You're the busiest guy in Oak Hollow."

"Yeah, well, I have a lot to prove." He set the chairs down in her garage and leaned them against the wall.

"You don't have to prove anything, Mark. If people don't see what kind of person you are, then it's their loss. Not yours."

He leaned back against the dead Expedition. "Yeah, well. That says easy, and does hard. But your endorsement means a lot."

She hadn't thought of her friendship as being an endorsement, but she supposed there was power in that, since she'd nearly been one of his father's victims. She wished it helped more.

"So are you okay about Craig?" he asked.

She shrugged. "Yeah. Tonight got my mind off him."

"Good." He smiled. "You're an awesome dancer."

She nudged his shoulder and looked up at him. "So are you."

Their eyes met, and she was struck at the paleness of his in the darkness. She had always liked his eyes.

Her heart pounded as she looked up at him, and her mouth suddenly went dry. She felt her face flushing under his gaze.

That shyness flushed over her again. "Thanks for carrying the chairs. You're my hero."

She saw him swallow, felt him turning to her. Then he was in front of her, hands in his pockets, his gaze feathering across her face.

He was going to kiss her—but he hesitated, giving her the chance to pull away, to make some excuse, to hurry inside.

Instead, she stood where she was, looking up at him as her heart stumbled.

Slowly, he lowered his face to hers. His hand came out of his pocket, and he touched her face, tipped her chin up to his. She closed her eyes as his lips touched hers. Her fears and grief melted away.

The kiss was sweet, soft, undemanding. But her heart slammed against her chest. She pulled back and looked up at him, surprised at her own reaction. He gazed back, his eyes probing, as if wondering if he'd made a mistake.

She smiled, and that hint of fear in his eyes faded. He grinned back at her.

"I'll see you tomorrow," he whispered.

She tried to think of something pithy to say, but came up with nothing. Swallowing hard, she whispered, "Good night."

"Lock up," he said as he left her garage.

She pulled the door shut and locked it, then stood in the dark for a moment, reliving that kiss, relishing the thrill of it. Knowing better than to think about it too much, she touched her heart and headed inside.

FORTY-SIX

KAY SPENT HER TIME AT THE PARTY ATTENDING TO ELOISE, who had become so ill that her skin had a deathly pallor. She was skinnier than Kay had ever seen her.

Eloise had trembled as she flirted with Sarah and Luke. When Eloise pulled Luke into her lap, Kay feared her bones would splinter under his weight. Yet there was joy on Eloise's face as she laughed with the children.

As she helped clean up after the party, Kay found Derek talking with some of the neighbors. She pulled him aside. "Derek, tell me about Eloise's cancer. She's getting worse, isn't she?"

He glanced at Eloise, talking with friends from her wheelchair. "I can't do any of the usual tests without an MRI and CT scan, but it's clear to me that her cancer has spread. She's got a lot of pain in her head, which tells me that it's probably made its way into her brain, and she's having chest and abdominal pains. From the sound of her lungs, I'd say it's there too. We haven't been able to do the chemo treatments every three weeks like she needs because we can't get enough in. The companies who make it have had to slow production, and they haven't been able to transport it. Then there's the money issue. No one can afford it. I'm hoping the government will do something about it soon."

Ironic, Kay thought, that the illegal drugs were getting in more easily than the lifesaving ones. Too bad Tamoxifen wasn't sold on the streets.

"But Kay, even if we could get the chemo, I doubt it would help her now. She's advanced stage four. The best thing I can do for her now is keep her comfortable until she dies."

Kay was stunned. "So she needs hospice care?"

"Frankly, yes. But the outage has put most of the hospices out of business."

She blinked back her tears and looked across the way to the frail woman. "How long do you think she has?"

"It's really hard to say, but I'd be surprised if she's still with us a month from now."

The news hit her hard, even though she had expected it. When Kay wheeled her home, she stayed and helped Eloise get ready for bed.

Eloise was grateful. "God has blessed me so much to have friends like you," she said. "Just think what this outage has done for us. Before, we didn't know each other well. Now we're like family."

As the woman got into bed, Kay pulled her blankets over her. Though it was still muggy and hot, Eloise seemed constantly cold.

"And those precious children you've taken in. What a joy to have them around. They're just precious. And that poor little Aaron has the weight of the world on his shoulders. I've been praying that he'll let God shoulder it with him. I can't wait to see what God makes of him."

Kay sat down next to her on the bed. "Eloise, how do you always have such a sunny outlook when things are going so badly for you?"

Wisdom twinkled in the woman's moist eyes. "Because so much is going right. I have twenty-five dollars that I didn't have a few days ago. Brad and Judith got me to the disbursement and kept me in the shade the whole time we were in line. Tonight we had a lovely celebration. And you're here now, ministering to me. How can I complain?"

Kay laughed softly. "I don't know, I always seem to find a way."

"Well, then, you need to sit down and make yourself a list."

"A list? What kind of list?"

"A list of things you're thankful to the Lord Jesus for. You'll see how many good things he's given you." She took Kay's hand and gazed into her eyes. "God told us to give him thanks *in all things*, and to praise him continuously. Even in our trials. There's power in that praise, Kay. You need to teach that to your children."

She smiled. "I have to get it through my own head first."

Eloise patted her. "Don't feel bad. I didn't teach my son that, either. Didn't know it then. But oh, if I had it to do over—I'd do so many things differently."

Kay felt as though she sat at the feet of someone who knew God so intimately that she should record every word. "What would you do differently, Eloise?"

She thought for a moment. "I would have made my son understand that I didn't need this big house and all the fine furniture. But I guess that's the mark of success in child-rearing—if they don't need you anymore."

Kay inclined her head and frowned at her friend. "Is it?"

She breathed a laugh, and that sadness fled. "No, it isn't, but like I said, what do I have to complain about? He's healthy and happy and has a life of his own. He's a good, good boy, Clark is. A trial lawyer up in Boston. He's very busy, you know." Her voice faded out. "I wish I could see him one more time. I think I have things yet to teach him."

Kay couldn't imagine dying without her children.

"Besides," Eloise added, her eyes growing moist. "I miss him an awful lot."

"Does he know how sick you are?"

Eloise dabbed at her eyes. "No, I didn't want to worry him. And I've only gotten one letter from him since the outage. I can see that God's working in his life through this. Maybe the Pulses have brought him closer to the Lord. God may be answering my prayers for his salvation, even as we speak."

When Kay left Eloise for the night, she started writing a letter to Clark. Doug came into the kitchen and peered over her shoulder.

"What's this?"

She told him what Eloise had said.

"She's so wise," he whispered. "Makes her seem richer than the rest of us. Even when she's losing everything ... even her life."

Kay sighed. "I don't want her to be alone, Doug. Either we need to bring her over here, or one of us needs to stay with her at night."

"We don't have any extra beds," Doug said, "but I suppose we could give her our room, since we couldn't get her up the stairs. One of us would have to sleep on the couch so we could check in on her at night."

It all seemed so complicated. She doubted Eloise would agree to it. "She'd be more comfortable in her own home," she said. "What if I slept over there at night? I'm not needed here after I get all the kids to bed."

"Not needed?" he teased, nuzzling her neck. "What about me?"

She kissed him. "You'll be all right."

His eyes turned serious. "I don't really like it," he said, "you and her over there alone. I wouldn't agree to it unless Jeff went with you."

"But she's been by herself all this time. We never worried about her then."

"You're right. God has protected her. But I'd feel better if Jeff was there with you, anyway."

"Okay, I'll tell him. I'll go pack an overnight bag, after I write a letter to her son."

"Her son?"

"Yes," Kay said. "It's time I let him know that if he doesn't come, he may never see his mother again."

FORTY-SEVEN

EARLY THE NEXT MORNING, KAY TOOK THE LETTER SHE'D
written to Clark to the post office.

"You're just in time," Mrs. Lipscomb said in her gruff
voice. "I was just heading to the train station, so it'll go out
today."

"Great!"

Mrs. Lipscomb checked the return address. "You Deni
Branning's mother?"

Kay nodded. "Yes, why?"

The postmaster went to a box and began digging through
the packs of mail.

"Knowing how your daughter pines away for her boyfriend, I try to pay a little more attention to your mail," she
said, "so here's the pack of it. Nothing from him, though."

"Thank you." Kay took the bundle, fighting back her
amusement at Mrs. Lipscomb's interest in their daughter's
drama. She flipped through the letters and saw one with the
return address of Tuscaloosa. Maybe it was from the Gatlin
family!

She hurried back out to the sunlight and tore into the
envelope.

Dear Mr. and Mrs. Branning,

*I'm writing to let you know that your letter to the
Gatlins didn't reach them. Six months ago we bought
their house and they moved to Atlanta, Georgia. Their*

218

address is below. I'm sorry it didn't get to its destination. I hope this helps.

The Andersons.

"Oh no!" She felt like throwing something. All that time wasted! Now she would have to start all over. What she wouldn't give for the defunct FedEx! Or better yet, a telephone with directory assistance. Mrs. Lipscomb came out the door, rolling her cart of mail to her truck.

"Mrs. Lipscomb, wait! I have to send another letter!"

The woman looked annoyed. "Well, let's have it."

"I haven't written it yet. Please, can I borrow an envelope and a stamp? I'll pay you back this afternoon, but I have to get this out today. It's to the parents of Jessie Gatlin."

Mrs. Lipscomb paused. "That girl that was murdered?"

"Yes. I just got her parents' address. I need to get it in the mail, to let them know what's happened."

"They don't know, huh?"

"No, they have no idea. And we haven't known how to reach them until now."

The woman turned and started loading the truck. "All right," she muttered. "But I don't have time to wait. Train's leaving. You can ride with me and write it on the way. Load your bike in the back while I go back in and get another load."

Kay did as she was told, then wrote feverishly until they reached the train station.

FORTY-EIGHT

Two weeks passed as Kay and Jeff slept each night at Eloise's house. The woman was getting sicker, and sleep was sometimes elusive. Tonight she had struggled to relax, despite the pain that gripped her. When Eloise finally fell asleep, Kay tiptoed back across the house and lay down on the couch in the living room. She tried to get comfortable, but she missed her own bed, the rhythmic sound of Doug's breathing, and the warm feel of his body next to hers.

Kay's sleep each night had been sporadic as Eloise retched and retched, and Kay sat with her, holding her head and cleaning her up. Fatigue ached in Kay's bones from the vigil night after night, while continuing to do her work at home during the day while other neighbors took turns being with Eloise. But her friend had offered her so much over the last few months. It was the least Kay could do to be there for her now.

Eloise had given Jeff the room upstairs that she had decorated for her son and his wife in case they ever came to visit. But they never had. Jeff managed to sleep through all the suffering downstairs, but Kay had called him once or twice to help when Eloise fell. He always responded quickly. But mostly she let him sleep, because he was usually exhausted from working so hard. The chicken coops were almost finished, and the chickens they had ordered would be delivered any day. Even Aaron had gotten caught up in the building, taking special pride in the structure at the back of their yard, and he looked forward to the eggs they'd be able to eat when the chickens started laying. She hoped they'd have the chance to experience the thrill of that before they found their relatives.

Kay watched the mail each time it was delivered, hoping for something from the Gatlin grandparents, or from Clark, Eloise's son. By now he'd probably gotten her letter informing him of his mother's condition. She supposed it was too soon to expect a reply, but time was running out.

Today, Eloise had thrown up blood and had seemed weaker and less responsive than ever before, yet she had some cogent moments. Eloise had no fear of her impending death, and if she was suffering, she never made it known. She had made her peace with God and she knew what her future held.

Now, trying to get comfortable on the couch, Kay wished for a light. She was so tired of the darkness. Kerosene was precious, so they conserved it. But she wouldn't have minded having a night-light tonight. They had started allowing Sarah to keep a pillar candle burning in Deni's bedroom so that if she woke during the night, she would remember where she was and wouldn't panic. Hopefully, it would chase away the ghosts that plagued her each night. Perhaps Kay needed to bring one over here for herself at night.

As if in answer to her mind's wanderings, a knock sounded on the front door. She jerked up and peered through the darkness. The knock was hard, determined, and she got up and pulled her robe on, held it at her throat and went to the front door to peer out the peephole. She couldn't see more than the shadow of a man—a big one—a stark silhouette against the moonlight.

She backed away from the door, careful not to make a sound. What would any man want, banging on this door at night? It wasn't Doug. He would have called through the door to keep from frightening her. No one else had any reason to be here.

Quickly, she ran up the stairs to get Jeff and tripped over the last step. Righting herself, she felt her way down the dark hallway.

"Jeff," she said, barely above a whisper. "Jeff, get up!"

She heard the bedcovers rustling. "What is it, Mom?"

"Someone's here," she said. "Get your gun."

She heard a few things drop in the darkness, but he turned on a flashlight then, chasing away the shadows. She breathed a sigh of relief at the light.

"Be quiet," she said. "He's knocking on the door. Should we answer it?"

He shrugged. "I don't know, Mom. What do you think?"

She took a few steps down the stairs. The man was still knocking. He wasn't going away.

"I don't know," she said.

Jeff was wearing nothing but a T-shirt and a pair of boxer shorts, but he stepped down the stairs in his sock feet, holding that shotgun to the floor. Just before they reached the bottom, she heard something rattling in the door. Whoever it was, was trying to pick the lock!

Fear constricted her throat.

"He's trying to break in," she whispered. "Jeff, stay back." She thought of taking the gun from him, aiming it at the door, and shooting before the person could make his way in, but suddenly the door flew open. Jeff raised his flashlight and his gun and Kay screamed.

"Don't shoot!" The man's hands flew to the air and he looked as startled to see them as they did him. "I'm Eloise's son, Clark."

It took a moment for the words to register ... then slowly Kay wilted, her hand on her chest.

"Oh, Clark! We almost shot you!"

"Tell me about it," he said. "I came as soon as I got that letter from one of the neighbors."

"It was from me," she cut in, extending her trembling hand. "I'm Kay Branning."

He had the build of a linebacker. Hard to believe that small woman could have given birth to such a man.

"How's my mother?"

Still breathing hard, she sat down and tried to catch her breath. "She's very ill, but still alive."

His voice cracked. "I'm sorry to come so late. I caught the last train into Crockett and I had to walk here. Since I'd never been here before, it took me a while to find the neighborhood. I'd have been here a lot earlier but I got lost."

"It's okay." She closed the door behind him and locked it. "I'm glad you're here. She'll be so happy to see you."

He wiped his eyes, and she saw that he was trembling. This wasn't the response she had expected from the cold son of Eloise. Was this the same man who had bought his mother a house then never come to visit her in it?

"Can I get you anything? Some water?"

"In a minute." There was a tremor in his voice. "First, I just need to see Mama."

"Of course. She's in here." She took the flashlight from Jeff, conscious that he was following her with that shotgun pointed down, just in case the man turned on her.

They stepped into Eloise's bedroom and shone the flashlight on her bed. Kay lit the candles on her bed table. Clark saw his small mother lying sick and scrawny on the bed, her eyes sunken in her sleep, her breathing hoarse and raspy. Tears flooded his eyes. He fell to his knees beside her bed and reached for her hand.

"Mama?"

Her eyes fluttered open and she looked up, trying to focus on him. Suddenly she realized who he was. "Clark?" she asked, as if she doubted her eyes.

"Yes, Mama, it's me."

"Oh, Clark." She rose up with more energy than she'd had in days, and he pulled her into his arms.

Eloise started to cry. Kay hoped she wouldn't get sick again and start throwing up. Mercifully, she didn't.

As Eloise and Clark held each other, talking softly, Kay and Jeff retreated to the kitchen. She lit a lamp and busied herself finding something for Clark to eat. Jeff sat at the bar, his hair messed up, the shotgun on the table in front of him.

"It's good that he came, isn't it, Mom?"

She blinked back the mist in her eyes. "Yes, it is. It was probably Eloise's dying wish to see her son."

"But won't it be sad for him to see her now when she's about to die?"

"I think it'll be healing," she said, "to know that they were reconciled before she died. It would be really sad if she died and he'd never made an effort to see her. No one should have to live with that kind of guilt."

"That's bad." He looked into the blackness just outside the kitchen. "Losing your mom, I mean."

She nodded. "Makes me miss mine a lot. My dad too. I hope they're doing okay."

He got up, came around the bar, and hugged her. "I'm glad I've got you."

She burst into tears then and pulled him into a tight hug. "I'm glad I've got you too, son. Thank you for being over here and protecting me and not complaining about it."

"Sure, no problem."

She found the loaf of bread someone had made for Eloise, and sawed off a piece. "So how are things with you and Mandy?"

"We broke up. She got mad at me for spending so much time rehearsing to play at the party. I figure if she doesn't understand my music, who needs her?"

Kay tried to suppress her smile. "I'm sorry about that. Can you work it out?"

"Maybe, when things settle down."

She breathed a laugh. "You think they ever will?"

"Probably not," he said, "but it's important, all the stuff we're doing."

"Yes, it is," she said.

As Kay moved around the kitchen, she felt a sweet sense of peace. Jeff was growing up. And she liked what he was becoming.

FORTY-NINE

*THE MONSTERS WERE OUT IN FULL FORCE TONIGHT. THEY
floated just above Sarah's head, inhabiting the clothes
that hung around her. Mama's closet was black-dark and
smelled of shoes, cigarette smoke, and sweat. She banged on
the door, begging to be let out.*

*Where was Aaron? What if Mama forgot she'd locked
her up? She'd have to stay in here with these monsters until
she came back and freed her. She screamed for her mother
and kicked the door.*

*Finally, it flew open and someone bent toward her. She
scrambled to her feet, reaching for mercy. But it was only
another monster, clawing her with long dirty fingernails . . .,
and it had her mother's eyes.*

SARAH'S SCREAMING WOKE DENI UP. THE CANDLE THEY
used as a night-light had flickered out, so she sat up and felt
through the darkness for the little girl who had burrowed
under the covers to the foot of the bed and was fighting to
find her way out.

Beth sat up. "Where is she?"

"Under here." Deni jerked the covers off the bed and
grabbed the child. Sarah wrestled her at first, but Deni held
her tight, whispering into her ear. "It's okay, sweetie. Deni's
here. You're with me, remember?"

The child stopped screaming, but she shivered against her. Deni sat down on the mattress and pulled Sarah into her lap. "That was a bad one, wasn't it?"

Sarah sucked in a sob and nodded. Her thumb went to her mouth and she laid her head against Deni's chest.

"She okay?"

She saw the shadow of Aaron standing in her doorway. "Yeah, I think she's fine. Just another bad dream."

"I can take her if you want me to."

Deni snuggled her closer. "No, she's fine. Just let her stay with me, okay?"

Aaron came closer to the bed and touched Sarah's back. He watched her for a moment as the child's eyes drifted shut. "I guess it's okay. Wanna stay with Deni, Sarah?"

"Uh-huh."

"Okay, good night."

Deni watched the boy retreat to his room. She smiled at the step of faith he'd just taken. Trust was growing. He was realizing he could share the burden of his siblings' well-being. She hoped he would sleep well with his distraught sister in Deni's care. It was about time.

Maybe before too long, Aaron would have the opportunity to become a kid again.

She sat on the edge of the bed and rocked Sarah with her body, the way she'd seen Aaron doing. She started to sing "I Can Only Imagine" softly against her curls, and she felt Sarah relaxing against her. She pulled the girl into bed with her, curled up in her arms.

"Don't leave me," Sarah whispered.

"How could I ever leave my sleeping bunny?" Deni kissed her forehead and held her as she fell asleep.

THE INVESTIGATION INTO JESSIE'S DEATH CONTINUED AS THEY waited for word back from the Gatlin grandparents. Glad for a diversion, the family tried to help Beth with the props and set for her play. It turned into a family effort, with all four of the Gatlin kids fully involved.

Jeff was writing the songs, and he and his band of amateur musicians began rehearsing for the performance. Every kid in the neighborhood had joined in the production, and Beth made sure everyone had a part.

Deni was proud of her little sister.

It was three months into the outage, and soon the teachers in the neighborhood who had agreed to hold school for Oak Hollow would be convening. The children would have to spend three hours a day in school (their classrooms would be their teachers' living rooms) after they had done the work they needed to do in their own homes and yards. Those teachers had offered Beth their full support in the production, in hope the children would bond before they were forced to sit in close quarters each day to learn. The play also served as a nice distraction for them, reminding them that they were kids and not just laborers in their parents' "fields."

Mark Green had built a stage for them to perform on out of an old flatbed trailer. Parents across the neighborhood got involved as well, making costumes and helping the children learn the songs.

When the day came for the big production, Doug, Jeff, and Mark rolled the stage and all the props down to the lake. Toy boxes and attics had been combed until everything they needed had magically materialized, with a little help and a little creativity.

When the big night came, the whole neighborhood turned out, just as they had hoped. Deni brought an extra lawn chair for Mark in case he had time to sit down after he got the stage and the backdrop into place. He had even fashioned a canopy on the stage and a curtain the kids could open and close. She had a feeling it would be used many more times before the outage was over.

This was one of the bright sides of the Pulses. Before the outage, Deni had only known her neighbors as faces behind windshields. Now they were becoming like family, and she enjoyed these gatherings. It helped with her loneliness.

Deni's mind drifted to Craig, and that old misery surfaced again. She hadn't heard a thing back from him since she'd mailed the breakup letter. There had been ample time for him to return something. It didn't matter, she supposed. Maybe he hadn't even had time to read her letter. Maybe it was sitting on his desk somewhere under a stack of congressional memos. Or maybe he'd read it right away, then forgotten what it said.

But her melancholy vanished when she caught sight of Mark. Since that kiss the other night, she hadn't seen him much. Now she watched him, waiting for a reaction when he found her. Their eyes met, and his smile lit up his face. Her heart felt suddenly lighter.

He signaled to her, asking her if the chair next to her was free, and she nodded and crooked her finger for him to come. He wove his way through the crowd and sat next to her.

"I think we got everything together in time," he said. "Man, I'm so glad it's a great turnout. Your sister really deserves this. She's worked so hard."

"I know," she said. "Who would have ever dreamed that Beth would be a playwright?"

"Not just a playwright," he said, laughing. "A director and producer and casting director and costume maker and songwriter and ticket salesperson and promoter and publicist."

"Funny thing about this outage," she said. "It's helped us each discover what we're good at. I never knew Beth was destined for Broadway."

"She didn't even cast herself for any of the parts," he said. "She's perfectly happy to be behind the scenes. That says a lot about her maturity."

"Yeah, she's grown up a lot. Haven't we all? The outage has taken a lot out of us, but some of us are better for it."

Mark's eyes grew introspective as he stared across the crowd. She wondered if he—with his father's death—felt a net loss or net gain.

He leaned back in his chair and she noticed, once again, what amazing eyes he had. They'd always been a bright blue. Even in high school, he'd been known for his beautiful blue eyes. Now that he'd become a man and his face was as dark as tanned leather, they looked even paler, like deep ocean water. There was peace in them, in spite of the things he'd been through.

A ten-year-old kid came out from between the curtains and began playing a guitar that was almost too big for him. When he finished, the crowd erupted in cheers of adulation, and grinning from ear to ear, he pulled the curtain open and the play began.

The crowd hadn't had such a good time since the neighborhood party, and they laughed raucously as the children remembered and forgot their lines. Aaron, Luke, and Joey played some of David's brothers.

Logan played David, and Jeff was Goliath. Deni knew they would never live down their mediocre acting debuts.

The play was over in less than thirty minutes, and as the children came out and bowed and Beth took her curtsy, the crowd went wild. Deni and Mark erupted out of their chairs in a standing ovation.

"You go, girl!" Deni cried. "That's my sister up there. Wheeew!"

It was Beth's shining moment, and little Sarah's too. In fact, everyone on the stage was a star tonight. The Gatlin boys smiled like heroes, and Sarah pranced for the crowd. It was too bad their mother wasn't here to see it.

As the applause died down and the crowd broke up, she heard her name called behind her.

"Deni!"

She turned and saw Chris walking toward her in her nurse's scrubs. Behind her, the setting sun was sending its last blast of glory. Deni had to shield her eyes.

"Chris, did you see the play?"

"No, I was working. Deni, I have a surprise for you."

There was someone walking behind her, but Deni couldn't see who it was. They grew closer ... she squinted into the sun ...

And there he was.

"Hey, babe, it's me!"

Craig stood there in all his glory, grinning like Harrison Ford when he found the Holy Grail.

"Craig!" Deni froze.

Then reality took hold, and she realized that he had come. She ran and threw herself into Craig's arms.

FIFTY

CRAIG HAD CHANGED.

He'd had an athlete's build before—he was a runner. Now he looked downright skinny. His hair was longer than she'd ever seen it, and he'd grown a beard. His clothes looked rumpled and worn, unlike the expensive Van Heusen shirts and pressed slacks he'd always worn before. More often than not, he'd worn a coat and tie as naturally as someone else might have worn a T-shirt and jeans.

But he looked so good. "I can't believe you came!"

He let her go and looked her over. "You look great. A sight for sore eyes."

"No, I don't."

"You do. I mean, really great. I've never seen you look better."

Her eyes glistened as she took that in. She could see in his eyes that he meant it. She had wanted so badly to hear that from him.

"How did you get here?"

"Train," he said. "I was so frustrated when you weren't home. You have no idea what it took for me to get here. I've been on a train for what seems like days, and it must have been a hundred degrees on that thing. And when I got here, I didn't know how to find your neighborhood. I got lost and had to find someone who could point me in the right direction."

"Did you walk from the station?"

"No, I brought my bike," he said. "They let passengers bring them aboard the train now, since that's the only way anyone has of getting around once they get to their destinations. But a lot of good it did me. Not like I could look your address up on MapQuest. Took me hours to find this place."

"I was checking on Miss Eloise," Chris said, "and I ran across him sitting in your front yard."

Deni hugged him again. "We were down here at the play. If I'd known you were coming, I would have met you at the station. I really never thought you'd come."

He rolled his eyes. "Yeah, I could tell that by your letter. Come on, Deni. What's with the Dear John? How could you think I don't love you?"

She glanced back at Chris and Mark. Mark stood looking at the ground with his hands in his pockets.

She turned back to Craig. "I was hurt that you hadn't come."

"Well, I'm here now." He glanced at Mark, and Deni followed his gaze.

"Uh ... Craig, this is Mark Green. He's a neighbor and an old friend from high school."

Mark planted a smile on his face and reached out to shake his hand.

Craig hesitated. "Green. The murderer's son?"

Mark pulled his hand back.

Deni caught her breath, stunned that he would say something so cold. She came to his rescue. "His father was the one, but he's not—"

"It's okay, Deni," Mark cut in. "Nice to meet you, Craig."

Craig shook hands, but as he did he looked Mark over. Deni wondered if Craig sensed the chemistry between them. She doubted it. It wouldn't make any sense to him.

He raked his hand through his disheveled hair. "I'm dying of thirst. I could guzzle that whole lake."

"Well, you don't have to," she said. "We have well water."

He wiped his perspiring face on the sleeve of his shirt. "Take me to it. I'm ready."

She slipped her arm through his and started to lead him to the well, but her mother's voice stopped her.

"Craig? Is that you?"

He smiled. "It's me, all right."

Her parents came toward them. Their smiles were strained, and she knew they weren't happy to see him. Still, her father shook his hand.

"Good to see you, Craig. You've come a long way."

"I had no idea how long," he said, "but I made it."

Deni thought of her own harrowing journey trying to get to him. She would have killed for a train. Beth came running up, unaware of his presence.

"Well, what did you guys think? Was that a success or what?"

Her mother swept her into a hug. "It was fabulous, honey! I'm so proud of you. I had no idea how talented you were, and everything went perfectly."

"Did you see when Sarah forgot her lines?"

"It was so cute."

Beth laughed. "Yeah, I was trying to whisper her lines to her from backstage. I know everybody heard me."

"My favorite part was when little Evie tripped over her costume and Leah Ward helped her up and made it into a big laugh so she wouldn't get embarrassed," Doug said. "I loved that."

"Excuse me," Craig cut in.

They all turned back to him.

"Hate to interrupt, but I'm dying of thirst. We were going to the well, Deni?"

Beth stopped gushing and looked up at him without recognition. Suddenly she realized who he was. "Craig?"

Deni grinned. "It's him, all right."

"What are you doing here?"

Deni's smile was triumphant. "He came just for the play."

"Huh-uh." Beth grinned. "You didn't know about the play, did you?"

He laughed. "No, but I wish I had. If only I'd gotten here a few minutes earlier."

Deni winked at her. "You did a great job, sweetie. I'm going to take him to get some water now."

As they started away, she glanced at Mark. He had turned his back and was high-fiving the kids coming off the stage. He seemed to have forgotten her, already.

Maybe that was best. Now that Craig was here, she supposed things would get back to normal. His coming had changed everything.

As they walked, he grinned down at her. "I wasn't kidding, you know. You look great."

"Guess the emaciated look becomes me. Dr. Atkins has nothing on the Pulses, does he? And there's nothing like constant perspiration to moisten your face."

"Nice tan," he said. "What do you do, sunbathe every afternoon?"

"Sunbathe?" She laughed out loud. "No way. My dad's a slave driver. I'm busy working out in the garden or hauling water to and from the house or sorting through garbage or riding my bike on errands."

His suggestion that all she had to do was lounge around stung her slightly, but she supposed it wasn't his fault. That was the kind of girl she'd been before the outage. Those days seemed like an eternity ago.

"So are your parents going to let me stay at your house?"

"Of course. You didn't think they'd put you out on the street, did you?"

"I didn't know. I don't think they like me all that much, and they probably worry we'll be sneaking around the hallways at night. You gotta admit they're a little rigid."

That irritated her, but she swallowed it. "They would never turn you away," she said. "They're not as rigid as you think."

Deni used the pulley to bring up a pail of water. He cupped it with his hands and drank it, then took another.

"Great water."

"Yeah, my dad and brother helped dig the well. Until then we got it from the lake."

He splashed it on his face and rubbed it around on his neck. "Man, I'd love to just dive in. Do you guys have a pool?"

"No. And I was really bummed about it at first, because it seemed like the families with the pools had it made. They could swim and get cool, and they could wash and had clean water to drink. But now all those pools are full of fungus and algae. Talk about gross. And the ones with the pools have less yard to plow. So I guess it's good that we don't have one." She raised up on tiptoe and kissed him again. His beard felt scratchy against her face. "I never thought I'd see you unshaven."

"I figured, why fight it?" he said. "Didn't have anyplace to plug my electric razor in and I ran out of razor blades and shaving cream."

"I thought you always said that a person who worked in politics could never have a beard. That people didn't trust politicians with hair on their faces."

"Yeah, well, I'm not running for anything," he said, "at least not yet. I'll shave before I make a run for Senator Crawford's job."

They walked back home and stepped into the darkness of the house. Heat assaulted them. It seemed so thick at the end of the day. Deni fixed him another tall glass of well water. He drank it, then collapsed on the couch.

"I have so much to tell you," he said, "but before I do, we need to talk about us."

She sat next to him. He picked up her hand and saw that she wasn't wearing her ring. "You know, this really bugs me. I'm sitting in Washington working my tail off trying to help run the affairs of this country at a critical time, stressing out about getting food and water and cash and electricity to the people, and I get this Dear John letter that knocks me off my feet. You have some kind of timing."

It warmed her that it had affected him that much. "I told you why I did it."

"Yeah, but it was unfair. I mean, it wasn't like I could just drop everything and take off after you. I'm a little more logical than that, and you know it."

"Your letters were so cold, Craig. Even after I told you what I'd been through trying to get to you."

"I was in a hurry when I answered it. I had a lot to do. The weight of the whole country is on us in Washington."

"How hard would it have been to say something sweet or kind to me? You sure had time to give me a travelogue."

He dropped his head back on the couch. "Again, unfair. I was simply trying to communicate. That's what you love so much, isn't it? Communication. I thought you'd want to know what was going on with me."

"It's the *way* you communicated that bothered me."

"See? There you go." He sat up straighter, mocking. "So let me get this straight. I should have written you poetry, drawn you pictures of little flowers and kissy-kissies all over it, and droned on about how much I missed you?"

She pulled her hand back.

"You're telling me that would have made things different? Better somehow? I thought you were bigger than that, Deni."

She got up and moved to a chair. "You know, I really don't know why you came."

"Okay, here we go." He sounded so battle-weary, so henpecked. She couldn't believe he saw her this way. He got up and took her hand, pulled her to her feet.

"I came because I love you, and I'm going to marry you. I won't let you break up with me."

It was that no-holds-barred determination that had first attracted her to him, and it served him well now.

He pressed his forehead against hers and lifted her left hand. Her heart sped up.

"So you might as well go put that ring back on. I'm not taking no for an answer. I've come too far, and I'm not in a good mood."

His take-charge mood sent a thrill through her. That slow grin crept back to her lips. Maybe he did love her, after all.

When he bent down to kiss her, her heart melted and all the anger of the past few weeks vaporized. He was here for her, and that was what mattered. She could get over the weeks that had passed and the letters that weren't warm enough. She could forget all the angry thoughts and feelings she'd had toward him.

He was here now.

She stroked his beard and broke the kiss. "I'm glad you came."

"Then you'll put the ring back on?"

She wished he didn't look so smug. "You knew I would when you came."

"It was a gamble, but I figured it was worth it." He hugged her so hard that he lifted her off her feet.

All that exhilaration she used to feel with him flooded back like the gates had burst.

"How long can you stay?"

"Long enough to marry you," he said. "Then I'll take you back with me."

FIFTY-ONE

DENI AND CRAIG WERE SITTING ON THE PORCH SWING THE
next afternoon when Mark drove his buggy — a VW pulled
by two horses — to the Brannings' house. It was packed full
of props from last night's play. Beth bounced out to unload
it. Her parents followed her to the car.

Mark offered Deni and Craig a wave as he got out and
opened the trunk. "How's it going?"

Craig didn't make a move to get up. "Pretty good," he
said.

Deni went down the steps to help, but by the time she
reached the car, the trunk was unloaded. She went to one of
the horses and stroked his mane. "Wish I had something to
feed you, boy, but I'm fresh out."

Mark seemed to ignore her for a moment as he handed
the props to Beth. "Did a great job last night, kiddo. I expect
great things from you."

"Thanks," Beth said. "I'm so glad it's over. It was chaos."

"But you're already thinking of the next one, right?"

She giggled. "I was thinking of doing Snow White."

"Well, next time, you have to play the lead," Mark said.
"You're a Renaissance woman, you know that?"

"Is that good?"

"It's good," Deni said.

Her parents and Beth carried the stuff into the house,
and Deni glanced up at the porch. Craig was swinging

237

gently back and forth, engrossed in a book of Chinese philosophy he'd brought with him.

Her parents thanked Mark again for all his help, and as they headed back inside, arms laden with the stuff he'd delivered to them, Mark came around to where Deni stood. Petting the other horse, he said, "So is everything going okay?"

She had trouble looking him in the eye. "Yeah. I can't believe he came."

"Told you he wasn't crazy." He went back to the trunk and she followed him. "So you're wearing the ring again, I see," he said in a low voice.

She looked down at it. "Yeah. He convinced me he really does want to marry me."

Mark was quiet for a moment as he opened his tool box and searched through it for something. Never finding it, he shut the trunk.

His eyes were cool as he turned back to her. "Well, that's good. I'm happy for you, Deni."

But he didn't look happy. He looked hurt.

"Look, Mark. I know what happened between us was …"

"Shh," he cut in. "You don't owe me anything. I'm fine. He seems like a nice guy."

As Mark got back into the VW and shook the reins through the windshield opening, Deni joined Craig again. She watched as Mark's horses pulled him toward the neighborhood entrance. About that time, a man turned the corner into Oak Hollow, swaggering like a drunken sailor.

"Oh, great. Here comes trouble."

Mark stopped him, and the two engaged in animated conversation through Mark's window.

Craig sat up and followed her gaze. "What?"

"That guy who's coming. He's Sarah's dad." She'd explained the situation to him last night. "What could he want now?"

"Does he know their money was stolen?"

"Who knows?"

They watched the two men talking. Mark seemed to be trying to turn the man away.

Craig got to his feet as Moe waved Mark's concerns away and headed into the Brannings' yard. He wavered slightly, and she realized he was drunk. Mark got out of his car and grabbed Moe's arm, but he jerked away and kept walking toward her. "Get ready," she told Craig. "There might be a fight."

Craig seemed ready, but she opened the front door and called her dad.

In seconds, Doug was out the door, clutching his rifle. They watched as Moe staggered toward them.

"What do you want, Moe?" Doug asked from the porch.

"I told you the other day, I want my kids."

"They're not your kids," Doug said. "Besides, their money's gone. It was stolen from them. We never got it, so if that's what you're after, you can just turn around and go home."

"I believe it was stolen from 'em," he slurred, "but you're the one stole it. Now you can cough it up or I can come in and get it myself, along with my daughter."

"I told you I don't have it," Doug said. "That neighbor of theirs, Edith, wound up taking their money, and then it got stolen from her. If you want it, you can follow the trail of thugs. But it's not here." He cocked his rifle and lifted the barrel. "So you need to go on, now."

Mark had followed Moe into the yard. "Come on, man. I'll give you a ride somewhere."

"I ain't going nowhere without my kid," he said. "Bring her out. She's my flesh and blood, and I want her."

Deni wanted to punch him. "Why? There's not another disbursement for three months. Just leave her alone."

"*You* leave her alone. She's mine!"

"You're not getting her," Doug said through his teeth. "Now get off of my property before I get mad."

For a moment, Deni thought Moe might call her dad's bluff. She had no doubt that he would shoot if he had to. She just hoped Moe wasn't armed. Craig moved closer to the door.

Even though the gun was aimed in his direction, Mark only moved closer to Moe. Touching his shoulder, Mark said, "Come on, pal. Let's go now. Nice and easy." Moe stood stiff as a statue, refusing to move. His eyes were locked with Doug's.

"Don't make me shoot you," Doug said. "It would be a waste of perfectly good ammo."

Deni reached for Craig's hand. His palm was sweating. Moe held her father's angry gaze for a moment, then finally let out a breath. He took a step back and pointed at Doug. "All right, I'm going, but I'll be back." Mark kept his hand on his back as he escorted him back to his rig.

He opened the car door and Moe climbed in. As the horse pulled them away, they finally relaxed.

Craig looked at Doug. "You think he'll be back?"

"Oh, I think so," Doug said. "I don't think we've heard the last of him, especially when there are more disbursements coming."

Doug stood watching until Moe was out of sight. Deni and Craig waited on the porch, and before long, Mark rode back into the neighborhood. He pulled in front of the Brannings' house and Deni leaned in his window.

"I dropped him off at a produce stand. He was a little tipsy. I know how he spent his disbursement."

"Thanks for taking him away," she said. "We appreciate it."

"No problem. But don't let your guard down. He'll be back."

He held Deni's gaze for a moment. She looked down, confused by the warmth rushing to her face. She felt guilty, as if she'd somehow cheated. She wondered if she should tell Craig that she and Mark had kissed.

"Let me know if you need me again," Mark said softly. "I'll do whatever I can."

"I think we've got it covered."

Deni jumped. She hadn't realized that Craig had followed her to the curb. His remark was thick with ownership, but Mark let it roll off him.

"Well, I'll see you guys later."

"Thanks, Mark. See you later." Deni watched as he pulled away.

After a moment, she looked back at Craig. He was watching her watch Mark. For a moment, she fully expected him to ask if there was something going on between the two of them. If he did, she'd have to tell him the truth.

But suddenly the door across the street flew open and Eloise's son flew out of her house. "Help!" he cried. "Help! Somebody get the doctor! Mama's not breathing."

Deni took off running. "I'll go get Derek," she cried, and ran through the yard to the doctor's house.

As she ran, she prayed that Eloise could be revived.

FIFTY-TWO

ELOISE'S SON — WHO HAD SCARCELY DONE A THING FOR HER while she was alive — built her coffin with his own hands. He got permission to bury her at a graveyard two miles away next to a church, and dozens of people from the neighborhood joined them in the walking processional to the burial.

Doug, Jeff, Brad, and two neighbors served with Clark as the pallbearers. They carried the coffin to the grave site with a borrowed horse and wagon. Kay made everyone dress up as much as they could, even the Gatlin children. She'd pulled old clothes out of the closet until she'd found something suitable for a funeral. And not just anyone's funeral, but Eloise's. She deserved their best.

Because Eloise's preacher was too far away, Doug conducted the service at graveside. Doug and Brad had dug the hole earlier that day, and they lowered the casket with ropes. Doug centered his funeral sermon on the Scripture that said, "Precious in the sight of the Lord is the death of his saints," and he read from Revelation 21 and 22 about heaven — which, he explained, Eloise was experiencing now. He told of all the times they'd talked about her love for Jesus and the fact that she had no doubt in her mind where she would be when she died.

"It was no big deal for Eloise to lose her electricity and car, her telephone, her air-conditioning. Her cancer diagnosis had taught her what was really important. And when it came to giving up her life, well, that was fine too. She had surrendered it to Christ a long time ago. And now she has it back."

Craig stood next to Deni, acting the part of a quiet mourner as they lowered her into the grave.

Doug asked each of them to grab a handful of dirt and toss it onto the coffin. Deni held little Sarah's hand as the little girl stooped to get a handful.

"Throw it in now, Sarah," she instructed softly.

Sarah dropped the dirt in. "Asha to asha, dirt to dirt."

Deni looked down at the child. She had said that before, when they'd had the little memorial for her mother. She had wondered then where she'd gotten that saying, but so much had been going on that she hadn't had time to think about it more. Aaron had suggested she'd learned it on TV, but was that true? She was three years old. How many of the programs had she watched that had funerals? And how would she remember such an obscure reference?

She made a mental note to ask her about it later and see if she could get Sarah to tell her where she'd learned it.

Clark wept as his mother's friends told him sweet stories about her life.

Eloise had left an important legacy. Deni hoped her son was man enough to embrace it.

"SO WHAT DID YOU THINK OF THE SERVICE?" DENI ASKED CRAIG AS they walked home.

He shrugged. "It was okay. Your dad did a good job. I guess you have to say *something* when someone dies."

Deni glanced up at him. "Dad was telling the truth, Craig. He was speaking from his heart."

"Yeah, I guess he was." He took her hand in his. "I guess some people just need something to believe in."

Deni was quiet for a moment. They'd had this conversation before, but not since she'd had her own transformation.

"You don't believe in anything?"

"I believe in myself."

She looked at the black-top road as they walked. "I thought that maybe the outage had changed things. It did for me."

He snickered. "If anything, it solidified my views. If there were a loving God, how could he allow something like this?"

"My dad thinks he allowed it because he *is* a loving God," Deni said. "That he was trying to get our attention and wake us up."

"For what?"

"To make us dependent on him."

Craig laughed. "Well, that would be worthless, since we're still in the dark no matter who we're depending on."

Deni grew quiet for a moment. She looked up ahead, saw Mark picking up little Luke and setting him on his shoulders.

"But God's provided for us in so many ways," Deni said. "I mean, we've got this beautiful house to live in, we've got a well, we've got a place to plant some food, even if it's not very much. We have neighbors and friends and a whole community we really didn't know before. And my family's closer than ever. We're learning things about ourselves that will make us better people."

"Yeah, and what about the people at that apartment complex? You think they have a lot of blessings too? And don't you think they were already dependent?"

"Maybe that's why God sent us to them. We're trying to help. Maybe that's his way of providing. They've survived somehow all this time. I think God's working in each of our lives, one by one. It may not be the same way in mine as it was in Aaron's or Luke's, but he's working nonetheless. And he took care of the children that whole time."

"By making them steal? You think if there's a God, he turned them into little criminals?"

Deni knew she'd never win an argument with him. He was too good at what he did. But the thought saddened her. If she married him, she would never be able to share the thing that had become the most important to her—her faith. The Bible warned not to yoke oneself with unbelievers.

She shoved that thought to the back of her mind. Sometimes God's laws were hard to keep, even when she wanted to. Besides, maybe by the time they married, he would be a believer.

She looked up ahead at Mark, loping with Luke on his shoulders. He related well to the Gatlin children, she thought. He knew what it was like to be the son of an outcast. Even Aaron liked him.

"Can I ask you something?"

Deni looked at Craig. "Sure. What?"

"Do you and that Mark guy have something going on?"

She tried to look shocked. "What do you mean? We're just friends."

He regarded Mark, his eyes narrowed. "I don't know. Every now and then I just get a feeling there's something more between you two. He's not the real reason you broke up with me, is he?"

That was just like him, to avoid taking blame by finding ulterior motives. "No, Craig. The reason I broke up with you was because of your letters. I told you that."

"But while we were broken up, did anything happen with you two?"

She was silent for a moment as she walked, but he didn't take his eyes off her.

"Deni, I asked you a question. I deserve an answer."

Finally, she stopped walking. "I was going to tell you," she said, "and we *were* broken up. I didn't do anything wrong."

His face went slack. "What happened?"

"It was just a kiss."

He groaned and took a step backward, shaking his head. "I should have known. Making me out to be the bad guy when all along—"

"I wrote and broke up with you *before* it happened, Craig. It wasn't planned. We were at the dance celebrating the disbursement and the well coming in, and we danced. He walked me home ... and we kissed. It was no big deal."

A red tint crept up his neck, to his ears, then made its way to his face. Whether it was from heat or anger, she wasn't sure. He looked up ahead, watched Mark taking Luke off his back and setting him on the ground. Then he lifted Sarah.

"I knew that guy had a crush on you."

She wanted to tell him that Mark was more mature than to have a crush on anyone, that their friendship was deep and abiding, and that he'd been there for her when Craig hadn't. But she didn't say any of those things.

"Craig, you don't have to worry. I think we were each as shocked as the other when we kissed. It hasn't happened since. But now that you're back, everything's normal again, and I can tell that Mark's already forgotten about it."

"Yeah, right." His jaw twitched. "No big deal to you maybe, but it is to me."

"So what do you want to do? Break up again?"

He shot her a look. "No, I don't want to break up, Deni. I think I've made that clear."

They walked in silence for a block or two, and Deni dreaded what would happen now. She heard Sarah screaming with laughter on Mark's shoulders, but she wouldn't let herself look at them.

Finally, Craig stopped again. "Look, nothing about this outage is normal. Let's just ... let's never bring it up again. How about that?"

Deni nodded, wondering if he could really do that. "Fine with me."

He pulled a handkerchief out of his pocket and wiped the sweat off his brow. "Do you think your dad has an extra razor?"

"I think he does."

"Would he let me shave?"

"Nope," she said, trying to be funny. "He has a no-shave rule in our house."

He looked at her like he thought she was serious.

"Kidding," she said. "He'll give you a razor."

He didn't smile. "It's been hot in Washington, but I think it's hotter here. I think it's time for this beard to come off."

She smiled. "I kinda like it."

"I liked it too," he said, stroking it, "but it is really hot. Besides, I think I'd like to look in the mirror and see a lawyer instead of a hillbilly."

"Hillbillies aren't the only ones with beards," she said. "It's a noble feature." She wondered if his shaving had anything to do with Mark's clean-cut features.

As they turned into Oak Hollow and walked toward their house, Deni noticed the sheriff's van sitting in front. Sheriff Scarbrough was on the porch talking to her parents, who must have just arrived home.

As they approached, her parents led him inside.

"We got the ballistics report back on the murder weapon," he was saying in a low voice. "It was a .38, just as we thought. But Aaron's stolen gun isn't the only one we're dealing with. Turns out Edith Stuart's gun was a .38 too."

Kay gasped. "Are you going to arrest her?"

"Already did, for robbery. She's in jail as we speak."

"Why not murder?"

"Because first we have to know the bullets we found in Jessie came from Edith's gun. If they did, we can charge her with homicide."

Deni hadn't expected that. Edith was conniving, but she didn't seem homicidal.

"But what would be her motive?" Kay asked. "Jessie didn't have any money. She didn't have anything."

"We're still working on that," he said. "We're hoping maybe the kids can help us."

"Sure," Kay said. "Come on in. We'll sit out back and you can talk to them there."

They gathered the Gatlin children around the patio table. Luke and Sarah sat together in the same chair, still dressed in their funeral clothes. Aaron stood with his arms crossed, like a sentinel guarding state secrets. Joey slumped in the chair next to him. Deni and Craig stood in the doorway, listening as her parents led the conversation.

"Aaron," Doug said, "Sheriff Scarbrough needs to ask you some questions."

Aaron's face tightened. "Okay."

Scarbrough set his foot on a chair and leaned on his knee. "Aaron, could you tell me if your mom had any kind of quarrel with Edith Stuart?"

"What's a quarrel?" Aaron asked.

"Did they fight or argue or anything like that?"

Aaron glanced over at Joey and they both shook their heads. "Sometimes. Not any more than anybody else."

"Was there anything of your mother's that Edith wanted?"

"She wanted our money," Joey said, "and she took it, that's what."

"No, I mean before the disbursement, when your mother was still living."

"They didn't get along real well," Aaron said. "Sometimes Edith screamed at my mom to make us shut up 'cause we made too much noise. Our TV was always too loud, Edith said."

"But sometimes it was her," Joey said. "Edith liked to play music really loud too, and she would have parties with people coming and going all night."

"The last time you saw your mother, had they had any kind of a fight?"

"I don't think so." Aaron squinted up at him. "Why are you asking us all these questions?"

"Because we're trying to find your mother's killer."

"And you think *she* did it?"

"She prob'ly did," Joey piped in. "Anybody who'd take our money like that, she probably is a killer. You should lock her up and never let her out."

"She is locked up right now," Scarbrough said. "I found a gun that's the same kind of gun that shot your mother, and we're working on proving that it's the one that killed her. There are a lot of guns like that and a lot of people own them ... including you. Despite our suspicions about Edith, it would still help us a lot to know where yours came from."

Aaron looked down at his feet. "I told you. It was in a Dumpster. But Edith probably is the one who killed Mama. She's mean as a snake."

Scarbrough didn't seem convinced. "Aaron, this is very important. People don't generally throw their guns in Dumpsters, and it seems odd that you would happen upon it like that. Why would you be digging in that particular Dumpster? Did you see the person who threw it there?"

"I dug in that one all the time, even before the Pulses. It was behind the pizza place, and sometimes they threw away hot pizza."

"But why would you have been looking through it after the outage, when the pizza store was closed?"

Aaron's cheeks flushed. "I thought ..." He glanced at Joey. His brother's eyes were on his own hands. "Well ... it was before the outage that I found it."

This was new. Scarbrough sat at attention. "You're sure? Because you told me earlier that you found it after the Pulses started."

Aaron squirmed in his chair. "Well ... I got mixed up on the time. I can't remember exactly."

Scarbrough waited for a long moment. Then he turned to Joey. "Joey, do you remember when he got that gun?"

Joey didn't look up. "No. I wasn't with him."

Scarbrough leaned in and touched the boy's shoulder. "Joey, look at me."

The boy looked up.

"Joey, it may be that the real owner of that gun was your mama's killer. None of you are gonna get in trouble for giving me a name. If you stole it from someone's home, or if you did something else to get it, I'm not going to charge you. I just need that name."

Joey just shrugged and looked at Aaron.

Aaron sat stiffer. "Thought you said Edith did it."

Sheriff Scarbrough shook his head. "I didn't say that exactly. She may have, but we can't rule out anyone else."

He questioned them a little more but got nowhere. Finally, he brought the interview to an end. "Okay," he said, "then I'll be on my way." He shook Doug's and Kay's hands and they led him to the door.

Before the kids got up, Deni took his chair. "Hey, Aaron," she said, "I have a question. Today at the funeral and before at your mom's memorial, when we put the dirt on the grave, Sarah said something. Do you remember that, Sarah? What did you say when you threw the dirt on?"

Sarah grinned proudly. "Asha to Asha, dirt to dirt."

Deni frowned. "Where did you hear that?"

"At a foonal."

"But *whose* funeral?"

"Nobody's funeral," Aaron cut in before she could answer. "She saw it on a cartoon or something. I don't know where she got it." He pulled Sarah out of her chair. "Come on, Sarah. You need to wash up. You're really sticky."

Aaron had never wanted to wash Sarah before.

Deni stopped them. "Wait a minute. Sarah, tell me where you heard that."

Sarah turned around, her curls bouncing. "At Mama's foonal," she said. "Not the one with the bush. The other one."

"The other one?" She looked from Aaron to Joey. They both looked down at their feet, not wanting to meet her eyes.

"She doesn't know what she's talking about," Aaron sneered. "She's always making stuff up."

"Huh-uh," Sarah said. "'Member when we had the foonal for Mama?"

Craig had gotten interested now, and he came and stood behind Deni's chair. "So, is she saying that you had a funeral for your mother before they found her dead?" he asked.

Aaron's face was turning red. "We figured she was dead, okay? That's all it was. We got tired of waiting for her to come home. And I felt bad for Sarah and Luke and I decided the best thing to do would be just to tell them she was dead." His hands were shaking as he slid them into his pockets.

"It didn't work. They forgot it as soon as it was done. Kept looking for her to come home and couldn't remember we pronounced her dead and gone. But no, she doesn't forget the stupid ashes to ashes."

Something wasn't right. Deni stared at him, trying to imagine a kid lying about his mother's death to comfort his siblings. It didn't even make sense.

Avoiding her eyes, he went inside, and she heard his footsteps going up the stairs. Joey stood still, looking into space as if remembering that day. Sarah and Luke were quiet.

"Why is Aaron sad?" Sarah asked.

"I don't know." Deni watched the three-year-old look toward the door her brother had gone through.

"Why don't you guys go play? I'll check on Aaron in a minute."

As the children went out into the yard and started to throw a ball, she looked up at Craig. He stood against the wall, arms crossed, wearing his lawyer frown. "What do you think?" he asked. "Do you believe him?"

She turned her palms up. "I guess it could be true. I mean, after a while when you get tired of waiting for somebody who never shows, you finally realize that you've got to declare an end to it."

He dropped into the chair across from her. "Are you talking about me or Jessie?"

She shrugged. "Just trying to relate, that's all. Trying to understand what would make little kids decide to have a funeral for their mom before they knew she was dead."

"It's kind of weird," Craig said. "Most kids would be in denial about their parents being dead. They wouldn't want to face it."

"Yeah, well, they didn't have the kind of parents you and I have. Their mother was neglectful, and she brought a lot of trouble and darkness into their lives. From the sound of Sarah's nightmares, I'd say there may have been more to fear from her being alive than dead."

When her parents came back in, Deni related the exchange to them. Her parents seemed suspicious.

Doug looked at Kay for a long moment, scratching his chin. Finally he said, "You don't think the children witnessed her murder, do you?"

Kay swallowed hard. "That thought just crossed my mind too."

Deni watched her dad processing the information, trying to decide what to do. "Should we tell the sheriff?" she asked.

"Tell him what? We don't know any more than we did before. And Aaron's sure not talking."

"Still," Kay said. "It might be something Scarbrough needs to know."

Doug finally agreed. "All right. I'll tell him. Maybe he can make some sense of it."

FIFTY-THREE

ELOISE'S SON CAME OVER THE NEXT MORNING AND HANDED Doug the key to his mother's home.

"I'll sell it eventually, when the outage is over. But for now, please just watch after it and make sure there's something to sell when the time comes."

"I'll be glad to," Doug said. "Don't worry about anything."

"And you can plow up her yard or do whatever you need to do, just like you were going to," Clark said. "I know Mama wanted to cooperate with the neighborhood in that. And, hey, if you find anybody who needs to rent the house or just live in it for a while until everything settles, let them. Just make sure they're people who won't trash it." He looked down at his feet, clearly struggling with his grief. "I really appreciate all you and Kay have done."

Doug put a hand on Clark's shoulder. "You okay?"

Clark's eyes misted and he tried to blink back tears. "Yeah, I'm fine. It was a good thing, me seeing my mother again. It would have been horrible to have had her die—" His voice broke and he swallowed hard. "To have her die without saying good-bye. I've been a terrible son, you know."

"No, not at all. You took care of her from a distance."

"Thought I was doing her a big favor to put her in that house, then never came to see her. I got so busy making money that I didn't have time to think about her."

"Don't beat yourself up," Doug said. "You came when it was important. You were here at the end."

Clark's moist eyes brightened a little. "Yeah, that's a good thing, or a God thing. I felt like the Lord was telling me that I needed to come and see about her after the outage, but I put it off. And then when I got your wife's letter and heard how ill she was, something just changed inside of me. I really appreciate you taking care of her all this time. The whole neighborhood ... you've all been great."

"She was a real blessing to us," Doug said. "A calm voice in a storm. She was the one with all the wisdom. She had already laid down her body at Christ's altar, yet she seemed richer than all of us."

"She was richer. And she passed that spiritual wealth on to me. It took my whole life, but I finally gave my heart to Christ too. I'll see my mother again someday."

Doug knew angels were rejoicing. "Then don't worry about it anymore. You gave her all she ever wanted before she died."

FIFTY-FOUR

THE BRANNINGS HURRIED TO FINISH THEIR CHORES EARLY on Monday so they could get to Sandwood Place to work on the cleanup and prepare to start on the well.

Craig tried to beg off, telling the family that he had some correspondence he needed to take care of, but Deni wouldn't hear of it.

"Come on, Craig, it's a family thing. We're all going to help. Besides, you need to see how these people live. It'll break your heart."

"We have poor people in Washington too," he said. "They're the ones who tried to burn down the Capitol. I can get along just fine without having to deal with that type again."

"That type?" Deni couldn't hide her disgust. "*What* type? Poor people?"

"They don't have to live like that," he said. "They could pull themselves up if they wanted to."

"Some of them may have been able to before the outage, but not all of them," she said. "And now it's utterly impossible." She sat down and pulled her dirty sneakers on. "I'm disappointed in you, Craig. I thought you had more social conscience."

"What's that supposed to mean?"

"It means that you shouldn't be working in government if you isolate yourself from the truth. There are people there who are trying to raise children, trying to do the right things, fighting to survive every day. Some of them are helping with the work. If we all felt like you, what kind of world would it be?"

He let out a long-suffering sigh and slammed his pen on the table. "Okay, Deni, you've made me feel like pond scum. I guess I'll go." He stormed upstairs to change clothes.

Guilt was a fine motivator. She was glad it had worked.

Ten of Doug's church members showed up to help—including Mark Green. They all rode bikes over together, and one of the men brought his horse-drawn wagon with all their tools piled in it. Deni and Craig doubled up on Craig's bike, trailing behind. Craig brooded at Mark's presence, but Deni pretended not to notice.

With Craig's arrival and Eloise's death—not to mention the Disbursement—it had been several days since they'd been there to work. To their surprise, the residents of the complex had finished cleaning up the garbage. Stacks of recyclables, washed and sorted, were stacked against the back wall of the building. They'd started a compost pile in an area that had been nothing but dirt before, and even though they didn't yet have a place to plant, one of the men pointed out that the compost might be something they could sell if they could make enough of it.

Some of the men were working on digging a pit in which to bury the rest of the garbage, but they had at least separated it into a mound. As soon as the pit was deep enough, they would shovel it in and bury it. Craig helped the men with the digging of the garbage pit, while Deni and her mother wheeled uprooted bushes and saplings from the site where the well would be. Craig and Mark worked side by side, in seeming competition with one another. But after a while, Craig raised his hands in surrender. "I have to rest," he said.

"No problem, man," Mark said, and kept working as if there wasn't an option.

Each time Deni emerged from the trees, she looked for Craig. He never went back to work. Instead, he was talking to the people who stood around. Talking—that was what he was good at. He would make a great politician. Too bad those talents weren't useful at the moment.

When the pit was finally deep enough, they shoveled the garbage in. The residents cheered as they began to cover it with the loose mounds of dirt. Craig joined in then, shoveling the dirt in, but she could see in the redness of his face that he was out of his element. Most guys she knew loved the outdoors and the sheer brute strength required in such a task, but Craig seemed resentful each time he sank his shovel blade in the dirt.

At one point, little Luke strayed too close to where they were working, and Craig swung around and yelled, "Hey, kid, stay out of the way, or you'll get hurt!"

Deni caught her breath at his harsh tone. Luke looked crushed and slunk away. Mark stopped working and rescued the child. "Over here, Luke. I've got a job for you." He busied him stacking the cardboard boxes they were using for the reusable items.

Deni's gaze followed Mark as he stooped with Luke, showing him how he wanted the boxes stacked and praising him for his efforts. It was a far cry from Craig's irritable outburst.

She turned and saw Craig leaning on his shovel, watching the others work again.

One of the women who lived on the first floor got her small children involved in helping Luke. The skinny kids worked on their piles with pride and contentment.

The stench was already fading as the garbage was buried. Feeling a mighty sense of accomplishment, Deni steered her wheelbarrow back into the woods.

"Hey, Deni."

She turned and saw Craig with his hands on his hips. "Are we leaving as soon as the garbage is buried, or does your family intend to work until dark?"

"Until dark," she said.

He huffed out a breath. "You've got to be kidding. Enough is enough."

Deni looked at the dirt covering his arms and shirt. Somehow, the rugged look wasn't as attractive on him as it was on Mark.

"If you don't want to work, you don't have to. Just quit. You know how to get to our house."

"Yeah and look like a complete jerk," he said. "I just don't *get* your family."

She wanted to say that they didn't really get him, either, but she didn't want to fight. "Just take a break," she said. "You've been working hard. Go sit down, drink something."

"Oh no," he said. "If mighty Mark can keep at it, so can I."

She recognized the jealousy in his tone, but it only made her angry. Ignoring him, she went back to work.

LATER THAT NIGHT, WHEN THEY HAD ALL RETURNED HOME AND cleaned up from the hard work, Deni went into her dad's study to work on this week's paper. By the light of an oil lamp, she pecked on the typewriter keys.

Craig came in and leaned in the doorway. He had shaved when they got home, and he looked more like the man she'd fallen in love with. The sun had done him good. He was getting a tan, though his cheekbones were burned, and without the beard, she realized she really did like his longer hair. "How can you do that now?" he asked. "Aren't you tired?"

"Exhausted," she said. "But I have to use all my free time, since I'm so busy during the day."

He came in and read the headline over her shoulder. " 'Gatlin's Next-Door Neighbor Arrested.' "

She kept typing, copying from the original she'd written last night. "I need to get this out tomorrow so that if anyone has information about Edith Stuart, they'll come forward."

"Assuming anyone reads it."

She stopped typing and looked up at him. "*Lots* of people are starting to read my newspaper. Everywhere I go people mention it to me."

" 'Newspaper' seems a little delusional, doesn't it? How many copies do you put out? Ten? Twelve?"

She bristled. "Fifteen, on bulletin boards in key places around town. But there may be thousands reading them."

He breathed a condescending laugh. "I just wouldn't try using it on a résumé if I were you."

His amused tone made her feel small. Her mind strayed to Mark's support of her paper—the typewriter he'd found her, the carbon paper he'd salvaged.

Craig didn't even realize he'd put her down. He put his arm around her, stroked her arm, and lifted her left hand to look at her ring. "I was thinking, Deni."

"Thinking what?"

"I can't stay much longer. Senator Crawford really needs me."

She sprang up, stricken. "You're going to leave? When?"

"I need to get back soon," he said. "I only came to get you. I don't want to set up housekeeping here with your folks. And as important as the work over at Sandwood Place is, and all the stuff you've got going on here, it's not my kind of thing. I'm better with helping the senator write bills that will help this country move forward. That's what my job is right now."

"So what are you saying? That the wedding isn't going to happen?"

His eyes twinkled. "Think again," he said. "I didn't plan to go back without you. I don't want to leave you again."

"Oh." It was what she had hoped to hear in the letters, just the kind of affirmation she needed. Now she wondered why it didn't thrill her. She tried to smile. "So when do you want to go?"

"I was thinking sometime in the next few days. How would you feel about a quick wedding here with your family, and then we take the train back to Washington?"

She thought of the beautiful wedding she had planned. It would have taken place next month. She would have worn her Vera Wang gown and all of her sorority sisters would have flown in for the occasion. It would have been so beautiful. But she didn't have the dress anymore, and her bridesmaids were scattered halfway across the country. She'd never get them all here now.

"It'll be great," he said. "Your dad can marry us."

"But he's not ordained," she said. "He just set up a house church. He's not allowed to officiate at a wedding."

"Then we'll get someone who is. Your old pastor or the judge or a justice of the peace."

She didn't like that idea. "And where will we do it?" she asked. "We can't very well do it in our backyard with it all tilled up. We could do it in a church, but it's dark in there, and even in daylight—"

"Come on, Deni. You're a problem-solver. This is doable, if you want to do it."

She looked into the flame flickering at the desk. What would it be like to leave her family now? She thought of little Sarah and her brothers, the project at Sandwood Place, the murder investigation. So much was unresolved. Could she really be happy with him in Washington? She swallowed and tried to think. "I'm not sure I'm ready to leave my folks, Craig."

He grunted. "Come on, Deni. You left them years ago. You've only lived back here a few weeks. They don't need you. They have your brothers and sister."

Her gaze drifted down to her ring. It represented so many dreams. But those dreams had changed. And so had she.

Craig lifted her chin and kissed her. "Come on, Deni. I'm ready to go home," he whispered. "I'm ready to start a life with you."

"But how?" She pulled out of his arms. "Without any power, we wouldn't be able to survive in your town house. We couldn't grow food. Where do you even get water?"

He shook his head. "Don't worry about it. We'll get a place closer to the Senate Building so I can get back and forth. I'll get the food that's brought in for the senate staff. We'll be well provided for."

She tried to imagine that. "But what will I do?" she asked. "I'd be alone most of the time, without a job or anything."

"You can take care of our house. You've gotten good at that kind of thing."

"Not by choice," she said. "It's different when it's a team effort, for a real purpose. We do what we can to survive. I'd be all alone there."

"You wouldn't be alone. You have lots of friends there."

The friends she had made during college had probably gone back home to their families as soon as the trains started running. She doubted there were many still there, but even if there were, that seemed like so long ago. So much had happened. Before the outage she had been ready to sever her ties with her parents and start a new life of her own. But things were so different now.

Still ... she had longed for weeks for Craig to come and get her, to take her back with him. Did she really want to hesitate? Maybe she was just tired.

"It's just that I always hoped for a pretty wedding with a beautiful dress. A little more time to plan. At least I could have *some* of my dreams."

"We'll do that later," he said, "after the outage is over. We'll have a big shindig and get all dressed up and you can wear the veil and the whole bit. How's that sound?"

Not good, she thought. "It wouldn't be the same, Craig."

"No, it wouldn't, but *nothing's* the same. *Everything's* changed. We might as well get over it." He leaned down, pressing his forehead against hers. "Think of it, Deni. We can get married and get on that train and go back to where our lives are supposed to be. And trust me, when the lights start coming back on, they're going to come on in Washington first. You'll be the first one in line to get Katie Couric's job."

The thought of her pre-outage plans began to fill her up again. "It is the right thing, isn't it?"

"Of course it is," he said. "It's always been the right thing."

FIFTY-FIVE

DENI'S PARENTS WERE GETTING READY FOR BED WHEN SHE knocked on their door.

The burning candles had the scent of mulberries. Her parents were sitting on the bed, her father leaned back against his pillows, and her mother sitting Indian-style in the center of the bed facing him. Deni felt guilty stealing this time from them, when they had so little time to talk alone.

"Mom, Dad, can I talk to you for a minute?"

"Sure," her mother said, turning around on the bed. She patted the mattress, inviting her to join them.

Deni sat, kicked off her shoes, and pulled her feet under her.

"What's wrong?" The shadows on her father's face accentuated the concern she saw there. She hated to give him one more thing to worry about.

"I just wanted to tell you that I've made a decision."

She saw the dread passing over her mother's face. "What is it?"

"Craig needs to get back to work. He wants us to get married in the next few days so I can go back with him to Washington."

Doug sat up straight, those shadows moving down his face. "What's the rush?"

"Craig came here just to get me, Dad. Now he's got to get back. He has important work to do."

The candlelight caught the glisten of tears in her mother's eyes. "But we haven't had time to plan for it," she said. "That doesn't even give us much time for you to pack. Why can't you wait a week ... two weeks? A month? Why don't you just plan to get married on your original wedding date?"

"Because he doesn't want to sit here for another month."

"Then he could go back without you," Doug said, "and you could go to him on the train. Or he could come back before the wedding, and we could do it right."

She picked at a thread on their bedspread. "I'd miss him too much. I don't want to wait. I want to get married now, with my family here to celebrate it with us. Besides, it's too expensive going back and forth."

Doug looked flabbergasted. "So you want to get married *now?*"

Kay got off the bed and looked down at her. "Deni, you need to think through this. You're settling for something. This isn't like you."

"Mom, everything we've done since the outage has been settling for something. Nothing's the way it should be. I've watched you and Dad make the best of things, and I'm trying to do the same thing. Even though I can't have the beautiful wedding I'd planned, I can still get married."

"But maybe you *can* have the beautiful wedding." Kay got on her knees on the mattress and knelt in front of her. "Deni, we could find you a dress. Every woman in Oak Hollow has her dress boxed in her closet. Someone would let you borrow everything you need. We could have a gorgeous outdoor wedding by the lake. It could be everything you'd hoped, if you'll just wait."

"I have waited. I've waited months to be with Craig, and now I can be. I don't want to be separated from him again."

Her father got off the bed, raked his hand through his hair. "Deni, *he's* the one determined to go back. If he loves you, if he doesn't want to be separated, let him stay."

"He has a career, Dad. He didn't lose his job because of the outage like 99 percent of America did. He's needed. This is who I'm marrying."

"That's what I'm afraid of," Kay said.

Deni looked at her mother, stunned. "What do you mean?"

Kay's voice was low, as if she feared Craig might overhear. "Are you sure he's the one you want to spend your life with?"

She couldn't believe they were still skeptical, even after he'd come all this way for her. "Of course I am, Mom."

"But, honey, you broke up with him three weeks ago. You said he wasn't right for you."

"But I misunderstood everything. I jumped to conclusions. It's what I do. He came. I didn't think he loved me, but he does, and he wants me to be with him."

"So you're going to abandon everything and just take off with him?" Doug asked.

Deni rolled her eyes. "Dad, I was going to do that anyway before the outage. I can't live with my parents the rest of my life."

"I didn't expect you to, but I was hoping you would at least stay here during the outage. If you're so far away in Washington, we can't help you if you get into trouble. People need their families right now. And how are you going to survive?"

"We'll survive right along with all the other senators and their staffs. And God's not going to let me starve after he's brought us this far."

Kay went into her bathroom and came back with a hand towel. Dabbing at her eyes, she said, "He's not right for you, Deni."

"Mom, he's my fiancé!"

"No, I'm sorry. I have to say it. There are things wrong with this union. I had seen it before, but I didn't know until he came here how bad it was."

Deni got to her feet and gaped at her mother. "What do you mean, *how bad it was*? He's a great guy. I love him."

"Deni, he's going to make you miserable."

Her mouth fell open. "Mom, that's awful. It's not true."

Kay's lips were tight. "Deni, you're a Christian now. He's not. The Bible tells you not to be unequally yoked."

"But you were going to let me marry him before. How come it's a problem now?"

"We had doubts then too," Doug said. "But it's so clear that he's not a Christian ... and you are."

She bristled. "You have no right to judge him."

"Deni, I'm not judging him," Doug said. "I'm repeating what he told me. I've tried talking to him about Christ, but yesterday he told me point-blank that he doesn't buy into the whole religion thing. He said that he doesn't even believe in God."

He had her there. She wished Craig had kept his mouth shut. He had just made things worse. "That doesn't make him an awful person."

"No, it doesn't. It just gives him different goals, different priorities, different values. How can you share your life with someone who doesn't share your most basic, core beliefs?"

"How are you going to raise your children?" Kay asked.

She threw up her hands. "He'll let me take my children to church," she said. "And I'll lead him to Christ eventually."

"Fine. But don't marry him until you do," Doug said. "Deni, you know what the Bible says about marrying someone who doesn't share your faith. God commanded that for a reason. It's important. God wants to bless you, and he knows what problems you'll encounter with a man who doesn't share your goals and values. I'm worried about Craig's character."

"Oh, that is totally absurd," Deni cried. "He's got great character."

"Think about the way he's treated the kids. I want you to think about how hard he worked today. While everybody else was slaving away, he was finding ways to get out of it."

"So he's more comfortable behind a desk than swinging a shovel. That doesn't mean he's wrong for me."

Kay hung her head and stared at her feet, as if searching for another argument. When she looked up, defeat had changed her face. Tears rolled down her cheeks. "We're worried about you, Deni. We want you to be happy. We love you."

"This isn't about you loving me," she said. "This is about you wanting to control me. You just don't want me out of your grip."

Doug stepped between them. "Don't talk to your mother like that, Deni."

It was just like him to change the subject. She took a deep breath and lowered her voice. "I'm twenty-two years old. I know what I'm doing. I'm not going to be able to convince you to like Craig. You've never liked him and that's been pretty clear from the beginning. But the fact is, I'm an adult and I'm going to marry him, and I came in here to tell you that I'm leaving on the train in a few days. I'd like to get married here if I can have your blessing."

Doug just stared at her. "I can't bless this marriage, Deni. It's wrong."

Astonished, she faced off with him. Did he really think that would make her change her mind? Digging her heels in, she said, "Then maybe we'll just get married in Washington."

Her parents were speechless. It was like a chess game. She felt like saying, *checkmate.*

But her father got the last word. "Maybe that would be best."

She stood searching for something to say in return, something that would put a knife through his heart. But nothing came to her.

And then she realized that it was her pride speaking, making her want to hurt them as they were hurting her. The fight drained out of her.

She opened the door, and without saying another word, stepped into the darkness of the hall.

FIFTY-SIX

DENI LAY IN BED THAT NIGHT, STARING AT THE CEILING. Little Sarah lay curled up next to her like a kitten, and Beth slept on the other side, the soft sound of her breathing percussing lightly in the quiet. Candlelight flickered on the wall, dancing in the shadows, a night-light for little Sarah. Thoughts of all the things Deni needed to do before she left with Craig paraded through her mind, demanding her attention. She wished she could get up and make a list so she wouldn't forget anything.

He's not right for you, Deni. He's going to make you miserable.

Her parents were so wrong. She tried to picture her life with Craig ten years from now. She saw herself in an evening gown at a political fund-raiser, laughing and introducing people, her husband dapper and sophisticated as he networked his way around the room. She could be a good political wife. She'd be like Maria Shriver, holding down her own career while campaigning for her husband. They would have a wonderful life, and her parents would see how wrong they'd been.

Besides, she knew she could lead Craig to Christ, maybe even before they tied the knot. He was a logical person, after all. He had seen how God had provided for them. He just needed persuading.

Do not be yoked together with unbelievers. For what do righteousness and wickedness have in common? Or what

267

fellowship can light have with darkness? What harmony is there between Christ and Belial? What does a believer have in common with an unbeliever?

She had read those words from 2 Corinthians 6 a thousand times since she'd given her life to the Lord, searching for loopholes, looking up the original Greek in her father's concordance, reading the commentaries on his bookshelves. But how many ways were there to say *do not?*

But didn't those verses start with the premise that Craig was wicked? No, of course he wasn't. She wouldn't have fallen in love with a wicked person. But then another verse drifted back into her mind.

There is none righteous; no, not one.

Except for the blood of Jesus that washed away her sins, wasn't she wicked, herself? Hadn't she been so caught in her sins that they dragged her across the country in the hands of a killer? Hadn't she been in bondage to sin, before Christ set her free?

Craig just needed to be set free.

New urgency rose up inside her, and she told herself that she needed to talk to him now. It couldn't wait until morning. She would reason with him tonight, and by the time morning came, he would be a new creature.

Then her parents would approve.

Quietly, she got dressed and glanced back at the bed. Sarah and Beth slept undisturbed.

She slipped out of her room and padded up the carpeted hall to Beth's room, where Craig slept.

The door was closed, so she tapped on it, then turned the knob and slipped it open. She pulled it shut behind her, so she wouldn't wake anyone else. She saw him lying there on top of the covers, wearing a T-shirt and a pair of running shorts. She hated to wake him up, but his soul needed saving. He would thank her later.

She lit the lamp beside his bed, then knelt on the floor and stroked her fingers through his hair. "Craig? Wake up, honey. I need to talk to you."

He stirred, then forced his eyes open. Squinting in the light, he said, "What is it?"

"Wake up," she said again. "We need to talk."

"About what?"

"About us. Our marriage."

He rubbed his eyes and sat up. "Can't it wait? What time is it?"

"I don't know," she said.

"Deni, whatever it is can wait. I'm tired."

"I'm tired too," she said. "But this is important. The most important thing in your life."

Finally, he sat up and raked his hands through his hair. "This better be good."

She suddenly found herself groping for the right word. "Craig, my parents are worried about me marrying an atheist. The truth is, I'm worried too."

He rolled his eyes. "Tell me you didn't wake me up to talk about religion, Deni."

"Not religion," she said. "Christianity. There's a difference. Craig, something changed in me when I was on the road trying to get to you. God showed me what a rebel I was."

"Come on!" He got up and walked across the room, got his watch, and put it under the light. "It's two a.m. What's wrong with this picture?"

"Craig, listen. God showed me where my sin had taken me, and even though I had gone my own way and was completely disobedient to him and my parents, he rescued me and provided for me."

"How can you be disobedient when you're twenty-two years old? You're not a child, Deni. Your parents can't demand obedience if you're an adult."

She wondered if he'd heard anything she'd just said. "Craig, this isn't about my parents. Listen to me. I'm talking about my relationship with God. There was a brick wall between myself and him because of my sin. But Jesus saved me from my sin, just as surely as he saved me from the hands of a murderer."

"I thought you told me your *dad* saved you from the killer."

He wasn't listening. "Craig, God was there, working. He provided people to help me along the way—food, water, and yes, he helped my dad get to me. Don't you understand what I'm saying?"

"Of course I do, Deni. I'm not an idiot."

"But do you believe that it was God who helped me? Do you believe that Christ changed me?"

He looked at her for a long moment and sighed. "I see some changes in you, yes. But we've all changed since the outage." He looked down at his bare feet. "Deni, if you want to believe in Jesus, that's fine. It doesn't bother me at all. I can respect your beliefs if you can respect mine. Two independent adults, deciding to spend their lives together. That works for me."

"But Craig, my Christianity is who I am."

"Great," he said. "It'll make you unique. I have nothing against Christians. But I don't like being proselytized, Deni. I have my own mind, and my own beliefs."

"But that's just it, Craig. You don't believe in ... anything."

"I believe in myself," he said. "It's always served me well before."

She sat back on the bed, looking up at him, knowing that she had struck out. He arrogantly believed he didn't need a savior. That was why Jesus had said, "Blessed are the poor in spirit." Those who were poor in spirit knew they were buried in sin.

And only Jesus had done something about it.

On the road running from death itself, she had been poor in spirit. But Craig never had been.

Her heart sank, and she knew she had to make a decision. But when he leaned down and kissed her, that resolve and determination inside of her melted. And her desire to spend her life with him swirled anew inside her.

She'd deal with his salvation later. They had the rest of their lives.

She heard a noise outside the door ... a click ... a creak. She pulled out of his kiss. "Did you hear something?"

He shook his head and tried to pull her back, but she slipped away, tiptoed to the door, and looked out into the hallway. She could see nothing in the darkness, but she stepped into the hall and listened. She heard a creak again at the bottom of the stairs. She stepped onto the stairwell. Peering down the stairs, she saw a flashlight beam sweeping across the living room floor, searching . . .

She sucked in a breath and stepped back into the shadows. This was not Sarah or her father or Jeff. It was someone else . . .

She ran back to Craig. "Someone's in the house!" she whispered. "Call your dad."

"I can't. He'll hear me. He might have a gun."

Craig seemed glued to the floor. "Are you sure you heard something?"

"Craig, I saw a flashlight in the living room. Hurry, you've got to do something!"

He looked around. "Does Jeff have a gun up here?"

"Yes!" She hurried out of the room and felt her way up the hall into Jeff's room. His shotgun lay beside his bed, and she picked it up and chambered a round.

Jeff sat bolt upright in the bed. "What are you doing?"

"Jeff, there's somebody in the house," she whispered.

He sprang up quickly, grabbed the shotgun out of her hand. "Where?"

"Downstairs. We can't get to Mom and Dad without him seeing us."

"Okay," he whispered, pushing her behind him. "Stay here."

But she followed him back into the hall. Her eyes had adjusted to the darkness now, and she saw Craig standing in his doorway.

"Get in the bedroom with the girls, Deni," Jeff ordered in a whisper. "Close and lock the door." She hurried around him, but didn't like the idea of sending her little brother down there without backup.

He glanced back at Craig. "Craig, go close my door so Logan won't hear, and close the boys' door—quietly. I don't want them waking up and making noise."

Craig did as he was told. Deni stepped into her room and bumped the table that held her pillared candle. The candle toppled over onto the glass top, and she quickly snatched it back up. The flame went out, leaving them in darkness. Maybe it was good that the thief wouldn't see the light.

She kept the door cracked enough to watch Jeff as he crept down the stairs. Craig came back and saw Deni standing in the doorway.

"Come on, Deni." He pushed her into the room and closed himself in with her. "Let's lock the door like he said."

"Craig, you've got to go out there and help Jeff. He could get killed!"

"I don't have a gun," he said through his teeth. "What am I going to do? I think it's better if I stay here and protect you."

She heard the covers rumpling. "What's going on?" Beth whispered.

"Shh. There's someone in the house. Be quiet. Don't wake up Sarah."

Beth got up and hurried across the carpet. "Call Dad!"

"We can't. But Jeff's going down with his gun."

Her heart hammered as she opened the door again and peered out. She heard Jeff's slow footsteps creak on the steps.

God, please protect him!

Craig tried to pull her back from the door, but she resisted.

Suddenly a gun went off, followed quickly by another shot. Deni jumped back and screamed. Downstairs, she heard her mother screaming. Deni started to run out, but Craig held her back.

The front door slammed.

"Dad, are you all right?" It was Jeff's voice, loud and frantic.

The only answer she heard was her mother's screams.

FIFTY-SEVEN

DENI BURST OUT OF THE ROOM AND STUMBLED DOWN THE stairs. Her father was on the floor, and in the light of her mother's flashlight beam, she saw blood soaking his shirt.

"Daddy!" she screamed.

"He's shot!" Kay dropped the flashlight and pressed her fist against his wound. "Jeff, run to get Dr. Morton. Hurry!"

Her brother took off into the night.

"Mom, is it—is it bad?" Deni asked.

"Light the lamp." Her mother's voice was shaking.

Deni heard the others coming down the stairs, Luke crying at the top. Her hands trembled as she tried to light a match.

She heard Beth sobbing. "Daddy?"

"I'm okay," her father rasped.

But Deni didn't know if that was true.

DEREK'S EXAMINATION OF DOUG CONFIRMED THAT HE was, indeed, okay. "The bullet grazed his ribs. I can't X-ray them, but I can feel that at least two are broken."

Deni finally took a full breath. *Thank you, Lord.*

Doug sat up. "I can feel it too."

"This wound is going to need a lot of TLC," he said. "I'll bandage it up, but we'll have to watch it to make sure

273

it doesn't get infected. Doug, you'll have to favor that side for the next little while. Let the pain guide you."

Doug winced as Derek began cleaning the wound.

"Can't you give him something for pain?" Kay asked.

Derek shook his head. "Normally I'd say yes, but my house was just broken into. Whoever did it broke the lock on my drug closet and stole the drugs."

Doug gaped at the doctor. "Are you serious? How long ago?"

"Just before your break-in. Cathy heard something that woke her up. She thought it was our cat, but when she got to the living room, she heard the front door close. She got me up and we found the closet door open. I was getting ready to go for the sheriff when Jeff came over."

"Do you think it was the same person?" Kay asked.

"If not, it's a huge coincidence. Did you see him, Doug?"

He shook his head. "It was dark, and he was shining the flashlight beam in my eyes. But I think I shot him. I heard him grunt when he got hit."

"You hit him?" Kay asked. "Are you sure?"

"I can't be positive, but there would be blood. He went out the front door."

Deni followed Jeff as he took the flashlight and shone it on the floor in front of the door. Sure enough, there were blood drops.

"You got him, Dad," Jeff said.

"Well, I couldn't have gotten him too bad, because he got away."

Kay came to look. "Well, he'll be easy to identify. He won't be able to hide a gunshot wound for long."

"I need to go after the sheriff," Jeff said.

Kay stopped him. "I'm afraid for you to go out there. What if he's still there? He has a gun, Jeff."

"Well, somebody has to go." Jeff looked up at Craig, standing on the stairs. "Craig, you can go with me."

Deni looked up at Craig, half-expecting him to find a way out.

Suddenly, Aaron ran down the stairs, almost knocking Craig down. "Is Sarah down here?"

"No, she's still asleep in my bed," Deni said. "She missed the whole thing, thank goodness."

"No, she's not! She's not there."

"*What?*" Deni asked.

"She's gone!" he shouted.

Kay sucked in a breath. "No, she's not!" She started up the stairs. Deni followed her. When she got to the room, her mother shone the flashlight on the bed. It was empty.

Deni grabbed the flashlight and began calling for her as she shone it under the bed. "Sarah? Honey, where are you? It's okay. You can come out." She checked under the bed, in the closet, the bathroom. "*Sarah?*"

"She's not here!" Aaron cried.

Immediately, the family sprang into action, searching every nook and cranny of the house for the child. When they were sure Sarah was gone, Kay uttered the words they had all begun thinking.

"That's what he wanted! He came to get Sarah!"

FIFTY-EIGHT

THE TREES HAD ARMS AND HAIR THAT BLEW WILDLY AS THEY hunkered over, coming for Sarah, reaching for her, grabbing her. She screamed and fought off those groping arms, the thorny fingers, the stinging hair that ripped across her skin. She saw the face of her mother, demonlike, with slime dripping from her teeth and poison words flying from her mouth. And just as she thought that one of them would slam her down, something stopped it all. Her mother fell backward and the trees vanished, leaving her in darkness. And the darkness smelled like sweat.

SARAH WOKE SUDDENLY. IT HAD BEEN ANOTHER NIGHTMARE, only this time she wasn't in Deni's bed but in the arms of a man she almost recognized, a man with bad breath and rough hands that covered her mouth and kept her quiet.

He was carrying her as he ran through the trees. She felt the wind blowing across the leaves and saw the branches reaching down just like in the dream. She tried to scream, but something was wrapped around her face, tight over her mouth. She tried to call out for Aaron, for Joey or Luke or Deni, or Mr. Doug or Miss Kay, but she couldn't get the words out.

No one could hear her. And he was taking her farther and farther away from help.

FIFTY-NINE

IT WAS ALMOST THREE A.M. WHEN DOUG HEARD
Scarbrough's van rumbling into the neighborhood. Brad,
had gone with another neighbor to wake the sheriff after
hearing the gunshots.

Scarbrough came in with three deputies and did a perimeter search for anything the perpetrator had left behind.
They took samples of the blood from the floor, dusted for
prints, and tried to trace his steps up the stairs to Deni's
room, where he'd gotten Sarah.

"It wasn't hard to find Sarah, since that was the only
room with a night-light burning," he said, coming back
down the stairs. "He probably gagged her so she couldn't
scream."

"But was he holding her when he shot me, then?" Doug
asked, panicked. "Is it possible I shot Sarah instead of him?"

Aaron almost exploded. "No! She wasn't shot! You
didn't shoot her, okay? She's all right. She probably got away
and right now she's trying to find her way back to us. We
have to go look for her!"

Jeff stopped the boy from heading out the door. "Aaron,
there are people out with flashlights looking. The other deputies are out in their cars. But you have to stay here, because
we don't want anyone else to get hurt."

"I won't get hurt!" he cried. "I'll kill whoever has her! I
bet Edith broke out of jail. She's trying to get even!"

277

"She didn't break out, son," Scarbrough said. "She's still there."

"Besides, I don't think it was a woman," Doug said. "I couldn't see the person very clearly, but whoever it was was bigger than me."

"What about Moe Jenkins?" Scarbrough asked. "He's already threatened to take Sarah."

Kay muffled a sob. "Yes, it probably was him. But why? What good would it do him to take Sarah now, when there's not another disbursement for three months?"

Scarbrough looked at the boy. "He probably wants a ransom. If it's him, we'll know soon enough. He'll get a demand to you. And there may be a blood trail." He stroked the boy's rumpled hair. "Don't worry, son, I'm gonna round up as many men as I can find to help us look. If I have anything to say about it, we'll have her back by morning."

Doug didn't like his helpless feeling. "Isn't there something we can do in the meantime?"

Scarbrough turned back at the door. "Yeah, there's something you can do, all right. You can pray for that little girl."

SIXTY

"IT WON'T DO NO GOOD TO PRAY." AARON'S TEARS STUNG his eyes, and he smeared them with the heel of his trembling hand. "God won't listen to me."

Doug sat on the couch in the lamplight, clutching his bandaged side, and trying to stay strong for the distraught boys. "Come here, son. Sit down."

"No!" Aaron cried. "We're just wasting time. I have to go find her."

"Aaron, it is useful to pray," Kay cried. "Prayer is all we've got. God knows where Sarah is, and he has lots of angels who can protect her. The Bible says that the angels of children always see the face of God. That means he gives them special attention."

"He never gave *us* special attention," Aaron bit out. "And there's no reason he'd give it to us now. He probably hates me. He'd never do anything I say."

He started for the door, but Doug called, "Aaron, you can't leave! Sit down!"

"I can't!" he screamed. "You people think you're in charge of her, but you're not, okay? I am! I'm the one who's always took care of her! I'm the one who promised her I wouldn't let nothing happen to her! But I did—" His voice cracked off, and he wilted against the door. "I did let something happen. I never shoulda let her sleep with Deni. I never shoulda let her out of my sight. We were better off in our apartment. At least nobody kidnapped us there!"

Doug came and stooped in front of him. "Son, I'm as upset as you are—"

"No, you're not! If you were, you'd have stopped him! You'd at least be out there looking for her, not expecting nobody else to do it! If she was yours you wouldn't be just sitting here."

Doug realized Aaron was right. He'd hesitated too long already. He thought back to a few weeks ago, when Deni vanished. He had left that very night to go after her. Nothing could have stopped him.

Only a bullet was stopping him this time, but aside from losing a little blood and breaking some ribs, he would be all right. But Sarah might not.

"Okay, Aaron. You and I will go look for her."

Kay threw herself in front of him. "Doug, can I speak to you in private, please?"

He recognized the panic in her tone. He told the boy to wait, then went into the study and closed the door. It was dark—but they didn't take the time to light a lamp. He could see her dimly through the moonlight coming through the window.

"Doug, you cannot go out there!" Her voice wobbled. "You've been shot. You've lost blood. You need to be at home. Please, don't go!"

He sighed. "Kay, I know we can't go chasing Moe Jenkins through the dark woods, but Aaron needs to feel that he's doing something. I know the sheriff and his deputies are doing a lot more than we can do. But let me take him out just for his own state of mind."

"Where will you go?"

"I don't know. But Jeff can stay here and guard the house in case Moe comes back."

She finally backed down, but not without more tears. "All right, but so help me, if you get hurt again, I'll kill you!"

He pulled her into a one-armed hug and kissed her forehead. "It'll be okay, honey. You guys just cover us with prayer. Maybe we'll find Sarah before they get too far."

DOUG AND AARON WALKED OUTSIDE AND TRIED TO DECIDE WHERE
to start. The air was cool, and the moonlight was bright enough
for them to see where they were going. Aaron stood in the middle
of the street, looking up and down, as if trying to think like the
kidnapper.

"I used to go through there," Aaron said, pointing into the
woods next to Eloise's house. "There's kind of a path. We used to
hide our empty boxes there."

Doug followed him between the houses to the woods. Shining
his flashlight, he tried to find a path. If there was one, it was
small and hard to see at night. He imagined Moe Jenkins running
through here wounded, with a bag full of drugs, a gun, and a fighting little girl in his arms. Didn't seem likely. "If he had a bike,"
Doug said, "he probably didn't have to cut through the woods."

"But Jeff got out there pretty quick," Aaron said. "He woulda
saw him if he rode off on a bike."

"Not necessarily. Jeff came to me first. That gave the kidnapper
time to get away. He very well could have ridden off on a bike."

"But holding Sarah? She woulda been fighting, unless she was
hurt."

Aaron stood there for a moment, staring at the woods. He was
sweating and his face was tight, every muscle rigid, as he turned
that over in his mind.

A light emerged from the woods, a flashlight beam between
the trees.

"Doug, is that you?" It was Brad's voice.

"Yeah," he said. "Have you guys found anything?"

Brad came out of the woods. "Not yet. If he was here, he got
away before we started looking." He eyed Doug. "You okay, man?
Shouldn't you be taking it easy?"

"Not until Sarah's found. Wish we could do an Amber Alert.
Let everybody know to be looking for her."

"We can put up some signs, but no one will see them till
morning."

Aaron started back across the street. "We can't wait until morning. We have to find her now!"

"Where are you going?" Doug called.

"To get a bike."

Doug opened the garage, and they mounted their bicycles and rolled to the end of the driveway as Jeff closed and locked it again.

"I don't know which way to go," Aaron said. "Where does Moe Jenkins live?"

"Follow me. I've been there."

Doug rode in the lead, the weight of his body pulling on his wound. He tried to lean on the bars with his good arm and kept his other arm against his broken ribs. "The sheriff is probably over there right now, but we can go see if they've found him. Maybe they already have Sarah."

They rode quietly through the dark streets.

The air was cooler than it had been and smelled of embers still smoldering on outdoor grills. The streets were abandoned except for stalled cars on the sides of the road.

The sky was cloudy, and the moon was hazy and cast little light, as though the sky were in cahoots with the evil invading their lives.

Doug shivered, and pulled his arm closer to his wound. He glanced at the boy. Aaron still had tears on his face, but a look of grim determination had hardened his young features. Doug's heart ached for him.

Doug kept his eyes open, but prayed aloud as he rode. "Lord, we need your help. I'm asking for angels to surround and protect Sarah. God, please keep the kidnapper from hurting her. And keep her from being frightened. Show us how to find her."

Aaron just kept his eyes fixed on the road ahead of him.

Doug glanced at Aaron. "Aaron, why do you think God's mad at you?"

The boy didn't look at him. "I don't think, I know. He's punishing me."

"But why? Is it the stealing?"

He rode for a moment without answering. Finally, he said, "Yeah, the stealing. And other stuff."

Doug wished he could see Aaron's face better. "What other stuff?"

"It doesn't matter," he said. "I can't undo what's done."

"No, you can't. But you can be forgiven, Aaron. The Bible says that if you confess your sins, Jesus is faithful and just to forgive us for our sins."

"That doesn't work."

Doug caught his breath. "Of course it does. Why would you think it doesn't?"

"Because I did that, and he's still punishing me. Some things are too big ..." His voice trailed off.

"Too big ... for what, Aaron? Too big for him to forgive?"

Aaron shrugged.

"Aaron, you know God has provided for you and your family through some pretty rough stuff. He led you to our house, so we would learn about your situation and take you in. Don't you believe that?"

The boy's face was intent on getting there. "I guess. Maybe."

"That means he loves you. He's watching out for you. He can forgive you for whatever you've done, Aaron."

Aaron snapped his chin up. "Oh yeah? Then how come Sarah got kidnapped, huh? How come God would do this if he doesn't hate me?"

"Aaron, there are things going on that we can't see. But I can guarantee you that God is greater than any evil, and he's in control. And he doesn't hate you. He loves you. And he loves Sarah too."

"Well, if this is what his love looks like, then I hate *him*, okay? I hate him for doing this to Sarah. If there's a God and he didn't stop this, then I hate him!"

Doug was quiet. He knew that nothing he could say could change the boy's mind. Instead, he prayed silently for God to make himself known to Aaron, and for Aaron to see that God answered these prayers, so he could understand how much he was loved.

But even as he prayed, Doug knew that God sometimes had plans that humans couldn't fathom. *God, you can stop this if you will. Please, Lord, deliver her just like you delivered Deni. For your name's sake, let Aaron see answered prayers.*

At Moe Jenkins's apartment, they saw the headlights from the sheriff's old vehicles illuminating the building. Residents stood outside in their pajamas and robes, watching the activity around his apartment. "See? The sheriff's already here," Doug said.

They made their way to the sheriff's van. Doug pushed through the crowd of deputies standing around him. "Scarbrough, have you found Sarah?"

Scarbrough looked annoyed to see them. "Guys, what are you doing here? You were shot tonight, Doug. You should stay home."

"I had to look for my sister," Aaron said. "Did you find her?"

"No, not yet, son."

Aaron looked crestfallen. "Where's Moe? What did he say?"

"Moe's not at home, and his neighbors haven't seen him since the disbursement. We're searching his room right now, but so far there's no sign of Sarah."

Aaron got off the bike and let it fall to the ground with a crash. "I want to go in."

"No, Aaron," Doug said. "You stay back now. This is police work."

"But you have to ask them who his friends are! Where he might have gone. Somebody knows something!"

"We're asking them all those questions, son," Scarbrough said. "Come here. You and Doug can sit in my van and wait until we're finished searching his room. We'll let you know the minute we find anything."

Aaron started to cry again, his face twisted and his lips purpling in his grief. But he climbed into the van and watched through the window as the police did what they had to do.

SIXTY-ONE

DAYLIGHT FINALLY BROKE, BUT THE SHERIFF AND HIS
deputies were no closer to finding Sarah. Doug's wound
pulsed pain through his trunk, and his head ached. Aaron's
eyes were red and swollen, and he looked like he needed to
lie down and sleep for a while.

But he still carried the weight of his little sister's life on
his shoulders.

Doug had only felt this helpless one other time in his life.
He mussed the boy's hair.

"What do you say we go home and get something to
eat? Get some water to bring with us? Then we can set out
again."

Aaron nodded. "Yeah. She might be thirsty when we find
her."

The sheriff put their bikes in his van and drove them
home, lecturing them all the way about leaving police work
to the professionals. But Doug knew Aaron didn't hear a
word. When you loved someone who was in trouble, reason
had little to do with it.

They stayed home for half an hour, time enough to eat
a slice of the homemade bread Kay had baked and fill up
water jugs to take with them. Then they rode to the homes
of every friend of Jessie's that Aaron could think of. No one
had seen Sarah. Most seemed alarmed at the news of her
disappearance. A couple of them gave them leads on where
Moe Jenkins might be, but those leads came up empty.

Finally, Doug convinced Aaron to return home with him for a little while to see if the sheriff had come by with any information. Secretly, he hoped the boy would agree to rest for a while, because the pain was starting to get to Doug. He needed to lie down, take whatever analgesic Kay had in the medicine cabinet, and give his injury a chance to heal.

Then he'd get up and look for Sarah some more. The innocent little girl was in grave danger, and Doug wouldn't rest easy until he found her.

SIXTY-TWO

Hours passed with no word on Sarah. Deni paced the house with her mother, too frazzled to do the usual chores that kept the family going. But they needed water, and since Jeff was needed to guard the house in case the kidnapper made another appearance, the job fell to her.

Craig had gone back to bed a little while ago, and was sleeping as if he hadn't slept in days. He seemed traumatized by the events of last night, as if *he'd* been the one to get shot. He'd slunk around brooding for hours afterward, not saying a word, and staying out of her family's way.

Deni rolled the containers of water home, fighting her disappointment at Craig's reaction to the break-in. She would have expected him to be a man—to take the shotgun out of Jeff's hand and head down to take care of things himself. Instead, he'd let the sixteen-year-old walk into the line of fire, and Craig had cowered in her room with the girls. Now, he couldn't even step up and help with the chores.

Would she feel safe with him if she married him? In her own home, she knew that her father would do anything it took to protect his family—risking his own life. The man she'd once thought was wimpy and weak had proven to be a man of toughness and courage. Even her little brother Jeff had grown into a good protector. He didn't back away from a threat to their family, and he didn't wait for anyone else to come forward and protect them.

Was she being too hard on Craig? She had cowered behind that door too, and she hadn't grabbed the gun out of Jeff's hands and insisted on leading the way down the stairs. But she would have, if she'd had to.

Even her own courage at setting out across the country seemed stronger than Craig's. He'd waited for the safety of the train to come to her. Was that wisdom—or just lack of passion?

Maybe she *was* being too hard on him. Maybe he was just prudent. He had a different way of reacting to crises. Not a worse way. Just different.

But as she pulled the water back up her driveway, she had to admit her disappointment in her fiancé. He wasn't adding up to be the man she'd thought he was.

SIXTY-THREE

THE KIDS HAD EATEN NOTHING BUT BREAD TODAY, BECAUSE
Sarah's disappearance had kept Kay so preoccupied. Doug
and Aaron had been gone for hours, and Kay feared where
their search might take them. Doug's injury was still fresh,
and last night he had lost a lot of blood. He wasn't in any
shape to hunch over his bicycle—he had two broken ribs
and a wound that could break open.

Then again, they had to find Sarah. Whatever it cost,
they had to rescue the child.

When the knock sounded on the front door, Kay rushed
to open it, hoping it was the sheriff with good news. But a
couple she'd never seen before stood there instead. The man
had a shotgun hanging from a sling on his back and a suitcase in his hand.

"Mrs. Branning?"

Her hand went to her hair. She couldn't even remember
if she'd brushed it today. "Yes?"

The man who looked about Doug's age reached out to
shake her hand. "I'm Allen Gatlin. And this is my wife,
Marie."

It took a second for the last name to sink in, but then she
caught her breath. "The grandparents?"

"Yes. We came as soon as we got your letter."

What timing! She burst into tears. How could she tell
them that Sarah was gone? Unable to speak, she let them
into the hot house, hugging both of them.

289

"I'm so sorry," she choked out.

"Sorry for what?" Marie pulled back, looking up at her with a mixture of compassion and concern. She was a small, attractive woman—not much older than Kay—with short brown hair and big, warm eyes. "Where are the children? Don't you have them?"

She wiped her face, trying to pull herself together. "Joey and Luke are out back."

The Gatlins didn't wait another second. They shot to the back door and looked out into the yard. The children weren't working today. Luke and Joey sat in the dirt at the back of the yard with Beth and Logan. Beth was talking, and they were all listening with rapt attention.

"Luke and Joey are the ones on the—"

"I know which ones they are," Allen cut in. He rushed out the door and into the yard. "Joey? Luke?"

The children looked up. Luke showed no recognition, but Joey slowly got to his feet.

"It's Grandma and Pop," Marie said. "Do you remember us, Joey?"

He regarded them cautiously and took a step toward her.

"Oh, I know you do!" She swept him into a hug.

Allen picked up Luke and kissed him on the cheek. "I'm your Pop, Luke!" He squeezed the boy so tight that Luke squealed. The man broke into tears. "I thought I'd never see you again."

He put Luke down and reached for Joey. "Hey, Pop," Joey said as he went into the man's arms. The boy began to cry with them as they all embraced. Luke grinned uncertainly.

Kay stepped toward them to break the news, but before she could get the words out, Joey blurted it out. "Sarah's kidnapped."

Marie gasped. "What?"

Allen swung around to Kay. "Is this true? What happened?"

"We don't know for sure, but we think it was her father." Standing frozen in the yard, she told them everything. The cruelty of their situation didn't escape her. Luke and Joey sat in their grandparents' laps as they took in the news.

"Aaron is out with my husband looking for her," Kay said. "They've been gone all day."

Marie buried her face in her hands. "We came just in time."

Heartbroken, Marie told Kay about their history with Jessie. When she'd gotten pregnant for the second time in high school, they'd tried moving to Tuscaloosa to get her away from her friends. But when their rules for her behavior had been too restrictive, she took her babies and fled back to Crockett. Several times they had found her and court-ordered her into drug treatment, hoping to save her life, since her destructive lifestyle was a danger to herself and her children. During those times, the children had stayed with them. They'd had them for almost a year when Aaron and Joey were babies. Each time Jessie had gone into treatment, she had bided her time until she was discharged, then gone right back to her drugs. They told Kay that they'd spent over a hundred thousand dollars on treatment programs for their daughter. But she had never made the decision to change her life, so it had all been a waste.

When Luke was born and Jessie was still using drugs, they had finally initiated a lawsuit to get custody of the children. At that point, Jessie had moved without leaving a forwarding address, and they hadn't been able to find her. Detectives they'd hired had traced her to Tennessee, but by the time they'd found her address, she'd moved again. Six months ago, the Gatlins had moved from Tuscaloosa to Atlanta so that Allen could accept a promotion with his company. They'd tried to notify Jessie of the change of their address through an e-mail address they weren't even sure she checked anymore. But they'd never found her, and they hadn't heard from her in over three years. They didn't know she had gone back to Crockett, and until the letter from Kay, they hadn't known that there was another child. Sarah was a complete surprise to them—their first granddaughter, whom they might never get to see.

When at last Doug and Aaron came home, Kay watched the reluctance on the boy's face as he went to his grandparents. It was clear he was having trouble processing all the things his mother had said about them. But after a while, he seemed relieved that they were here to help.

The reunion couldn't have come at a better time.

DOUG AND KAY LEFT THE GATLINS ALONE WITH THE KIDS TO GET reacquainted, and Doug collapsed onto the bed. Sweat poured from his forehead even though the night was cool. His breathing was labored.

Kay checked his dressing. "Should I call Derek, honey? You don't look good."

"I'm okay," he said. "Just give me a few minutes to rest." He took her hand and pulled her down next to him. "Kay, where is she?"

She shook her head. "I don't know. We've been praying all day, Doug. They've got to find her soon."

He closed his eyes and pressed his fists against them. "I should have been guarding the house. I should have heard him sooner."

Kay took his hand and kissed it. "Doug, you did hear him. You may have stopped him from killing us."

"He didn't want us dead," he said. "He needs us alive so we can pay him to get her back."

"But there hasn't been a ransom note."

"There will be." He hoped he was right. If there was, Moe would be motivated to keep Sarah alive. "Aaron won't be able to handle it if anything happens to her. He's almost at the end of his rope now. He's only nine."

A knock sounded on their bedroom door and Kay called, "Come in."

Deni came into the room. Jeff, Beth, and Logan trailed behind her, and Craig brought up the rear. "Mom, is Dad all right?"

"I'm fine," he answered. "Come here."

His children all came to the bed. Logan and Beth climbed up on it next to him and Kay. Jeff and Deni stood over him. Craig hung back at the door.

"You don't look fine," Deni said. "Dad, you look really sick. You're not taking care of yourself, and if you don't stop going all over the place to look for her, then you might get an infection and die."

"Yeah, Dad," Jeff said. "I'll take Aaron and his grandparents to look for her, and you can stay here."

He tried to laugh. "I'm okay, guys. I'm just tired."

"Your gunshot wound doesn't hurt?" Logan asked skeptically.

"It hurts, but I can stand it."

"*And* you have broken ribs," Deni pointed out. "The doctor said for you to take it easy. You could puncture a lung or something."

"I can't take it easy right now. Sarah's still missing, and I have to do everything I can to find her." He settled his gaze on the ceiling. "I'm hoping she'll be found tonight. The police have several leads they're working on."

"So how are the Gatlins doing?" Kay asked Deni.

"Some tears," Deni said. "Really stinks, you know? Them coming all this way only to find out that their granddaughter has been kidnapped. But I think it's helping Aaron to have them here."

Doug took Deni's hand. "Since all of you are here, let's pray, why don't we?"

Deni took Jeff's hand, and the rest of them grasped hands. Craig remained at the door.

"Come on, Craig. You too," Kay said, reaching out a hand for him.

He looked reluctant, but he came and stood at the edge of the bed, between Jeff and Deni. They began to pray one at a time, speaking as they felt led. Craig remained quiet.

Silently, Doug sent up a prayer for him too, that God would work on his heart. It looked like he really was going to be a member of their family, and Doug needed to start thinking of him as a son ... whether he liked it or not.

SIXTY-FOUR

MOE JENKINS SNIPPED A TENDRIL OF SARAH'S HAIR, watched it fall to the floor. Too bad he couldn't sell it. He knew women who'd cut off an arm to have hair like this.

Careful not to wake the child, who had cried and screamed until he'd had to drug her with Dramamine, he snipped again and added another strand to the heap on the floor. She was too identifiable with that hair. And if his first plan didn't work, then he'd have to resort to plan B. And that meant the hair had to go.

He finished cutting her curls off, then gently brushed his fingers over the crudely cropped haircut. She looked like a little boy now. Perfect. He'd be able to walk or bike across town with her in broad daylight and no one would recognize her.

And the hair would add a great touch of drama to his ransom note. Kick up the urgency a notch or two.

He scooped the hair up onto a piece of notebook paper, then dumped it into a Ziploc bag that had previously held his dope.

He tried to think, but his brain was muddled. He'd taken too many painkillers to dull the pain of his gunshot wound. The bullet had grazed his waist, taking a chunk of flesh with it. *Focus*, he told himself. *Think*. Maybe he shouldn't alert them that he'd cut off *all* her hair. If they knew that, the police could sketch pictures of what she'd look like without it.

No, he'd only send one strand. That way they'd know he meant business and it would give them the drama he needed.

He took the rest of it out of the bag and dropped it on the warehouse floor. Then he got a clean piece of paper. Trying to steady his hand, he wrote out the ransom note:

If you ever want to see the kid alive again, bring $200 to the 10th Street Bridge tonight at 11:30. If I see police anywhere around, Sarah dies and you can bury her dead body next to that tramp of a mother of hers.

There. That ought to do it. He sat there and stared at it for a moment, aware of the irony that he would go to all this trouble for two hundred bucks. But he knew the Brannings probably didn't have more than that, and you couldn't get blood out of a turnip.

He figured the Brannings would have already spent some of their disbursement, but if they'd gotten enough for ten people—the six of them and the four Gatlin kids—that would have been 250 dollars. He didn't buy their story about the stolen money. No way they would have kept those brats for nothing. Two hundred dollars wasn't outside the realm of possibility, and if they didn't have it, they could get it from others.

Hopefully they cared enough about the kid to pay it.

If they didn't, he could go to plan B—move to another town and keep her until the next disbursement. She was his, after all. And if she gave him too much trouble, he could always go to plan C.

He could keep his promise to bury her next to her mother.

SIXTY-FIVE

THE SLEEPING ARRANGEMENTS WERE CROWDED TONIGHT. Though Aaron's grandparents had been offered that Eloise lady's house for the night, they had decided to stay at the Brannings' in case there was word from Sarah. They had pulled out the sofa bed in the living room, and Grandma and Pop were sleeping on that.

That made it difficult to sneak out without being caught. But Aaron had had plenty of practice; he figured he could make it.

He slipped off the bed without waking his brothers, then quietly got dressed. He had given sleep an honest try, but he couldn't stop thinking about Sarah. He imagined terrible things happening to her. What if she was locked up somewhere in the dark? He pictured a damp dungeon, or a cage like in *Hansel and Gretel*, and Sarah screaming until her throat was raw. She had such a fear of the dark after all those hours she'd spent in their mother's closet. What if that man had beaten her or worse? What if she was calling Aaron's name?

What if she was dead, lying somewhere in the woods like their mother?

Fears circled like vultures in his mind, keeping him from sleep. He had to go out and find her. Lying in bed had given him ideas. There was a house his mom had taken them to once, when she'd had to get her dope. The place had stunk worse than anyplace he'd ever smelled. They'd been cooking dope in a back room, and the place was full of crazed and heavy-lidded friends of hers, smoking from lightbulbs—or something like them. There were needles lying around and people with stripes up their arms, sitting in a dazed stupor.

Maybe Moe bought his dope there too. Maybe Aaron could find someone there who'd seen him and Sarah.

He went down the hall, careful not to make a sound, then stepped down each step. His foot creaked on the third step and he held his breath.

Maybe no one had heard.

He made his way to the ground floor, then headed for the front door. It was too risky to take one of the bikes, since he'd have to raise the garage door to get it out. That would surely wake the Brannings. And if he rolled the bike through the house so he could take it out the door without opening the garage, the *click-click-click* of the wheels would surely wake his grandparents in the living room.

No, he'd just have to walk. Quietly, he turned the dead bolt on the front door. It clicked too loudly. He stopped and listened, but no one stirred. Wincing with the effort of silence, he turned the knob and pulled the door open. The hinges squeaked.

"Aaron, where are you going?"

He swung around. He couldn't see who had caught him in the darkness, but it sounded like Pop.

"Nowhere. I was just—"

The flashlight came on, shining in his eyes. His grandfather came closer and closed the door back.

Bolting it, he said, "Aaron, come sit down with me. Let's talk."

"I wasn't doing nothing. I just wanted some air."

But his grandfather wouldn't listen. With a hand on Aaron's shoulder, Pop guided him to the study so they wouldn't disturb his grandmother. He was glad of that. He didn't need her freaking out too.

His grandfather lit the lamp and sat down knee to knee with him. His silver eyes were solemn, probing. "Aaron, where were you going?"

His mouth twisted. "Just to look for Sarah. I thought of some place she might be."

Pop's face softened. "Son, you can't go out into the night like that or something will happen to you too. Where would we be then?"

"But she's still out there!" he bit out. "You don't know her, but she's really little, and she can't defend herself—"

"I know that." The tears in his eyes backed up his words. "I've thought of nothing else all night. I couldn't sleep, either."

Hope lit Aaron's face. "Then come with me."

"Where?"

He wiped his face. "There was this house where Mama used to buy dope."

"You think Sarah's there?"

"No, but maybe somebody there knows Moe and can figure out where he took her."

His grandfather leaned forward and put his hands on Aaron's knees. "Son, we can't go to a crack house in the middle of the night. We could get murdered, and then what would happen to Joey and Luke? If something happens to us, who will look for Sarah?"

"But she's been gone so long!" Aaron's voice broke, and he dropped his face into his hands. "What if she's dead?"

The words fell like a cement block between them. "Aaron, we can't go out after her tonight. That would be foolish. But we can pray for her. I've been praying all night."

"I can't pray," Aaron said. "God doesn't listen to me."

His grandfather pulled back. The shadows moved down his face, making the lines in his skin look deeper. "You're wrong about that. Aaron, we've prayed for you for years. God's heard every prayer, and he's brought you back to us."

"That's because *you* were praying. Not because I was." He got up and went to the window looking out on the front lawn. He couldn't see much more than his reflection in the darkness. "He hates me, God does. He's punishing me for all the stuff I've done."

Pop came over and stood behind him. "Aaron, why do you think that?"

"Because," he said. "In church, Mr. Doug said that heaven is a perfect place, that God can't let sin in it. And if he hates sin, then he hates me."

"God doesn't hate anybody."

"Yes, he does. The Brannings read the psalms some nights after supper. I heard it myself one of those times. There's one that says God hates the wicked and the violent."

His grandfather turned him around and gazed down at him. "But Aaron, God just meant that he takes sin seriously. He doesn't overlook it. Then he tells us stories of people who did wicked and violent things, and he forgave them. Like King David. Did you know that there was a time when he was so wicked that he stole another man's wife, then had her husband killed so he could have her for himself?"

Aaron just looked at him. "David, from David and Goliath?"

"Yes. You know about him?"

"Beth wrote this cheesy play about him. It's a musical. We're talking really lame, but all the kids in the neighborhood were in it. Even me."

"Good. Then you know how close he was to God when he was younger, and how God worked in his life. But later on, he still let wickedness in and was responsible for a murder. How much worse can it be?"

Aaron swallowed. "God forgave murder?"

"Of course he did. And the apostle Paul was a murderer too. Do you know about him?"

Aaron tried to think, but nothing came to him. He shook his head.

"Paul turned out to be one of the greatest preachers who ever lived. He helped spread Christianity across the world, and he wrote a lot of the Bible. Before he gave his life to Jesus, he went around killing Christians for their beliefs. There's no telling how many he killed. Then God got hold of him and turned his life around, and he was sorry. God forgave him and used him to do great things,

Aaron. So you see? Nothing you've done, no matter how wicked you think it is, is too much for God. He tells us that if we confess our sins, he will forgive them."

Aaron stared at his grandfather, wondering if he could trust him. For so long, he'd believed his mother's stories about how they were out to get her and break up their family. But now he could see that wasn't true. Grandma and Pop really seemed to love them. Maybe Pop could be trusted about God too.

"How do you confess your sins?" Aaron asked.

"You just tell God what you did and tell him you're sorry."

Sorrow welled in Aaron's chest, and all his past deeds paraded like drunken dancers in his mind. His face twisted with his pain, and he tried to hold back his tears.

Pop stroked his hair. "Do you want to tell me what you're sorry for?"

Aaron sucked in a sob. "I can't. You'll hate me."

"Aaron, I could *never* hate you. Not in a million years. Why would you think that?"

The tragedy of his sin rushed up like floodwaters, trapping and drowning him.

"Because you're her daddy, that's why."

His grandfather stared at him, stricken. Tears rimmed his eyes. "Aaron?"

Aaron's sobbing grew harder. "Sometimes we do things we don't mean. Sometimes we're sorry but we can't tell nobody. And then God punishes us by taking our sister."

His grandfather reached out and pulled him into his arms, crushed him against him. "It's okay, son. I'll never hate you, and neither will God. You don't have to tell me what you did. Just whisper it to God when you're alone, and you'll see."

DOUG STOOD JUST OUTSIDE THE DOOR TO HIS STUDY, LISTENING to every word. The pain had gotten him up, and he'd come into the kitchen to get some water. That was when he'd seen the light in his study.

He stood in the shadows, listening to the boy's pain. As Aaron's words sank in, he tried to get his mind around them. What violence was the boy talking about? And why would his grandfather hate him if he knew? What did it have to do with Jessie?

Somehow, Aaron blamed himself for his mother's death. New questions ignited inside Doug. Did the boy have something to do with his mother's death?

Or had he merely witnessed it?

Doug peered into the study again, saw the pain on Allen's face. It was clear that he was thinking the same thing. But could it be true? Doug backed against the wall in the hallway, and breathed a quiet prayer for clarity. If the boy had somehow killed his mother ... what did that mean? And what should be done about it?

No, it couldn't be that. The boy would never have killed his mother. Not in a million years.

But as Doug went back to bed, the thoughts wouldn't leave his head. Aaron was hiding something important. Somehow, Doug would have to get it out of him.

SIXTY-SIX

DENI LAY AWAKE IN HER BED AS THE NIGHT TURNED INTO morning. Sleep seemed more and more rare for her these days. Her heart ached with all the tragedy in her life, all the turmoil, all the worry. The Bible said to be anxious for nothing, but how did someone stop worrying about the life of a little girl in mortal danger? As the first gray light of morning came through her window, Deni got up and prayed some more. Life had been so hard lately, so full of sadness. She wanted so much to put it all behind her, to stop the dreariness and the constant labor, the danger and the turmoil.

She wondered if things would be easier in Washington. Maybe there wouldn't be such hard work. Maybe Craig was right about getting the provisions that came in for the senators and their staff. Maybe she could even get a job in Crawford's office, filing or doing paperwork, and eventually, when the lights and televisions came back on, she'd be in the hub of broadcast journalism. She'd be one of the first on the scene to apply for the jobs.

But until they found Sarah, she couldn't even think about leaving. The thought of leaving even after Sarah was found hung like lead in her heart. What about her mother and father and sister and brothers? How could she bear going through the rest of this outage without them? It wasn't like she could keep in touch by the phone or computer.

Could she depend on Craig to fill the void left by her family?

Since Craig had come to town, he'd disappointed her in so many ways.

And now she just wasn't sure ...

SIXTY-SEVEN

WHEN MORNING CAME, DOUG FOUND AARON ASLEEP IN THE chair in his study, and Allen still awake. Allen got up when he heard Doug outside the door and followed him into the kitchen.

"Sorry we can't offer you coffee," Doug said. "It's a luxury we can't quite afford."

"If only that were the worst of our problems," Allen said.

Doug poured him some water and slid it across the counter. The man probably hadn't slept all night—the lines in his face were deep.

Doug kept his voice low. "Allen, I heard you talking to Aaron last night in the study. The things he said ... well, they kind of made it sound like he knows more about Jessie's murder than he's telling."

Allen stared into his water. "I don't know what you're talking about."

"When he told you that he had things to be forgiven for. Things about his mother."

Allen's eyes glistened as he met Doug's eyes. "You're reading way too much into that. He's a little boy. Surely you're not accusing him—"

"It's just that you should have made him tell you what it was. You shouldn't have let him keep the secret. We need to know if he had something to do with her death."

Allen got up and went to the door of the study, and made sure Aaron still slept. Quietly, he came back to Doug. "Now you listen to me," he said, just above a whisper. "My grandson is not a killer. He's a broken kid with a troubled past. He's lied and stolen to feed his family. He has a conscience, so he has a lot of things to feel guilty about. But murdering his mother is not one of them."

Doug hoped he was right. "I want to believe that too. But the next time he talks about it, you need to see it through. I know you want to protect him. So do I. But there's a murder investigation underway and we need to know what happened."

"All right, Doug. I hear what you're saying. If he's hiding something, I'll get him to tell me."

Doug knew he couldn't count on it, and he almost didn't blame Allen. He'd lost a daughter and maybe a granddaughter. He would cling to what he had left, even if it meant lying.

After breakfast, he and Allen went with Aaron to find the house where Jessie had gotten her drugs. Armed with his rifle and Allen's shotgun, they headed to the sleazy area between Crockett and Birmingham, where reports of murders, rapes, and shootings were everyday occurrences. The streets that used to be high-traffic seemed barren and abandoned now as men loitered in the streets. This area was much worse than the apartment complex where the Gatlin children had been living. Mangy, skinny dogs roamed, looking for food; men loitered on the streets watching as the three rode by. But Aaron wasn't afraid. Courageously, he confronted each group he saw before Doug or Allen could. So far, no one had admitted to seeing Moe or Sarah.

Aaron led them to the rundown house where his mother used to buy drugs. It was a rattrap with a rotting front porch and trash piled high in the yard. Doug swallowed his anger. How could Jessie drag her kids to a place like this?

The building had been condemned long before the outage, and the windows were boarded up. But the door was open. A terrible smell wafted out of it, and as he stepped into the doorway and gazed into the darkness, he saw three people through a haze of smoke. A man lay sleeping on a torn-up sofa, and another on a big red beanbag. On the floor, a girl sat rolling a cigarette, deeply engrossed in her task.

"Hello," Doug said.

The girl looked up. "You cops?"

"'Course not," Aaron said. "I'm Jessie Gatlin's boy. This is my grandpa and my foster father."

She finished rolling her cigarette. "What do you want?"

"My baby sister," he said. "I think Moe Jenkins kidnapped her."

That got her attention. "Moe Jenkins?"

Doug touched the rifle hanging from his back and stepped into the house. "You know him?"

"I might."

"Have you seen him in the last day or so?"

"I ain't seen him in weeks." She licked the paper and folded it over.

"Anybody here who might've seen him?" Allen asked.

She shrugged. "I don't know who all's here."

Clearly, Aaron took that as an invitation. He shot through the smelly living room and into the kitchen. Doug followed after him.

Two men sat on the filthy counter. One had a tourniquet around his arm and a syringe in his trembling hand. The other was counting change on the dirty counter. Doug grabbed Aaron's shoulder and kept him from moving toward them.

"I remember you," Aaron said to the one shooting up. "You knew my mama."

The man's lids were heavy. "Get outta here, kid. You don't belong here."

Doug agreed with him. "We don't want any trouble," he said. "All we want is Moe Jenkins. Have you seen him?"

The two men exchanged looks, then the heavy-lidded one popped his tourniquet loose. "I don't know nobody by that name."

"I think you need to be leaving."

The voice came from behind him. Doug turned. A scruffy man stood in the doorway, aiming his shotgun at Doug. He was bone-thin and the whites of his eyes were as yellow as the enamel on his teeth. The man chambered a round, and Doug moved his free hand to his wound.

Doug moved Aaron behind him, and his grandfather grabbed him. But Aaron wouldn't be silenced. "Look, I know you don't like to rat each other out and that's fine. We won't tell the cops nothing about you. I just want my sister!"

The girl from the living room came to the other door, as if curious about the tension.

"We don't know nothing about her, kid," Yellow Teeth said. "Now get out."

Doug didn't like being a drug addict's bull's-eye. But Allen blocked the door where the girl stood.

"Some of you have children," Allen said in a raspy voice. He turned to the girl. "Are you a mother?"

Her face slackened. "Yes."

"Then think of that tiny three-year-old girl in the hands of a maniac." His voice broke, and tears filled his eyes. "I've lost my daughter. I don't want to lose my granddaughter too."

There was silence in the room. No one moved.

The man with the gun had steely eyes. "Empty your pockets," he said.

"We don't have any money." Doug pulled his pockets inside-out. Aaron and Allen did the same.

"Then we don't have no information. You got ten seconds to get out of this house."

Doug raised his hands. "Okay, put the gun down. We're going."

But Allen still wouldn't budge. "You people have families somewhere. People who love you and want better for you. People who are praying for you to come home."

Doug shot him a look. This wasn't the time for a sermon about the social perils of drug abuse.

But Allen went on. "You had a choice. You came here of your own free will. You chose where you are. But little Sarah didn't choose. She's the hostage of a man who's not in his right mind." He looked from one to another of them, beseeching. "You're not zombies, you're human beings. You're worth more than this. And you can still feel something for a little girl who's in jeopardy."

The man with the gun wasn't impressed. "Ten … nine … eight …"

Finally, Allen gave up, and led Aaron through the living room and to the front door. Doug followed, fully expecting the boy to erupt and run back in.

"Five … four … three …"

Doug shoved both of them out the door.

Aaron was drenched with sweat and breathing hard. "They know where she is. All of them or some of them, they know. We've got to make them tell us."

"Son, they have a gun," Doug said.

"I don't care!" Aaron screamed. "Let them kill me!" He started to sob. Doug reached for him, but he wouldn't be comforted.

Tears spilled onto Allen's cheeks as he cried, "God, help us!"

In a low voice, Doug said, "It's dangerous here. We can't stay. We'll get Sheriff Scarbrough to come back and shake the place down. That's the best we can do right now."

Aaron's eyes flashed, and he turned on him. "My sister is missing!" he shouted. "She could be dead. I'm *sick* of burying people." The words shot straight to Doug's heart. "My mother was mean, even to Sarah. She deserved to die, but Sarah doesn't!"

The words stunned him. Allen straightened and turned to the boy.

"You've never said that before," Doug said. "That your mother was mean."

The boy was falling apart, and his voice was hoarse with his ranting. "She went psycho sometimes. That last day, she came home all high on something and started beating us all up. And when she hit Sarah and locked her in the closet, I couldn't take it anymore …" His voice faded as if he realized he'd said too much.

The girl in the house stepped out on the porch and looked at the boy.

Doug just gaped at him. "What did you do, Aaron?"

Aaron smeared his tears. "*Nothing!*" he cried. "*Nothing.* I didn't do nothing. I just distracted her and she came running out after me. At least I got her away from Sarah before she bloodied her nose like she did Luke's."

As the boy raved, the events of Jessie's last day began to take shape. Aaron *had* had something to do with his mother's death, as Doug had suspected. Had Aaron shot his mother in self-defense? Was he Jessie Gatlin's killer?

Before Doug could put the thoughts together, the woman hurried off the porch, looking furtively over her shoulder. She headed straight to the frantic boy, tears welling in her eyes. "I saw your sister," she said.

Aaron sprang to attention and Doug caught his breath.

"You did? Where?" Aaron asked.

"Came by here yesterday," she said. "The little girl was asleep and he said she was his kid. I didn't know he had a kid, but then, they looked alike so I figured it was true."

"Where did he take her?" Allen demanded.

"He got a key from somebody. I heard him say something about the old Firestone building over on Lime Street."

Doug's heart raced. "Lime Street. I know where that is."

She stood there a moment, glancing back at the door. "I had to tell you," she said, wiping a tear. "I'd want somebody to if it was my kid." She swallowed and touched Aaron's shoulder. "Your mama may not have acted like it, but she loved you. She bragged about you all the time, the way you took care of things. Sometimes she cried because she knew she was doing wrong."

"Then why didn't she quit?" Aaron bit out.

"Because the dope ... it had her in chains. Took over her mind."

The girl's mouth trembled as she got out the words. Doug looked at her, thinking she may have once been pretty, but now her skin was dry and drawn, and fine wrinkles dug into her face. Was she describing her own bondage as well as Jessie's?

The girl folded her arms in front of her, and her mouth trembled. "You don't mean that when you start out," she said. "You don't expect to trade in your kids for a fix. You just want to control how you feel for a little while, then the next thing you know it's controlling you."

Allen's face contorted with the pain of her words. He looked at her with the sadness of a father watching his child self-destruct. "There are places where you can go to get help," he said. "Find them. Don't let the drugs win."

She made no promises. Wiping her face, she went back inside.

Aaron just stared at the door, his face blotched with his pulsing emotions. Allen touched the boy's head and pulled him against him. Aaron pressed his face into his Pop's chest and sobbed into his shirt.

Then he pulled away and grabbed his bike. "We have to hurry."

Doug threw his leg over his bike. "Let's go tell the sheriff what she said."

They got across town in record time and alerted the sheriff. He gathered his deputies and headed to the building. Doug, Allen, and Aaron followed on their bikes. They held back a safe distance as the team of armed deputies went in. The three of them stood, breath held, waiting for the sound of Sarah's cries, praying she would run into their arms.

Instead, the officers came out empty-handed.

Scarbrough's frustration rippled in his voice. "They were here, all right. We saw small footprints on the dirty floor. And this." In his gloved hand was a pile of Sarah's locks.

Aaron went crazy. "He's got my sister! You've gotta find him!"

"He left before we got here, but we'll go back to that house and find who gave him that key."

"We'll come with you," Doug said.

"No." Scarbrough's voice brooked no debate. "Go home and take the boy. I don't want him in the middle of all this."

Doug had to agree. It could get uglier than it already was.

As they rode back home, tears rolled down Aaron's red face. Doug knew that keeping him home would take a monumental effort.

SIXTY-EIGHT

It was growing dark by the time they got back to their garage, and Doug had begun to feel the effects of his wound and his sleepless night. They pulled their bicycles into the garage, closed and locked it. Deni met them at the door.

"There's a ransom note, Dad! With a lock of Sarah's hair!"

Aaron shot inside. "Where?"

Deni handed it over. "Some kid said a man paid him a nickel to deliver it to our house. It came about half an hour ago."

Aaron took the envelope and pulled out the tendril of hair. He swallowed hard, then pulled out the letter and held it under the light. Kay came in with Marie and the kids. Marie's eyes were swollen and red.

Allen read over Aaron's shoulder, then wilted. "He wants 200 dollars, tonight at 11:30."

Aaron's face came alive. "And he'll give her back?"

"Maybe, maybe not," Doug said.

Aaron snatched the note away. "I want to take it to him. I want to take the money."

"No," Doug said. "That's out of the question. I'll take it."

Aaron stood straighter. "But she's my sister! Besides, you're already hurt."

"I'll take it," Allen cut in. "She's my granddaughter."

"No," Aaron said. "Moe doesn't know you. He'll think you're the cops. And Sarah doesn't know you, either."

"It has to be me," Doug said. "I know them both. He's probably expecting me."

"It could be a trap," Kay blurted. "You shot him, Doug. He may just want to get even. We have to get Sheriff Scarbrough."

"No!" Aaron cried. "I won't let you. He said he would kill her. We have to do it his way."

"We can't trust him, Aaron," Doug said. "He's a criminal, a kidnapper."

"I don't care! There's a chance that Sarah's okay."

Doug turned to Jeff. "Son, go to the sheriff's department and send someone after Sheriff Scarbrough."

"No!" Aaron screamed. "You can't do that! He said he'd kill her!"

Doug stooped in front of the boy. "Aaron, listen. We'll do this smart. We'll have the police hiding. He won't see them. He'll think we did it his way."

"What if he knows? What if he's watching the house and he sees the sheriff coming? What if he kills Sarah?"

Doug thought that over. The boy was right. He looked up at Jeff, who waited in the doorway. "Jeff, tell the sheriff to meet us behind the abandoned Shell Station on Keisler Street in an hour. Ask him not to bring his van. It'll attract too much attention." He took the ransom note from Aaron's hand. "Take this to him."

Jeff took the note. "What about the money, Dad? We don't have two hundred dollars."

Doug shook his head. "We still have one hundred dollars of our money."

Allan pulled out his wallet and counted his own bills. "I have thirty dollars. How are we going to get the rest?"

Doug took the thirty dollars. "Maybe the sheriff can come up with it. If not, we'll start asking the neighbors."

"I'll ask him," Jeff said, then he hurried out to find the sheriff.

"I have to take the money to him," Aaron said. "I've always took care of her. I'm not afraid of criminals and mean people. I kept my mother off her, didn't I?"

Doug exchanged looks with Kay. He couldn't let that comment go. Not now. It was too important. He sat down at the table, pulled Aaron into a chair and looked at him, his face close to his.

"Aaron," Doug said gently, "I want you to tell me what happened that day when your mother locked Sarah in the closet and bloodied Luke's nose."

Aaron's face tightened. "Nothing happened."

"Then how did you know your mom wasn't going to hurt the kids more?"

He looked at his dirty hands. "Because she wasn't, that's all. I just knew."

"*How* did you know?"

Allen intervened. "Doug, this isn't the time."

But Kay was hearing all this for the first time. Frowning, she looked down at the boy. "Aaron, do you know who killed your mother?"

Aaron's face seemed to swell with restraint. He pressed the heels of his hands against his eyes. "No, I don't know anything."

"Aaron," Doug said, "you told me before that your mom was chasing you. Did you run into the woods?"

Kay caught her breath and shot an alarmed look at Doug. Deni slowly sat down.

Allen and Marie were quiet. Beth and the kids came into the room. Kay cleared her throat. "Beth, take the children and go play upstairs, okay?"

Beth nodded quietly and gathered Joey and Luke, but Joey refused to go. "I'm staying," he said. "This is my business."

Beth took Luke upstairs with her.

Joey stood looking at his brother. "She had the shower rod and she was hitting us with it," the younger boy said.

Aaron sucked in a deep breath, and his lips curled with his words. "She was coming at me and I was running in the woods, deeper and deeper ..." He looked at his grandparents and shook his head. "She was just dope-sick, and she took something that made her crazy."

Kay's hands covered her mouth.

"She didn't know I had the gun," Aaron said. "But I did. I found it in her purse and I got it out so she couldn't hurt nobody. And I turned it on her and I told her to leave me alone or I would shoot. She didn't stop coming, and the gun was shaking so bad I didn't know if I could pull the trigger. But I aimed at her legs." He sucked in a breath. "I thought if I shot her there, she wouldn't die but she would stop. So I pulled the trigger." He squeezed his eyes shut.

Silence hung over them. Doug felt sick. Not only had the boy carried the weight of his family, but he'd also carried this ...

"I didn't mean to kill her," he cried. "I only meant to stop her. I didn't want her to die."

Joey started to sob. "You killed her?" The seven-year-old was shaking as he stepped toward his brother. "You told us you found her dead, Aaron! You told us a lie."

"I didn't mean to," he cried. "She was still yelling when I left her there, still cussing at me and telling me to come back, hollering for me to call the ambulance. I thought I just hit her in the leg. I thought she could walk. She got up and was dragging her leg behind her, and I ran and locked the door and wouldn't let nobody open it. But she never came."

He wiped his runny nose across his arm. "The next day I went back looking for her and she was laying there, blood all over her head, everywhere." He squeezed his eyes shut. "I didn't even think I *hit* her in the head. And I couldn't tell nobody because if they put me in jail, who would take care of Joey and Luke and Sarah?" Wailing, he looked up at his grandparents. "That's why God hates me. And you prob'ly hate me too!"

Allen knelt in front of the boy. "No, son," he whispered. "We love you."

"I had to leave her there 'cause I was scared to go back." His grandmother pulled him into her arms, and he didn't resist.

Doug let the movie roll in his head. Aaron shooting, running away ... finding her dead the next day. Telling his siblings she was dead without letting them know how ... holding a funeral without the body, just so they'd have closure.

But there'd never been closure for the boy.

No wonder he thought he couldn't be forgiven.

SIXTY-NINE

AARON DIDN'T LIKE WAITING. MR. DOUG HADN'T WANTED him to have anything to do with the plans for the ransom drop, and had insisted that he stay home. His grandparents hovered over him, not letting him out of their sight. But as time grew close, his mind worked to find a way to escape. If Doug or the sheriff messed things up, maybe *he* could convince Moe to give Sarah back.

Besides, the painkillers Moe had stolen from the doctor's house might make him careless; he might make mistakes. What if Moe caught a glimpse of the deputies hiding in the trees, waiting to arrest him? What if he got away and took it out on Sarah? What if the drugs made him violent?

Before they locked up the garage for the night, Aaron made Joey get one of the bicycles and hide it in the bushes.

Aaron couldn't shake his grandparents even for a moment, and when he told them he was tired and wanted to go to bed early, they didn't buy a word of it.

"I'll lie down with you," Allen said. "I'm tired too."

Aaron just stared up at him. "I don't really like sleeping with nobody else."

His grandfather gave him a sad smile. "Aaron, you sleep with your two brothers every single night. You wouldn't be planning to sneak out, would you?"

He felt his cheeks getting warm, but he shook his head. "No, I'm just tired, that's all."

"Fine. But tonight I'm going to sleep with you."

Aaron had no choice. But he waited, wide awake, for Pop to fall asleep. Unfortunately, his grandfather never closed his eyes.

Aaron's mind raced. He sat up in bed.

Pop looked over at him. "What is it, Aaron?"

"I have to go to the bathroom."

He saw the hesitation on Pop's face. "Okay. Go and come right back."

He thought of running down the stairs and out the door, but Pop followed him into the hall. Aaron went into the bathroom and closed the door, locked it. A windup clock hung on the wall. He grabbed the flashlight they kept by the sink and shone it on the numbers. It was eleven o'clock. Thirty more minutes before the drop. He still had time.

There was a window over the toilet. He stood on the commode lid and quietly unlocked the latch. Slowly, he pulled the window up. It made little noise.

He leaned out into the night air and shone the flashlight, looking for a way down. He couldn't jump from the second story, but in the moonlight he could see that part of the roof extended under that window.

By the time Pop realized he was gone, he'd be on his way.

Carefully, he slid out the window and tiptoed across the roof. He climbed down the lattice under Jeff's window and hit the ground. He found the bike where Joey had hidden it and took off toward the bridge.

It took him fifteen minutes to ride to the Tenth Street Bridge. There was a park next to the bridge with picnic tables and playground equipment; a wooded area surrounded the park. He got off his bike before he reached the park and rolled it into the trees. Then he peered toward the bridge.

There was a half-moon tonight, not enough to illuminate the bridge, but he saw a flashlight beam underneath it. He stole closer, staying in the darkness, and saw that it was Mr. Doug who held the light. He stood under the bridge, pacing back and forth, holding the money in a bag under his arm.

Except for the wind whispering through the trees, the place was quiet. Moe might suspect that people were watching, ready to pounce, but he wouldn't see anyone.

Aaron moved closer, careful to stay among the trees. By now, he knew that deputies were probably hidden in the trees too, waiting for Doug to leave the money. As soon as Moe showed up, they'd surround and capture him and force him to tell them where Sarah was. He hoped Moe brought her with him.

He stole toward the bridge, staying in the shadows.

His eyes scanned the night, searching for movement. A bead of sweat trickled down his temple. If only he had some of those infrared glasses like they had in the movies.

"Well, well."

The voice startled him, and Aaron swung around. Before he could make out who it was, a hand closed over his mouth. He tried to scream, but the man wrapped him up tight against him. He heard a gun cock, felt the barrel against his forehead. "This is just about too good to be true."

Aaron recognized Moe's voice and knew he'd made a mistake. The man clamped his arm around Aaron's neck. "Scream and I'll break your neck," he whispered.

Aaron stopped fighting, knowing Moe could do it. His breath came in constricted gasps.

"Now we're gonna walk down under the bridge real slow," Moe whispered against his ear. "They think I'm a fool, that I don't know they got cops all over this place. But it don't matter now, 'cause I got me another hostage."

Aaron closed his eyes, knowing he'd just ruined everything.

SEVENTY

DOUG HEARD SOMEONE COMING AND TURNED TOWARD THE sound. A flashlight beam blinded him, and he couldn't see who was behind it.

"That you, Moe?" he asked, squinting into the light as he shone his own light toward him.

As the beam moved closer, he saw that it wasn't just Moe. He had Aaron with him. The arm that held the flashlight was clamped under Aaron's chin, and Moe held a gun against the boy's head. Panic choked Doug.

Moe's laughter cut through the night. "Thought you'd outsmart me, did you? Thought you'd surround the place with cops and I wouldn't know."

How had Moe gotten Aaron? Had he gone to the house? Had he hurt Kay or the kids? He tried to steady his voice. "All we want is Sarah. You can have the money. Just let Aaron go."

Moe laughed again. "You think I'm insane? Had a hostage dropped into my lap, and you think I'll just let him go?"

Dropped into his lap. What did he mean? Had Aaron come here on his own?

"So has everybody got it?" Moe yelled out, his voice echoing over the night. "I've got a nine-year-old hostage. Try anything, and I'll kill him. Now toss me the money."

"Don't do it!" Aaron choked out. "Get Sarah first."

Doug's heart beat in his throat. "Where is she?"

Moe rammed the barrel of the gun into Aaron's head. "I know it's dark, but you ain't blind. I call the shots."

"If that gun goes off, you'll be dead before you hit the ground, Moe. There are twelve guns aimed at you right now."

Moe turned his flashlight off. "Hope they know I won't go down alone. Turn off your light."

Doug hesitated.

"I said turn off the light!"

Moe was getting more agitated, and Doug feared the gun would go off. He turned off the flashlight.

"Now the money."

Doug didn't know what to do. If he gave Moe the money, maybe he'd let the boy go. But what if he didn't? What if he took him with him? Then they'd have two children in danger.

He tried to see through the darkness. Where were Scarbrough and his men? The plan had been to surround Moe and capture him, but they hadn't counted on this new turn of events.

Making the decision, he tossed the bag so that it would fall three feet from Moe's feet. Holding Aaron, Moe couldn't reach for it.

"Pick it up!" Moe shouted.

Doug stepped forward and bent down to pick up the bag. As he came up, he swung his fist upward, knocking Moe back. Moe lost his footing, and Doug lunged for the gun.

It fired into the sky.

Aaron threw his head back and struggled against Moe's grip while Doug fought for the gun.

"Freeze!"

Suddenly they were surrounded, guns pointed at Moe's head. He stopped fighting. Doug kept his hand clamped around Moe's wrist, holding the gun pointed at the sky.

Scarbrough moved closer. "Drop the gun, Jenkins."

Moe's hand opened, and Doug took the gun and backed away. Sweat drenched his shirt, and he couldn't catch his breath.

"Let the boy go," the sheriff said.

Slowly, Moe released Aaron, and the boy stumbled away.

"Get down on the ground, hands over your head."

Moe slowly bent down, trembling. Doug kept the pistol trained on him as he hesitated before hitting the ground. Alarm bells went off in Doug's head as Moe jerked up his pant leg, exposing another pistol in a holster around his calf.

Moe grabbed the gun and came up firing.

SEVENTY-ONE

DARKNESS THREW EVERYTHING INTO CONFUSION, AND Doug grabbed Aaron and hit the ground. Gunfire rang in the air. When it stopped, he looked up and saw flashlight beams shining on Moe, who lay slumped on the ground.

"Aaron!"

Doug saw Allen running toward them, horror on his face. "You could have been killed!"

Aaron began to scream. "He didn't tell us where Sarah is! Make him tell us!" He ran to the limp body and pushed the sheriff aside. Grabbing Moe's bloody shirt, he screamed, "*Where's my sister?*"

The sheriff checked his pulse. "Too late now, son. He's dead."

Allen pulled him off. "It's okay," he said. "We'll find her!"

"No, we won't!" Aaron threw himself at the sheriff. "You shouldn't have killed him before we found her. *Where is she?* My sister's still lost! You've got to find her!"

"I think we have, son." Scarbrough pulled a set of keys out of Moe's pocket. A tag on the keys said U-Store-It.

Doug caught his breath, and Aaron got to his feet.

"Jones, Anderson, and Black," Scarbrough said, "you three stay here and work the scene. The rest of us are heading to the U-Store-It in my van."

It was crowded in the van, with seven deputies, who came in case Moe hadn't been working alone. All the way there, Aaron kept sobbing heart-wrenching, death-grieving sobs, as if he knew they would find his sister too late.

Doug took Aaron's hands and forced the boy to look at him. "Aaron, let's pray. God's listening."

Aaron nodded and closed his eyes.

Doug started. "Father, we're begging you—"

But Aaron cut in. "God, you don't have to like me, but I know you like Sarah—"

Doug opened his eyes, surprised that the boy had taken over the prayer. Aaron's eyes were squeezed shut, and he muttered his prayer through wet, purple lips. "—because she hasn't done nothing wrong. I'm sorry I shot my mama, but don't punish Sarah. Please forgive me and save her. Please don't let her be hurt."

Allen wept into the boy's hair as he held him.

Doug wiped his own eyes. *Please God, answer his prayers. Show him that you hear.*

They reached the storage buildings and the team piled out. They jogged down the aisle, checking the markings on the front of each garage door. When they found number three, the sheriff unlocked the padlock. Slowly, he raised the door.

"Sarah?"

Doug waited a moment, straining to see in the darkness ... then heard a high-pitched scream.

Sarah was alive!

Scarbrough turned on the flashlight, illuminating the terrified child. Aaron rushed in. "It's me, Sarah! It's me! It's okay, buddy. It's me."

Doug reached the opening of the garage as the groggy child threw her arms around her brother's neck. Her little curls were cropped off close to her head. She looked like a different child.

But she was safe and whole.

Aaron got to his feet and picked her up. She was almost as big as he, but he held her firmly, stroking her short hair. "It's all right now," he was saying. "God helped us find you. And Moe can't hurt you no more."

SEVENTY-TWO

THE LITTLE GIRL WAS FRAGILE AND AFRAID TO SLEEP, BUT SHE was also hungry and thirsty and glad to be back with her brothers. Her grandparents got to know her as she slowly came out of her shell, and when dawn broke, Deni felt the need to go into her bedroom closet, get on her knees, and thank God for saving Sarah's life.

As she prayed, she heard someone coming into her room.

"Deni?" It was Craig's voice.

"In here!" she called. He opened the door and looked inside. "What are you doing in here?"

She sat back on the floor and wiped the tears off her face. "I was praying. Thanking God for answering our prayers for Sarah."

"Oh."

She patted the floor next to her. "Want to pray with me?"

"Nope."

Disheartened, she got up and came out of the closet. The first light of morning was breaking into her room. Soon she'd have to go get water and help her mother fix something for breakfast. It wouldn't matter that none of them had slept that night.

Craig dropped into the chair by her window. "Deni, I haven't wanted to bring this up the last couple of days, because you were all upset. But we're sticking with the plan, aren't we?"

"What plan?"

"To leave in a couple of days."

She just stared at him. "I can't leave right now. Things are in too much turmoil."

"They've been resolved. The girl's been rescued. You're not needed here." He propped his chin on his hand and gazed at her. "Look, I know this is hard for you. But I have to get back by next week."

"My parents have been through a lot, Craig. It wouldn't be fair to take off like that. I want to wait until I have their blessing on our marriage."

He sighed and took her hands. "Deni, I understand your compassion. It's one of the reasons I love you. But I have to get back to work or I'll lose my job."

"No, you won't. You're always telling me how valuable you are to Senator Crawford. He wouldn't fire you because of this."

He rubbed his jaw. "Maybe I've exaggerated my value to him. But he needs me now. The country is in crisis. And if I don't come back he'll have to replace me."

"Then go back without me, and I'll come later."

He got up and looked out the window, shaking his head. "You wouldn't come."

"What? Of course I would."

"No, you wouldn't. I'd leave here and your parents would talk you out of it. They never have liked me. And then that Mark guy would move in on you—"

Warmth surged through her at this new vulnerability. She touched his back, kissed his shoulder. "Craig, you have to trust me."

He turned and looked down at her. "It's not about trust. You're just stalling. I'm giving you a week, Deni. That's all."

Deni had never liked being told what to do, and she really hated it now. She backed up, staring at him. "Craig, you're not my father. You can't lay down the law with me."

"I will be your husband. What happened to all that Christian submission bunk? Or is that one of the rules you ignore, unlike the one about being unequally yoked—or whatever it is you call it."

That stung. "Maybe you're right. Maybe I'm not ready to be married."

He stared at her with tight lips. "Maybe you're not. If you don't come with me, the wedding's off, because I can't afford to take time to come back and get you again. I don't know what grand gesture you're looking for from me, but I came."

"Noted," she said.

He stormed out of her room, and she heard him clomp downstairs. Fuming, she refused to go after him. She heard a door slam and through her open window, heard the garage door coming up. She looked out as he leaped on his bicycle and took off.

Where in the world was he going?

Fury raged within her. She ran down to the garage, jerked the door back down, and hooked the locking mechanism so it couldn't be opened again.

Her mother came to the door and looked out. "Who's leaving?"

"Craig," she said.

Her mother looked confused. "Where did he go?"

"I don't know."

"Is he coming back?"

"He must be. He didn't take anything with him."

Kay grunted. "Well, did you two have a fight?"

Deni stormed back into the house. "I don't want to talk about it."

She went back into the closet and wept her heart out. Getting on her knees, she prayed for her future. She asked God to show her whether she was wrong, whether she should leave her parents and cleave to her husband-to-be. If she was going to marry him, was she supposed to start submitting to him already, when everything seemed so wrong? Could she really submit to someone she couldn't respect?

She wanted to marry him, but not like this.

And then she thought of being without him again, of him getting on that train and riding off to Washington. Would she ever see him again?

She didn't know Senator Crawford well, but he seemed like a compassionate person. Surely he would understand.

But it didn't matter, because he wasn't going to wait. He had laid down the timetable. She had a week to decide whether she was going to marry him and leave.

She couldn't get married here, not with her parents feeling the way they did. She would have to get married in Washington, without them to support her. She'd have to learn to be a wife on her own, without having her mother to call for a recipe or to vent about an argument she and Craig had had. Her dad wouldn't be there to help her move in or repair the things in their new home that would need fixing. And Craig sure wasn't handy.

She would miss Beth and Jeff and Logan, and the Gatlin boys and little Sarah. And she would miss Mark.

She thought of the way Mark had been with the children, when he'd helped Beth with the backdrop and all the props of the play. He'd been with the volunteers who'd gone out looking for Sarah after she'd been kidnapped. Craig had decided to sleep instead.

But it was Craig's ring she was wearing. She'd made a promise to him. She just had to decide if she could keep it.

SEVENTY-THREE

TWO HOURS PASSED WITH NO WORD FROM CRAIG. MOST OF the family had gone to bed after the grueling night, but Deni couldn't nap. Where had he gone? He'd left his suitcase and taken nothing with him except for his bicycle. She wondered if something had happened to him along the way. New worries crept up inside her. Was he hurt? Maybe he had been mugged or murdered for his wallet or his bike. Why else would he stay gone in a strange town all day?

When he finally returned about midmorning, she almost threw herself at him. "I'm so glad you're okay. I thought something had happened to you. Where did you go?"

He was drenched with sweat. He looked angry and stepped back from her, pulling two tickets out of his pocket. "I went to the train station. I got us tickets to leave on the train a week from today. Are you going with me?"

Anger flushed her cheeks, but she tried to force it down. "I don't know," she said. "I have to pray some more about it. You shouldn't have spent the money until I told you for sure."

As she expected, he tried to strong-arm her. "Pray all you want," he said, "but realize this is a life-altering decision. You go with me, we get married, we spend our lives together. You don't go with me and it's over between us. It's as simple as that."

With that, he stormed up the stairs. She let him go and sat there staring into space, too numb to even feel the rage she knew she should feel.

It wasn't supposed to be like this. When she left home with him, she was supposed to feel giddy, excited, eager to start a new life. She wasn't supposed to be resentful and sad.

But those were the times she lived in. Leaving and cleaving had taken on new meaning.

Maybe she just had to get used to it.

SEVENTY-FOUR

SARAH WOULD NEED COUNSELING FOR THE THINGS SHE'D experienced with Moe, but thankfully, there seemed to be no physical abuse. Still, her nightmares would continue for some time.

The day after Moe's death, Sheriff Scarbrough showed up at the door to talk to Aaron. The boy met him with his chin held high, a look of resolve on his face, as if he expected to be arrested for his confession.

"Sit down, son," Scarbrough said.

Aaron did as he was told. Looking down at his hands, he said, "I know what you're here for."

Scarbrough's expression softened. "Aaron, look at me."

He looked into the sheriff's dark eyes.

"You didn't kill your mama, boy. There were two bullets—one of them in her head."

"No, I only shot once."

Scarbrough nodded. "So you said. I assumed both bullets were from the same firearm. I was wrong."

"What do you mean?" Doug asked.

"I just got the ballistics report back on the second bullet. The one through her head was from Moe Jenkins's gun."

Aaron gasped.

"Are you serious?" Deni asked.

"Absolutely. After Aaron shot her in the leg, Moe must have come along and found her. He finished the job."

Aaron just stared at him for a moment, dumbfounded. "You mean ... it wasn't me?"

"No, son. You shot her in the leg, but she would have recovered from that."

The rigid tension in Aaron's bones seemed to melt and his face twisted. A tear stole out of his eye. "'Cause I didn't mean to kill her," he said again. "I didn't really want her dead. I just wanted her to stop."

Allen let out a heavy sigh and hugged the boy again. "We know you didn't, Aaron. We know why you did it. At least now you know you didn't cause her death."

"So you're not gonna arrest me?"

"Not after all that's happened, Aaron. No point in it."

Aaron let that sink in for a moment. "Then ... I guess God forgave me too, huh? Just like Pop said. Since he heard my prayers and answered them and stuff."

"You bet he did," Doug said.

A slow smile worked its way into the child's eyes, but it would be a while before the edge of sadness gave way.

Allen got to his feet and shook the sheriff's hand. "I think it's time for us to plan our trip home. We'll take the kids back to Atlanta. We're ready to get on with our lives. We've got a lot of healing to do."

ALLEN AND MARIE DECIDED TO TAKE THE SAME TRAIN THAT would take Deni and Craig away.

But Deni still couldn't make up her mind. She had talked to Chris about it, and as much as her best friend hated to see her go, she encouraged Deni to put the love of her life first.

But that was just it. She wasn't sure Craig was her soul mate.

She'd watched for Mark every morning as she went to the well to draw water, but he'd made himself scarce for the last few days.

As the day approached, Craig turned on the charm, and she began to think that being in Washington might be better than she'd thought. Things would be easier there. Wouldn't Craig see to that?

No more backbreaking labor, no more slaving for every meal they ate.

Or was she just being naive?

There was something good about what she'd been doing these last few months. Something noble about working with her hands. And she'd enjoyed getting closer to her family.

But she was twenty-two and she had to leave sometime.

Finally, she agreed to go.

THE MORNING BEFORE THEY LEFT, DENI FOUND MARK SITTING at the well, as if waiting for her. He wore a white baseball cap and a yellow tank top, and his strong arms were crossed.

"I was hoping to see you," Deni said. "Have you been avoiding me?"

His smile seemed fragile. "Not exactly. Just trying to stay out of the way. I get the feeling Craig doesn't appreciate our friendship much. And who can blame him?"

"Yeah, I guess."

"So ... you're going, huh?"

"Chris told you?"

He nodded and swallowed hard. "I've been praying for you."

She leaned on the well wall and gazed into the water. "We're leaving tomorrow."

For a moment there was silence. Finally, she looked at him.

His eyes glistened and his cheeks blotched red. "Why so soon?"

Her throat felt tight. "Craig has to get back. He's needed there."

"Chris said he gave you an ultimatum."

"That's right. Either I go with him or it's over."

"Seems a little harsh. I mean, he's asking you to pack everything you own and take off forever. With so much going on, you haven't had time to think about it with a clear head."

If only Craig could see that. "I tried to tell him that, but he said it's now or never. To him, I'm just too much of a mama's girl, tied to the apron strings."

The lines between Mark's eyes deepened. "I call that family loyalty. Being there for the people who need you."

"I know, but what good am I as a wife if I can't even leave my parents?"

He turned and leaned his elbow on the well's post and looked into her eyes.

"You did leave your parents, Deni. You've been gone for the last four years. He knows that. You don't have a problem with separation anxiety. It's just a weird time. Not everyone *has* family. Those who do should be allowed to be close to them."

He made so much sense. Her heart swelled as she looked at him. "I told him. I tried to make him understand."

"So why are you going?"

She turned away. "Because I want to marry him," she said. "We have plans. We have hopes and dreams. And maybe when I get on that train, I can leave all these worries behind. Everything's so hard and depressing. Maybe if I start over new with him, we can have a life that's not so hard."

"I don't think you're going to be happy, Deni." The words came out cracked.

Tears rimmed her eyes. "But you don't know Craig. He hasn't been his best here. He's really a great guy. He makes friends everywhere he goes. He's so smart, and he has so much promise."

"As a politician, maybe, but does he have promise as your husband, as the father of your future children, as your companion?" He turned her to face him. His eyes were piercing, undebatable, as he held her tearful gaze. "Deni, I'm saying this as your friend. Forget whatever happened between us. This isn't about me wanting you for myself. I just don't see Craig making you happy."

"Well, can any human being ever make us happy?" she asked. "I mean, don't we have to let God fill all the voids in our lives?"

"In a way, yes," Mark said. "But Deni, God gives us spouses to comfort us and keep us company, and to help us through life. I don't like thinking of you stacking up disappointments for the rest of your life."

She wished she hadn't come here. This was just confusing her. "But he will be there for me. If I didn't believe that, I wouldn't go. He's a statesman, a loyal public servant, an all-around great guy." She knew her words were weak.

"Deni, he's probably really great. Some day he'll run for president, and I might vote for him. But we're talking about you."

She put her back to him and started drawing out the water. "You're wrong," she muttered as she worked the pulley. "We'll have a happy life, just like we planned."

He stood behind her, silently watching as she pulled up the water and emptied it into her container, then lowered the bucket for more. When she'd filled her container, she finally looked at him again. He was standing there with his hands in his pockets, gazing at her through those deep eyes that seemed to read her every thought.

Finally, she sighed. "We can say good-bye or . . . not."

He took off his cap, raked his fingers through his hair. "I'll miss you, Deni. I really wish you wouldn't go, but if you do, you can always know that I'll be praying for you, every single day."

The sweet words were more than she could bear. "Thank you, Mark." She reached out and hugged him.

His arms felt like home. Why didn't Craig's? He held her for a moment, not letting her go. Against her ear, he whispered, "If you marry him, Deni, it has to be for life. You know that, don't you? It's a covenant before God. You have to mean it. There are no safety nets, no easy ways out, no back doors."

She squeezed her eyes shut and nodded.

"Promise me you'll pray about this really hard. Promise you'll ask God."

"I have," she whispered.

He kept holding her. "Promise you'll listen to what he's saying."

"I will."

He let her go, and she saw the tear escaping down his cheek, but he quickly wiped it away. "I have to go now," he said.

She didn't want him to leave, but he started walking away. "Bye, Mark."

He stopped and turned back. "Be happy, Deni." He got the words out, then didn't look back again.

SEVENTY-FIVE

SHERIFF SCARBROUGH BREACHED PROTOCOL AND GAVE them a ride to the train station. It took two of the department vehicles to get all of the Gatlins and Brannings there, but Deni was glad she didn't have to find a way to carry her luggage on a bicycle.

Her mother had been weepy all morning, wiping her eyes and trying to stay strong, but she had gently and kindly helped Deni get packed.

They said their good-byes as the Gatlin children climbed onto the train, two cars back from where Craig and Deni would sit. Marie Gatlin held her little granddaughter close to her, stroking her short hair as Sarah sucked her thumb. Already they'd bonded like mother and daughter, and Deni knew the child would be all right. She cried as she kissed Sarah good-bye.

"Bye, Deni."

"Bye, sweetheart. I'm gonna miss my little sleeping bunny." Sarah smiled and hugged her. Deni bent and hugged Luke, then Joey, and finally Aaron. "You're a good man, Aaron Gatlin," she said.

The smile in his eyes told her that was what he needed to hear.

Craig pulled her away. "Time to go, babe."

Deni hesitated. She turned back to her family. Even Jeff and Logan said teary good-byes.

When she got to her dad, he hugged her so tightly that he lifted her off her feet. Then she reached for her mother.

She didn't think she could bear letting her mom go. "I want you to be happy, honey," Kay choked out. "I really do." Her mother touched her face, and Deni saw the resolve in her eyes. Her mother was strong—stronger than Deni had ever been. She would be fine.

But Deni wouldn't.

"Cut the apron strings," Craig muttered.

Kay let go and shot Craig a bitter look. "Take care of her, Craig," she said. "She's precious to us."

He looked annoyed. Taking Deni's hand, he led her to the platform and waited for her to step up.

Deni looked back at her mother, saw her wilting against her father.

Craig's voice was impatient. "Come on, Deni. You don't have to drag this out."

She looked up at him through her tears. "This is hard," she said. "I don't know if I can do it."

"Deni, the train is going to leave."

She stood there a moment, struck by the biggest decision of her life, weighing how deeply she would grieve for her family versus how much she loved Craig.

And suddenly, she wasn't sure it was worth it.

"I can't," she said.

He gaped at her. "What do you mean? Deni, get on this train."

"I'm not going." She slid the engagement ring off her finger and put it into his hand. "I love you and I'll miss you," she said, closing his fingers over it. "I'm sorry it can't work out, but this isn't the right thing and it's not the right time."

Only then did Craig realize she meant it. "Deni, you're just having a little separation anxiety. It'll pass."

"No, it won't." The train's whistle blew. "My luggage!" she cried to the worker at the cargo car. "Those red bags. I need them back!"

The man grabbed them and tossed them off. Craig came off the platform. "Deni, do you realize what you're doing?"

"No," she said. "I'm confused, Craig. But I'd rather be confused here than there."

"All aboard!" the engineer called.

Craig stood frozen, his mouth open. "Deni, this is crazy!" The words sounded brittle, hollow. His face changed and that cocky assurance melted into fear. "I don't want to leave you."

Hope flared inside her. "Then don't."

He looked back at the train as they began closing the cargo car. "Deni, I told you, I have to go. This isn't fair." He stepped back up, as if to show her he could.

Panic gripped her.

Craig saw it in her face and reached for her. "Come on, Deni. I'll make you happy, I promise. Just get on the train."

But she didn't make a move to take his hand. Instead, she stepped backward, shaking her head. "I can't go, Craig. I'm so sorry."

"And I can't stay."

Her face twisted as grief overcame her. For a moment she expected him to throw up his hands and disappear inside the train. But he didn't. Instead, his face softened, and he jumped off the platform and pulled her into his arms. She clung to him with all her might, praying he would change his mind.

Finally, he released her. His own eyes glistened as he went back toward the train. It started to move, its wheels slowly rolling, the steam engine doing its soft *chug-chug*.

Then he stepped back onto the train.

This was it. She looked up at him through her tears, wishing things could be different, but knowing they couldn't.

"I love you, Deni," he called over the steam engine. "Despite what I said, it's not over!" Then he turned and went inside. She stood still and watched through the windows as he moved through the car to his seat. He looked back at her out the window and touched the glass.

She pressed a kiss into her palm and blew it at him as the train took him away.

SEVENTY-SIX

IT WAS LATE AFTERNOON WHEN DENI FOUND MARK IN HIS backyard, splitting firewood. Dirty from a hard day's work and sweating with exertion, he swung the ax easily.

"Mark?"

He turned around and caught his breath at the sight of her. "Deni!" Mark dropped the ax. "I thought the train was gone by now."

She shook her head. "I changed my mind. I'm not going with him."

He let out a breath and put his hand on his heart. Eyebrows raised, he asked, "Not ever?"

She looked down at her feet, knowing she couldn't make promises. "I don't know. Ever's a long time. All I know is I'm not going now. I gave him back the ring." Those tears assaulted her again, and she felt like a fool. Why had she come here when her emotions were so raw? She should have waited.

But Mark closed the distance between them and pulled her into his arms. "I'm so sorry," he whispered against her ear. "I know how hard this must have been. Are you all right?"

She savored the comforting feel of his arms around her. He made her feel safe. "I will be."

After a moment he loosened his hold, and she stepped back, holding his gaze for a long moment. His eyes were probing, searching her heart. But she had no answers, and she could make no promises.

"I just wanted to come tell you," she said. "I thought you should know."

He brushed back the hair from her eyes. Her heart skipped a beat as his fingers lingered on her skin. Pleasure sparkled in his eyes. "I'm glad you didn't go." His voice wavered. "I hated the thought of losing one of my only friends."

She appreciated his sensitivity, not to demand more of her. He was too wise for that, she thought. Too trusting of God's timing. And that gave Mark a peace that other men only pretended. She loved that about him.

"Well, I have to get back and help with supper," she said.

Quietly he walked her to the gate, and as she started down the sidewalk toward home, he called after her. "Welcome home, Deni."

She looked back over her shoulder. He was smiling softly, and she smiled back. It lifted the weight of her grief and chased the shadows from her heart.

Restoration was on the horizon ... and healing was on its way.

A NOTE FROM THE AUTHOR

Two weeks before the release of *Last Light*, I faced a power outage of my own. My state of Mississippi was ravaged by hurricane Katrina, and I found myself living through some of what my characters were experiencing.

Though I live 120 miles from the coastal areas that were devastated, and my home wasn't damaged, I wound up without electricity or telephones. Gas stations couldn't pump until the electricity was restored, and once it was, lines quickly formed, with a three-hour wait to fill up cars and generators.

Food spoiled, and the spoiled people (like me) who were used to summer hibernation in our air-conditioned homes were suddenly drenched with perspiration and trying to get cool. Some had contaminated drinking water. Some had trees in their living rooms. And some, farther south, didn't have living rooms at all.

While the government was condemned for FEMA's response and the world seemed paralyzed with panic, an amazing thing happened. Christian people sprang into action. In their hurry to fill the needs of those around them, they found themselves guided by the Holy Spirit's direction, falling into step with the God who was caring for those he loved, when they barely had enough time to think.

A great example of that was at Pass Road Baptist Church in Biloxi, Mississippi. Still standing in the midst of massive devastation, that church became a distribution center for supplies for the victims. Christian people who had lost their own homes showed up each day to sort, stack, and collect tons of supplies being donated from around the country, and they were distributing them to the hurting and hungry families lining up in their cars.

There weren't many church members able to tithe, since the suddenly homeless were also suddenly jobless. So another church farther north committed to paying the salaries of the staff and helping to support the work going on in that place. Mission groups from all over the country began a pilgrimage there to help out in any way they could.

It wasn't just that church, either. Teams of Christians were cutting fallen trees away from homes, mudding out sheetrock, showing up at sites of devastation, and doing for free what others were charging thousands to do. In my own church in central Mississippi, Christian doctors and nurses ministered to hundreds of evacuees who needed medication and medical equipment. Those who couldn't go south spent hours a day cooking for the shelters, washing clothes and towels and sheets, visiting with the lonely who sat on their cots. An evacuated nursing home brought its weak, frail, elderly, and sick to our church gym. Those who had to be carried and wheeled off the buses were revived and cared for, and later were able to walk back onto the buses that took them to their new facilities.

I realized, as all that was happening before my eyes, that this was what I wanted to convey in this series. That each of us is put in place for a particular time in particular circumstances and prepared in a particular way, not knowing what God will need us for. Some of us have experienced tragedies and crises with no answers from God about why he would drag us through such pain, only to find that it qualified us uniquely to do some mighty work of God when the time of someone else's crisis came. And that's how the body of Christ works.

I wanted to make sure that my readers understood that we're here for such a time as Katrina, or Rita, or September 11, or the Oklahoma bombing, or a mining disaster, or our neighbor's cancer, or a parent's grief, or a widow's sorrow. And when we face our own disasters, there will be people there for us. Because when Christendom is really working, that's what it looks like.

This message is for me as much as my readers. I pray that I will not whine when God strengthens me through trials, and that I will let him prepare me for what lies ahead—those things for which he made me. Those times when I can be Christ to someone who may never have met him and show them the love of the Savior who can lift their burdens.

And I pray that when that time does come, I'll see the blessing in that crisis, and it won't be wasted on me.

READING GROUP GUIDE

1. Consider the conditions in which we find the Gatlin children. Was it right for Aaron and Joey to steal in order to feed themselves and their siblings, Luke and Sarah?
2. The new Oak Hollow well symbolizes many things for the neighborhood community. What connections are there between the well and the community's circumstances?
3. How do the circumstances of Aaron Gatlin's life lead to his original assumptions of the Brannings?
4. What impact do the Gatlin children have on the Branning family? Physically and emotionally?
5. React to Craig's letters to Deni. How would you feel reading those letters? What would your reaction be? What's now in store for Deni's future?
6. Disbursement day comes for the community of Oak Hollow. What is the first thing you would invest your $25.00 in? What would the benefits or consequences to those purchases be?
7. How will the disbursement help the citizens? What are some negative aspects to this new source of money?
8. In Night Light, the community of Oak Hollow learns to celebrate again. Why is it important to celebrate the small things in life? How do the celebrations affect the neighborhood as a whole?

9. Doug and Kay Branning spoke some harsh realities to their daughter Deni regarding faith and her fiancé. Would you have spoken up? What would be the consequences, both good and bad?

10. Identify the climax of the story. How does the Branning family react? What happens to the Gatlin children? What are the effects?

11. Aaron Gatlin struggles to receive forgiveness. What are some factors that lend to his struggling? How does forgiveness finally reach his heart?

12. Many changes have occurred for the Branning family and their neighbors since the Pulses started. What are some of the more dramatic changes? What has not changed for the family?

13. God calls us to share our gifts with others. Where would your gifts be most useful in your community? Does it take a catastrophe to really see the best and worst of people?

THE RESTORATION SERIES

In the face of a crisis that sweeps an entire high-tech planet back to the age before electricity, the Brannings face a choice. Will they hoard their possessions to survive—or trust God to provide as they offer their resources to others? Terri Blackstock weaves a masterful what-if series in which global catastrophe reveals the darkness in human hearts—and lights the way to restoration for a self-centered world.

An Excerpt from *TRUE LIGHT*

PROLOGUE

ON MAY 24, CIVILIZATION AS WE KNOW IT COMES TO AN end.

Plumbing doesn't work because the water treatment plants run on electricity. Trucks and trains don't run, so stores run out of food. Generators are rendered useless. In this major meltdown of life, people are stranded where they are, with no transportation, no power, and no communication. Crime runs rampant as evil fills the void, and desperation becomes the only moral guide many people recognize.

Eventually, word makes its way to Crockett, Alabama, that the event was caused by a star—a supernova named SN–1999—which is emitting electromagnetic pulses every few seconds. With no assurances of when the star might burn itself out and allow them to rebuild, people are left with a choice: will they hoard what they have until it all runs out, or will they share with those around them who are in need?

The Brannings, an upper middle-class Christian family, struggle to maintain their faith in the midst of the world's new challenges, and learn the lesson of giving of themselves ...

Even when it threatens their survival.

ONE

THE BUCK FELL WITH THE FIRST SHOT, AND ZACH EMORY couldn't help being impressed with himself. From his deer stand, it looked like an eight- or ten-pointer. If the weather stayed cold, he'd be able to make it last for several weeks' worth of meals.

He climbed down from his deer stand and pulled up the collar of his jacket. It was so cold his ears were numb, and his fingers had begun to ache. But it was worth it. Even in the pre-outage days, Zach had spent many mornings sitting in a deer stand freezing to death, just for sport. Now it was a matter of survival.

He jogged toward the animal that lay dead twenty yards away. His brother Gary would be crazy with envy. They had a competition going, and Gary was two up on him. Zach hoped Gary had heard the gunshot and would come to help him move the deer. It would take both of them to lift it into their rickshaw.

He bent over the buck. Ten points. And a perfect shot right through the heart. His dad would finally be proud, and if he was lucky, his mother would drag herself out of bed to get a look.

He heard footsteps behind him and turned to see a man emerging from the trees, walking toward him. Zach squinted, trying to place him. He'd seen him before, but he couldn't remember where.

"Did I score or what?" he asked as the man came closer. "He's a ten-pointer. Got him in one shot, right through the ticker!"

The man didn't look like he'd come to celebrate. He stopped about thirty feet away ... and raised his rifle.

Was he going to shoot? Zach's hands came up, as if that would stop him.

The gun fired—its impact propelling Zach backward, bouncing him onto the dirt.

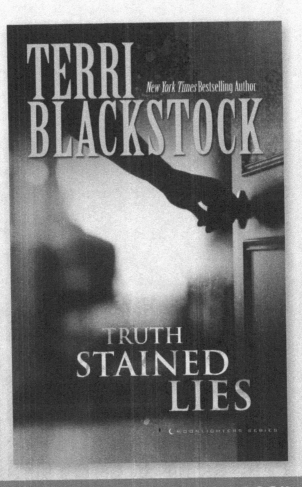

About the
Author

Terri Blackstock is an award-winning novelist who has written for several major publishers including HarperCollins, Dell, Harlequin, and Silhouette. Her books have sold over 6 million copies worldwide.

With her success in secular publishing at its peak, Blackstock had what she calls "a spiritual awakening." A Christian since the age of fourteen, she realized she had not been using her gift as God intended. It was at that point that she recommitted her life to Christ, gave up her secular career, and made the decision to write only books that would point her readers to him.

"I wanted to be able to tell the truth in my stories," she said, "and not just be politically correct. It doesn't matter how many readers I have if I can't tell them what I know about the roots of their problems and the solutions that have literally saved my own life."

Her books are about flawed Christians in crisis and God's provisions for their mistakes and wrong choices. She claims to be extremely qualified to write such books, since she's had years of personal experience.

A native of nowhere, since she was raised in the Air Force, Blackstock makes Mississippi her home. She and her husband are the parents of three adult children—a blended family which she considers one more of God's provisions.

Terri Blackstock, a *New York Times* bestselling author, has sold over six million books worldwide. She is the author of numerous suspense novels, including *Intervention*, *Vicious Cycle*, and *Downfall* (the Intervention Series), as well as the Moonlighters Series, the Cape Refuge Series, the SunCoast Chronicles, the Newpointe 911 Series, the Restoration Series, and many others. (www.terriblackstock.com)